Nursing and Informatics for the 21st Century – Embracing a Digital World, 3rd Edition, Book 3

Nursing and Informatics for the 21st Century – Embracing a Digital World, 3rd Edition is comprised of four books which can be purchased individually at www.routledge.com:

Book 1: Realizing Digital Health – Bold Challenges and Opportunities for Nursing – ISBN: 9780367516888

Book 2: Nursing Education and Digital Health Strategies – ISBN: 9781032249728

Book 3: Innovation, Technology, and Applied Informatics for Nurses – ISBN: 9781032249803

Book 4: Nursing in an Integrated Digital World that Supports People, Systems, and the Planet – ISBN: 9781032249827

Nursing and Informatics for the 21st Century – Embracing a Digital World, 3rd Edition, Book 3

Innovation, Technology, and Applied Informatics for Nurses

Edited by
Connie White Delaney, PhD, RN, FAAN, FACMI, FNAP
Charlotte A. Weaver, PhD, MSPH, RN, FHIMSS, FAAN
Joyce Sensmeier, MS, RN-BC, FHIMSS, FAAN
Lisiane Pruinelli, PhD, MS, RN, FAMIA
Patrick Weber, MA, RN, FIAHSI, FGBHI

Foreword by Deborah Trautman, PhD, RN, FAAN
President and Chief Executive Officer,
American Association of Colleges of Nursing

Foreword by Kedar Mate, MD
President and CEO,
Institute for Healthcare Improvement

Foreword by Howard Catton
Chief Executive Officer,
International Council of Nurses

A PRODUCTIVITY PRESS BOOK

First published 2022
by Routledge
605 Third Avenue, New York, NY 10158

and by Routledge
2 Park Square, Milton Park, Abingdon, Oxon, OX14 4RN

Routledge is an imprint of the Taylor & Francis Group, an informa business

© 2022 selection and editorial matter, Connie White Delaney, Charlotte A. Weaver, Joyce Sensmeier, Lisiane Pruinelli & Patrick Weber; individual chapters, the contributors

The right of Connie White Delaney, Charlotte A. Weaver, Joyce Sensmeier, Lisiane Pruinelli & Patrick Weber to be identified as the authors of the editorial material, and of the authors for their individual chapters, has been asserted in accordance with sections 77 and 78 of the Copyright, Designs and Patents Act 1988.

All rights reserved. No part of this book may be reprinted or reproduced or utilised in any form or by any electronic, mechanical, or other means, now known or hereafter invented, including photocopying and recording, or in any information storage or retrieval system, without permission in writing from the publishers.

Trademark notice: Product or corporate names may be trademarks or registered trademarks, and are used only for identification and explanation without intent to infringe.

ISBN: 9781032249810 (hbk)
ISBN: 9781032249803 (pbk)
ISBN: 9781003281016 (ebk)

DOI: 10.4324/9781003281016

Typeset in Garamond
by Deanta Global Publishing Services, Chennai, India

Dedication for Connie White Delaney

Responding to the urgent and powerful invitation for community, partnership and collaboration, this *Nursing and Informatics for the 21st Century—Embracing a Digital World*, 3rd Edition is dedicated to all individuals, organizations and informaticians who are co-creating futures, health and healthcare. May these co-created informatics-anchored futures radiate the brain of intellect and wisdom, the brain of heart and compassion, and the action brain of impact, voice, caring and awakening!

Dedication for Charlotte A. Weaver

Reflecting these painful times, this dedication goes out to all our frontline nurses and fellow healthcare workers who have taken care of us all around the globe at the risk of their own lives and well-being. We owe you.

Dedication for Joyce Sensmeier

To my husband and life partner, who has faithfully supported my informatics journey, encouraging me to take risks along the way and congratulating me on every success. Thank you for believing in me.

Dedication for Lisiane Pruinelli

To those who battle every day for a better world … 'I don't write a book so that it will be the final word; I write a book so that other books are possible, not necessarily written by me.' —Michel Foucault

Dedication for Patrick Weber

For the sake of the population, the empowerment of nurses worldwide is the best effort to improve disease prevention and promote good health. Thank you to my co-editors and all the authors for their work on this book series.

Contents

Foreword by Deborah Trautman ix

Foreword by Kedar Mate xi

Foreword by Howard Catton xiii

Preface xv

Acknowledgement xxi

Editors xxiii

Contributors xxvii

Introduction xxix

1 **Top Informatics Trends for the Next Decade** 1
   JOYCE SENSMEIER

2 **Canadian Health Outcomes for Better Information and Care: Making the Value of Nursing Visible through the Use of Standardized Data** 17
   PEGGY WHITE, LYNN M. NAGLE AND KATHRYN J. HANNAH

3 **Consumer-Generated Whole-Person Health Data: A Structured Approach** 39
   ROBIN AUSTIN, SRIPRIYA RAJAMANI AND KAREN A. MONSEN

4 **Sensors and the Internet of Things** 61
   THOMAS R. CLANCY

5 **Applied Data Science** 81
   LISIANE PRUINELLI AND MAXIM TOPAZ

6 **Understanding the Foundations of Artificial Intelligence: Data, Math and Machine Learning** 95
   TRACIE RISLING

7 Artificial Intelligence for Nursing and Healthcare: Potentials and Cautions 113
MARTIN MICHALOWSKI AND JUNG IN PARK

8 Artificial Intelligence-Based Model for Monitoring Pressure Ulcer Changes in Bedridden Patients: A Case Study from Taiwan 131
USMAN IQBAL, CHUN-KUNG (ROCK) HSU AND YU-CHUAN (JACK) LI

9 Telehealth and Virtual Care 147
ELIZABETH A. KRUPINSKI AND KIMBERLY D. SHEA

10 Simulations-Based Care Delivery 169
CYNTHIA SHERRADEN BRADLEY, JOANNE DONNELLY AND NELLIE MUNN SWANSON

11 Case Studies in Applied Informatics during COVID-19 189
BRENDA KULHANEK

Index 203

Foreword

When the nation's nursing school deans voted to endorse *The Essentials: Core Competencies for Professional Nursing Education* in April 2021, new competency expectations for tomorrow's nurses came into focus. Driven in part by the need to ensure consistency among graduates of entry-level and advanced-level nursing education programs, one area receiving special emphasis across roles is nursing informatics. As we considered how best to prepare professional nurses to thrive in the future, the need for providers to 'use information and communication technologies and informatics processes to deliver safe nursing care to diverse populations in a variety of settings' (Essential 8.3) was affirmed as a key competency expectation.

Over the past 20 years, informatics increasingly has been a focus in nursing education, given the rapid rise in the use of technology to guide healthcare delivery and clinical decision-making and the need to critically consider all available data when engaging in evidence-based practice and precision healthcare. Basic informatics competencies are foundational to all nursing practice.

Reaching this point in the evolution of our understanding of informatics would not have been possible without pioneers in the field. The authors of *Nursing and Informatics for the 21st Century—Embracing a Digital World*, 3rd Edition—Connie White Delaney, Charlotte A. Weaver, Joyce Sensmeier, Lisiane Pruinelli and Patrick Weber—stand among the world's leading authorities on health informatics, data science and digital health. Committed to enhancing the scholarship of discovery, these nurse leaders are known internationally for their trailblazing work that has been known by such authorities as the Alliance for Nursing Informatics, American Medical Informatics Association, International Academy of Health Sciences Informatics and the Healthcare Information and Management Systems Society. Their pedigrees are undeniable, their thought leadership profound.

The publication of this expansive resource comes at a time when nursing is once again divining its future into the next decade. In addition to the re-envisioned AACN's *Essentials*, which is setting a new standard for nursing education, recent National Academy of Medicine reports on *The Future of Nursing* and *Implementing High Quality Primary Care* point the way forward for nursing practice, research priorities and interprofessional engagement. All these paths demand a greater understanding and reliance on informatics as a driver of innovation and impact. Further, healthcare's move to address pressing social needs, including a shared desire to achieve health equity, gain insight into the social determinants of health, expand consumer access to data and attend to global health concerns are all considered within the context of digital technologies and applied data science as part of this new book series.

Nursing and Informatics for the 21st Century—Embracing a Digital World, 3rd Edition will be of great interest to nurses and other health professionals in the US and globally who are eager to learn more about leveraging automated systems and emerging science to sustain health and improve healthcare delivery. This book series serves as an important resource for practice leaders, nurse researchers, systems analysts, healthcare consumers and graduate students looking to explore opportunities for innovation that develop at the nexus of nursing science, emerging technologies, critical thinking and patient-centered care.

As we look to a future with nursing education that is more competency-based, informatics will be front and center. For faculty wishing to keep pace with the latest thinking on contemporary nursing education and practice, this essential resource will help to inform your understanding about the value and reach of informatics and may also generate new ideas for developing experiential learning opportunities using artificial intelligence, telehealth, simulation and other leading-edge technologies. These emerging tools and practices are transforming nursing roles as well as the skills and knowledge needed to manage care remotely. This comprehensive work will help lead conversations to inspire future generations of nurses to explore how best to leverage nursing informatics in their research, practice and leadership roles.

Deborah Trautman, PhD, RN, FAAN
President and Chief Executive Officer
American Association of Colleges of Nursing

Foreword

Walk onto any clinical service unit in a modern hospital, and you will realize that clinical practice today is a fully socio-technological phenomenon—entirely reliant both upon a nurse's compassion and upon our technology's capacity to supply information and services just in time. Technologies are no longer working their way into health and healthcare—they are already integral to both. But the promise of these incredibly exciting digital therapeutics, diagnostics and monitoring systems depends on, just as more conventional medicines have for decades, the human systems required to implement them. This interface—between nurses and the digital information that can make care more effective, efficient, and reliable—is at the heart of 21st-century nursing informatics.

Years ago, the field of quality improvement in healthcare started with a simple premise—we could work on those human processes to take the fruits of clinical science—medications, new diagnostic assays, vaccines—and more reliably deliver them to patients to create lasting health effects. It is time for a complementary agenda—quality and reliability sciences must now be applied to improve the delivery of proven digital therapies and diagnostics. Just as we created reliable workflows that delivered antibiotics that would prevent sepsis deaths, so too must we create workflows that will leverage new data sources and technologies to improve the way we care for patients. Digital will change healthcare just as antibiotics have, but neither will achieve impact without implementation methods that ensure that the 'medicine' gets to the patient.

This is crucial because of the incredible potential of technology and data to improve care and outcomes. Consider how good artificial intelligence (AI)-guided diagnosis and triage have become: for some clinical conditions, AI now gets diagnostic and treatment accuracy over 90% right compared to clinicians in urgent care environments. These technologies won't replace the nurse or the physician, but they can radically affect the capacity of a clinician to see patients. If much of the time-consuming fact-finding, differential diagnosis, care plan documentation, and charting can be done by an AI-guided automated assistant, nurses can spend much more time caring for patients.

Realizing technology's transformative potential in nursing requires a comprehensive understanding of how to turn data into information; information into knowledge; knowledge into wisdom; and wisdom into applied practice. This book series is essential to such an understanding. This new edition is a detailed and exhaustive exploration of the myriad contexts, approaches, challenges and success stories of how effective informatics can improve every dimension of health, including the fiercely urgent dimensions of needing to improve access to care and ensuring health equity.

For those new to the field of informatics, this series contains an illuminating history of the rapid and profound changes in digital health over the past decade. And for those with deep experience in the field, there are chapters detailing both what's happening at the cutting-edge and what the future holds. Anyone who wants to improve nursing practice in the modern era needs to read this book series and heed its calls to action.

Kedar Mate, MD
President and CEO
Institute for Healthcare Improvement

Foreword

As the COVID-19 pandemic has so painfully shown us, it is hard to accurately predict the future. While the temptation is to spend time and effort on futurology—it can be hard to resist—our time is probably better spent on trying to prepare flexibly for what is coming next and, in some way, help to shape it.

What seems certain is that digital health will feature in our futures and that nurses are in a prime position to take advantage of the benefits it can bring. In fact, as we have seen, recent developments in digital health are some of the few positives to have come out of the pandemic.

Finding ways to deal with the pandemic brought about a rapid increase in access to digitally enhanced care, whether it be through the use of videoconferencing for consultations and telehealth or through increased access to massive amounts of data that were previously buried and heavily guarded in the depths of healthcare organizations' information technology systems. The issue now is understanding the data and using it meaningfully to improve services and reduce costs.

While only a year or so ago it would have been correct to say the future is digital, we can now say that, in many parts of the world, digital health is already here and that it looks like it's here to stay. We can see it in the development of nurse-led models of care and how the use of data and new equipment is changing the traditional, paternalistic models of care to more responsive ones that are personalized, faster, sustainable and more affordable.

The biggest challenge ahead will be to expand access to nursing informatics to all nurses, wherever they are so that they can provide equitable access to state-of-the-art care to people everywhere.

This is especially important as the world deals with and recovers from the COVID-19 pandemic. Nurse-led models of care, underpinned by access to data, are a big part of the solution as we strengthen our health systems for the post-pandemic world to come.

I am delighted to write this foreword for what is likely to be a very influential book series about nursing and informatics and how nurses can maximize the impact of digital health for the benefit of patients and their families and the health systems that they work in.

In the past, information technology has promised so much but often failed to deliver on its potential. If it is to fulfil its promise, it must be an enabler for people to be empowered, and it must improve access to services, the quality and efficiency of those services, and the patient's care and health outcomes.

For this to happen, the people on the receiving end of care need to be at the centre of the systems that are developed, and nurses must be involved in all stages of their design, development and implementation. In the past, we have seen how the ill-thought-out introduction of some systems has taken nurses away from direct care, to the detriment of their patients and the annoyance of the nurses.

Nurses do not want to spend hours in front of computer screens, as they have been required to in the past. They do not want to spend their time inputting data into counterintuitive systems that do not meet their requirements. What they want is quick and easy access to the information they need at their fingertips, in people's homes, at the nurses' station on wards, at the bedside and in the clinics where they work, in real time while they are interacting with their patients.

We see the power of technology and data-driven change across the globe, from low- to high-income settings, from the use of Apps on mobile phones to the adoption of sophisticated information systems and algorithms. But underlying it all is the continuing need for a highly skilled and educated nursing workforce. Whatever the future holds in terms of information technology, artificial intelligence and robotics, they will always be used in support of the compassion, the relationships and the dynamic human factors that only nurses can provide.

This *Nursing and Informatics for the 21st Century—Embracing a Digital World*, 3rd Edition shows the path ahead for our profession to become fully digitally enabled. I am sure it will prove to be an indispensable guide along the way.

Howard Catton
Chief Executive Officer
International Council of Nurses

Preface

While we commit to living in the 21st century and maintaining our open minds and hearts to the needs, wishes and wisdom that will inform our future, we have found the pace of change to be challenging in preparing this book series. Every day, new technologies and partnerships are in the social news media, and healthcare systems announce new digital health programs that push care out into the hands of patients and into the home. Additionally, these new care modalities and technology changes are occurring simultaneously with national and international policy mandates to address social injustices and inequities, equality in access to care, and planetary health. Tremendous innovation has transpired since the publication of this book's second edition in 2010. In that space of time, medical sensing devices and mobile technologies have become ubiquitous, permeating every aspect of our lives. Concurrently, the synergistic effect of new technologies and tools such as cloud data storage, application programming interfaces, artificial intelligence and machine learning are game changers in advancing digital health. Together with legislation and regulatory changes, the proprietary limitations of electronic health record (EHR) systems have been upended. The voice of the consumer and insistence on patient-centered, connected and readily accessible care have never had greater velocity, urging our unremitting attention.

Thus, in planning this third edition, we abandoned the previous framework of presenting an 'international snapshot of current state' on EHR adoption and nursing. Technology changes and new applications that extract data, apply AI systems, dashboards, and suggest care protocols made a primary EHR framework irrelevant. Increasingly, economics and policy mandates push healthcare systems to embrace a preventative, wellness and population health focus that requires new thinking toward advanced technology applications that extend services into clinics, community and the home. In the United States, reimbursement linked to Alternative Payment Models (APM) and 'value-based purchasing' with dependency on quality metrics require healthcare systems to collaborate with community resources and post-acute care providers. All collaboration, local to world-wide, demands exchanging and sharing information, as well as actively engaging individual patients and their families. A plethora of digital/mobile applications have emerged to fill this evolving 'non-acute care/non-EHR' space. As chapters from geographic areas spanning the globe describe, economic imperatives, mandates to deliver equal access to care in rural as well as metro areas, and the need to incorporate social determinants of health into care delivery have also driven the adoption of digital health solutions. Therefore, this third edition focuses on these new technologies and the care delivery models they make possible: thus, we gave this work the subtitle *'Embracing a Digital World.'*

Kristine Mednansky, Senior Editor from Taylor & Francis Group, LLC, asked us to consider a new edition, based on feedback from the readers of our previous works. Our full gratitude goes to Ms Mednansky for this series' existence. Her voice was the key driver for creating this work, the *Nursing and Informatics for the 21st Century*, 3rd Edition. Ms Mednansky ensured that this current work would meet the needs of readers in a variety of formats: electronic, print, and the option to purchase either an individual chapter or an entire book. Moreover, readers will note another major difference in the look and feel of the previous hardcover book: this work has been converted to a four-book series to deliver a resource that is more easily consumed. Our hope is that with this flexibility in access and usability, the work embodied in this collection of contributing authors will be widely read and extensively shared. We look forward to receiving your feedback on this novel approach.

This work is organized into a series of four books, each with 11 chapters: (1) Realizing Digital Health–Bold Challenges and Opportunities for Nursing; (2) Nursing Education and Digital Health Strategies; (3) Innovation, Technology, and Applied Informatics for Nurses; and (4) Nursing in an Integrated Digital World that Supports People, Systems, and the Planet. Each book in the series includes international contributors with authors from Africa and South Africa, Brazil, Belgium, Canada, China, England, Finland, Germany, Italy, Norway, the Philippines, South Korea, Sri Lanka, Switzerland, Taiwan, and the United States, as well as authors of additional exemplars from China, India and the West Balkan countries. Throughout this series, the wisdom of leading-edge innovators is interwoven with digital health applications, global thought leaders and multinational, cooperative research initiatives, all against the backdrop of health equity and policy-setting bodies, such as the United Nations and the World Health Organization.

We begin Book 1 of the series by introducing the paradigm of digital health, and its underlying technologies, offering examples of its potential use and future impacts. This introduction is followed by an in-depth look at the ethical considerations in digital health that nurses and informaticists need to understand, authored by an international team of nursing informatics leaders from Finland, Canada and England. The growing movement in consumerism and patient engagement is described in a collaborative research initiative between academia–government–industry. This chapter is bolstered by numerous exemplars, all illustrating the importance of the engaged patient enabled by new digital technologies with the goal of making possible comprehensive access to individuals' digital health information, regardless of system or location. Several chapters focus on the underlying need for terminology and data standards to capture the data necessary to enable new science and knowledge discoveries. Subsequent chapters outline the critical and urgent role that nurse executive leaders' play in advancing digital health, as well as the knowledge and skills needed to take advantage of new digital technologies. We follow with chapters on the role(s) of nursing informatics leaders in large, US health systems, as well as a global perspective from Brazil, Italy and the Philippines. To provide a clear understanding of the challenges facing the United Nations and World Health Organizations' goals for health equity and equality, we include a critical examination of South Africa's healthcare delivery system, technologies and nursing's role across these structural segments. We close Book 1 with a look at the information sharing needed to support true team care spanning multiple settings and systems.

Book 2 is dedicated to a deep examination of nursing education's best practices, strategies, and informatics competencies. The chapters included in Book 2 span nursing education and learning for applied critical thinking, including the use of technology, content, skills versus tools, the use of 'smart' systems for care delivery and the role of critical thinking as essential to nursing care delivery. These concepts are understood as a paradigm shift that must be incorporated into nursing and healthcare education. Best practices for workforce and degree-level education are presented in a description of Emory's Academic/Practice partnership focusing on disruption through nurse innovation enabled by all nurses and students having access to big data. This book closes with a review of innovative methodologies being used in simulation labs across the globe, including some uses of virtual and augmented reality simulations.

Book 3 defines the foundations of artificial intelligence (AI), machine learning (ML) and various digital technologies, including social media, the Internet of Things, telehealth and applied data analytics, all with a look toward the future state. The Applied Healthcare Data Science Roadmap is presented as a framework aiming to educate healthcare leaders on the use of data science principles and tools to inform decision-making. We focus particular attention on the cautions, potential for harm, and biases that artificial intelligence technologies and machine learning may pose in healthcare, with the role of advocate and protector from harm falling under the nurse's role. Book 3 concludes by outlining four case studies featuring innovations developed by nurses in response to COVID-19, which highlight the creative use of technologies to support patients, care providers and healthcare systems during the global pandemic.

We continue with a focus on the theme of enabling digital technologies in Book 4 as they are used to address planetary health issues and care equity across developing countries. Throughout the development of this series, the world has struggled with the core issues of equity in access to care, needed medical equipment and supplies and vaccines. Sustainability and global health policy are linked to the new digital technologies in the chapters that illustrate healthcare delivery modalities, which nurse innovators are developing, leading and using to deliver care to hard-to-reach populations for better population health. Social media use in South Korea for health messaging, community initiatives and nursing research are presented with additional references to other Asian countries. A US description of consumer engagement with patient ownership of all their medical records data is presented with the underlying technologies explained in simple, understandable terms. Additionally, we tapped experts to highlight the legal statutes, government regulations and civil rights law in place for patients' rights, privacy and confidentiality, and consents for the United States, the United Kingdom and the European Union. The next chapter in Book 4 is written by two participants of the 'Future of Nursing 2020–2030' task force who deliver an optimistic message. These authors recognize the work that needs to be done around health equity and equality and review nursing's role responsibilities to effect these changes. Their optimism comes from all the opportunities that social policy and enabling digital technologies make possible for nursing. The authors outline how these changes in care delivery models, the patient/provider role and dependence on digital tools all present opportunities for new nursing roles, access to expansive data resources for research with the exponential growth of our science base and for entrepreneurship.

We conclude this book series with a chapter written by the editors in which we envision the near future. We explore the impact that digital technologies will have on: a) how care is delivered, including expanding care settings into community and home; b) virtual monitoring; and c) the type and quantity of patient-generated data and how it is used to advance knowledge and care excellence. Ultimately these changes highlight the numerous ways that nursing roles and skill sets related to digital health are needed to support the global goal of equal access to health and care. We emphasize the necessity for partnering. We send the message that nursing, along with our transdisciplinary partners, is being called to lead and create unparalleled transformation of healthcare to person-centered, connected and accessible care anchored in digital health.

Acknowledgement

We share our deep gratitude with all of the persons, including care providers, researchers, educators, business and corporate leaders, and informatics experts in all settings, for requesting an update to the second edition of *Nursing and Informatics for the 21st Century*. Together, you recognized the value and synergy of nursing and informatics, the core function of informatics in shaping nursing, health and healthcare, and the reciprocal learning that a global perspective offers us. Thank you to Taylor & Francis Group, LLC, and especially Kristine Mednansky, Senior Editor, for giving us the opportunity to produce this third edition as a totally new body of work in this post-EHR era. But most especially, for your creativity and flexibility as we presented a book double our original plan. Thus, this third edition is presented as a four-book series enveloping *Nursing and Informatics for the 21st Century*. We are deeply humbled by the dedication, work and creativity of our contributing authors, many of whom formed teams that expanded across continents to be able to capture the fullest coverage and latest information. The contributors bring state-of-the-art knowledge, coupled with real-world practice and education. It is the integration of nursing and informatics knowledge and practice that will sustain our health, communities and planet. Last, we would be remiss not to say a deep thank you to Midori V. Green, our project manager par excellence, who kept us organized and on track through her diplomacy and hard work and without which we would not have made our deadlines.

In gratitude,

Connie White Delaney
Charlotte A. Weaver
Joyce Sensmeier
Lisiane Pruinelli
Patrick Weber

Editors

Connie White Delaney, PhD, RN, FAAN, FACMI, FNAP serves as Professor and Dean at the University of Minnesota School of Nursing and is the Knowledge Generation Lead for the National Center for Interprofessional Practice and Education. She served as Associate Director of the Clinical Translational Science Institute—Biomedical Informatics, and Acting Director of the Institute for Health Informatics (IHI) in the Academic Health Center from 2010 to 2015. She serves as an adjunct professor in the Faculty of Medicine and Faculty of Nursing at the University of Iceland, where she received the Doctor Scientiae Curationis Honoris Causa (Honorary Doctor of Philosophy in Nursing) in 2011. She is an elected Fellow in the American Academy of Nursing, American College of Medical Informatics, and National Academies of Practice. Delaney is the first Fellow in the College of Medical Informatics to serve as a Dean of Nursing. Delaney was an inaugural appointee to the USA Health Information Technology Policy Committee, Office of the National Coordinator, and Office of the Secretary for the U.S. Department of Health and Human Services (HHS). She is an active researcher in data and information technology standards for nursing, healthcare. Delaney is past president of Friends of the National Institute of Nursing Research (FNINR) and currently serves as Vice-Chair of CGFNS, Inc. She holds a BSN with majors in nursing and mathematics, MA in Nursing, PhD Educational Administration and Computer Applications, postdoctoral study in Nursing & Medical Informatics and a Certificate in Integrative Therapies & Healing Practices.

Charlotte A. Weaver, Ph.D., MSPH, RN, FHIMSS, FAAN is a visionary senior executive, now retired after 40+ years of experience in nursing informatics, patient safety and quality, evidence-based nursing practices and healthcare automation in acute, ambulatory and post-acute care. She created a breakthrough in the nursing educational curricula by introducing learning using an electronic health record (EHR) in virtual environments and pioneered the corporate-level, Chief Nurse Officer role. She also has Board Director experience in the public/non-profit healthcare sectors. With 15+ years of experience at the chief executive level in the corporate HIT industry and healthcare delivery organizations with Board-reporting responsibilities, her fields of specialization include EHR, health IT policy, post-acute care delivery in home health and hospice provider organizations. Dr. Weaver serves on a number of academic, healthcare systems and healthcare technology company Boards. She is a fellow in the American Academy of Nursing and the Health Information Management Systems Society (HIMSS). She is a frequent presenter at national and international conferences and has published extensively as a writer and editor. Dr. Weaver has a PhD in Medical Anthropology from the University of California, Berkeley and San Francisco, an MSPH in Epidemiology and a BA in Anthropology from the University of Washington, and a Nursing diploma from St Elizabeth's School of Nursing. She was a post-doctoral fellow at the University of Hawaii.

Joyce Sensmeier, MS, RN-BC, FHIMSS, FAAN is the Senior Advisor, Informatics for HIMSS, a non-profit organization focused on reforming the global health ecosystem through the power of information and technology. In this role, she provides thought leadership in the areas of clinical informatics, interoperability and standards programs and initiatives. Sensmeier served as Vice President, Informatics at HIMSS from 2005 to 2019. She is president of IHE USA, a non-profit organization whose mission is to improve our nation's healthcare by promoting the adoption and use of IHE and other world-class standards, tools and services for interoperability. An internationally recognized speaker and author of numerous book chapters and articles, Sensmeier achieved fellowship in the American Academy of Nursing in 2010.

Lisiane Pruinelli PhD, MS, RN, FAMIA is Assistant Professor and co-director of the Center for Nursing Informatics in the School of Nursing and Affiliate Faculty at the Institute for Health Informatics, University of Minnesota. She is a Fellow of the American Medical Informatics Association and a University of Minnesota School of Nursing Global Health Scholar. She serves as the co-chair of the Nursing Knowledge Big Data Science Initiative, co-chair for the Data Science and Clinical Analytics workgroup, and as an advisor board member for the International Medical Informatics Association—Student and Emerging Professional interest group. Previously, she served as a co-chair for the Midwest Nursing Research Society Nursing Informatics workgroup. With more than ten years of clinical experience in both transplant coordination and information systems development and implementation, she is part of a new generation of nursing informaticians focused on applied clinical informatics. Her expertise is in applying innovative nursing informatics tools and cutting-edge data science methods to investigate the trajectory of complex disease conditions suitable for clinical implementations. Her work aims to identify the problems and targeted interventions for better patient outcomes. Dr. Pruinelli grew up in Brazil, moved to USA in 2012 and brings an international and diverse perspective to her everyday work and life. She earned a PhD degree from the University of Minnesota School of Nursing in 2016, and a Master's of Sciences (2008), a Teaching Degree in Nursing (2002) and a Bachelor of Nursing Sciences (2000) degree from the Federal University of Rio Grande do Sul, Porto Alegre, Brazil.

Patrick Weber, MA, RN, FIAHSI, FGBHI is Founder, Director and Principal of Nice Computing, SA in Lausanne, Switzerland. He holds a MA degree in healthcare management and is a Registered Nurse with a diploma degree in nursing. Weber has been an active leader in the European health informatics field for over 30 years, serving as his country's representative to IMIA-Nursing for over a decade and has held numerous board-level positions in IMIA-Nursing as well. Weber is an active member and leader in the European Federation for Medical Informatics (EFMI) and has held numerous leadership positions including treasurer, vice president, president and past president over the past decades. He has served as the vice president of MedInfo 2019 at International Medical Informatics Association (IMIA) and vice president Europe, and is currently the IMIA Liaison Officer to WHO, Geneva. Within his own country, Weber leads the expert group for Swiss DRG quality control for medical coding and is President of the Oliver Moeschler Foundation leading pre-hospitalization healthcare emergencies. He is EFMI Leader of EU H2020 projects such as CrowdHealth, FAIR4Health and HosmartAI. He is the co-editor of *Nursing Informatics for the 21st Century: An International Look at Practice, Trends and Future*, first and second editions; *Nursing Informatics 2016 eHealth for All: Every Level Collaboration – From Project to Realization*; and *Forecasting Informatics Competencies for Nurses in the Future of Connected Health*. Weber is a founding member of the International Academy of Health Sciences Informatics and a member of the Board of the Swiss Medical Coding Association.

Contributors

Robin Austin, PhD, DNP, DC, RN-BC, FAMIA, FNAP, Assistant Professor, School of Nursing; Graduate Faculty, Earl E. Bakken Center for Spirituality & Healing; Co-director, Omaha System Partnership, University of Minnesota

Cynthia Sherraden Bradley, PhD, RN, CNE, CHSE, Assistant Professor, Director of Simulation, University of Minnesota School of Nursing

Thomas R. Clancy, PhD, MBA, RN, FAAN, Clinical Professor Ad Honorem, University of Minnesota School of Nursing

Joanne Donnelly, DNP, APRN, CRNA, Clinical Assistant Professor and Program Director, Nurse Anesthesia, University of Minnesota School of Nursing

Kathryn J. Hannah, C.M., PhD, DSc(hc), Professor (Adjunct) School of Nursing, University of Victoria

Chun-Kung (Rock) Hsu, MS, IT Department, Taipei Municipal Wan-Fang Hospital

Usman Iqbal, PhD, PharmD, MBA, FAIDH, AFCHSM CHM, Associate Professor, Global Health and Development Department, College of Public Health, Taipei Medical University

Elizabeth A. Krupinski, PhD, FSPIE, FSIIM, FATA, FAIMBE, Department of Radiology & Imaging Sciences, Emory University

Brenda Kulhanek, PhD, MSN, MS, RN-BC, NPD-BC, NE-BC, Vanderbilt University School of Nursing

Yu-Chuan (Jack) Li, PhD, MD, FACMI, FACHI, FIAHSI, Distinguished Professor, Graduate Institute of Biomedical Informatics, College of Medical Science and Technology, Taipei Medical University; Dermatology Department, Wan-Fang Municipal Hospital; President-elect, International Medical Informatics Association (IMIA)

Martin Michalowski, PhD, FAMIA, Assistant Professor, University of Minnesota School of Nursing

Karen A. Monsen, PhD, RN, FAMIA, FNAP, FAAN, Professor, School of Nursing; Director, Center for Nursing Informatics; Director, Omaha System Partnership, University of Minnesota

Lynn M. Nagle, PhD, RN, FAAN, FCAN, Adjunct Professor Faculty of Nursing, University of New Brunswick; Lawrence S. Bloomberg Faculty of Nursing, University of Toronto; Arthur Labatt Family School of Nursing, Western University

Jung In Park, PhD, RN, Assistant Professor, Sue & Bill Gross School of Nursing, University of California, Irvine

Lisiane Pruinelli, PhD, MS, RN, FAMIA, Assistant Professor, School of Nursing and Affiliate Faculty, Institute for Health Informatics, University of Minnesota

Sripriya Rajamani, PhD, MBBS, MPH, FAMIA, Clinical Associate Professor, School of Nursing; Affiliate Faculty, Institute for Health Informatics, University of Minnesota; and Informatics Project Consultant, Minnesota Department of Health

Tracie Risling, PhD, RN, Faculty of Nursing, University of Calgary

Joyce Sensmeier, MS, RN-BC, FHIMSS, FAAN, Senior Advisor, Informatics, HIMSS

Kimberly D. Shea, PhD, RN, FWAN, College of Nursing, University of Arizona

Nellie Munn Swanson, DNP, MPH, APRN, CPNP-PC, Affiliate Faculty, University of Minnesota School of Nursing

Maxim Topaz, PhD, RN, MA, Elizabeth Standish Gill Associate Professor, Columbia School of Nursing Data Science Institute

Peggy White, MN, RN, FCAN, National Project Director, C-HOBIC and Co-Lead, National Nursing Data Standards Initiative

Introduction

As digital health transformation continues to evolve, new technologies and innovations are emerging that will profoundly impact health and care delivery and transform the patient experience. This book describes key innovations in applied informatics and envisions how these new technologies will become an integral part of healthcare over the next decade. In Chapter 1, Sensmeier highlights the top informatics trends including personalized healthcare, telehealth, artificial intelligence, voice technology, predictive analytics and mobile device integration. The state of adoption, potential applications, benefits and challenges for implementation of these advances are explored. The importance of standardized data on making the value of nursing visible is the topic of Chapter 2. White, Nagle, and Hannah describe key strategies and learnings from the implementation of the Canadian Health Outcomes for Better Information and Care (C-HOBIC) initiative across Canada.

Informatics makes it possible to understand whole-person health from the consumer perspective, as outlined in Chapter 3 by Austin, Rajamani, and Monsen. They also highlight studies of consumer-focused technologies such as mHealth, demonstrating numerous benefits to personal and population health. Clancy in Chapter 4 defines the Internet of Things (IoT), proposing that it is enabling the transformation of health systems from a hospital-centric model to patient-centered care through its capacity to provide access anywhere along the continuum of care. Advances in sensor technology, wired and wireless networks and commercial acceptance of standards are also considered as accelerators of the adoption of the IoT.

The Applied Healthcare Data Science Roadmap is presented by Pruinelli and Topaz in Chapter 5 as a framework aiming to educate healthcare leaders on the use of data science principles and tools to inform decision-making. Using this approach gives nurse leaders the roadmap necessary to use real-world data to inform research, teaching and quality improvement and to achieve better patient outcomes. Chapters 6 (Risling), 7 (Michalowski and Park), and 8 (Iqbal, Hsu, and Li) explore aspects of artificial intelligence (AI) while sharing a vision for how this complex technology can become a catalyst for unprecedented transformation in health and care delivery, emphasizing that all nurses should include AI as a priority for professional development. Benefits, cautions and applications of AI are outlined, including a case study from Taiwan of an AI-based model for monitoring pressure ulcer changes in bedridden patients.

Krupinski and Shea in Chapter 9 provide an overview of key telehealth concepts and shares lessons learned during the COVID-19 pandemic that may pave the way toward regulatory and financial support for the future of virtual care. The evolution of simulation-based activities is described in Chapter 10. Bradley, Donnelly, and Swanson highlight examples of how simulation training can strengthen healthcare organizations dedicated to improving patient safety and quality of care. Finally, four successful case studies developed by nurses in response to the COVID-19 pandemic highlight the innovative use of technology to support patients, care providers and the healthcare industry during the global pandemic are described in Chapter 11.

Connie White Delaney
Charlotte A. Weaver
Joyce Sensmeier
Lisiane Pruinelli
Patrick Weber

Chapter 1

Top Informatics Trends for the Next Decade

Joyce Sensmeier

Contents

Introduction 1
Emerging Trends and Nursing's Role 2
Top Informatics Trends for the Next Decade 4
    Personalized Healthcare 4
    Telehealth 5
    Artificial Intelligence 7
    Voice Technology 9
    Predictive Analytics 10
    Mobile Device Integration 11
Conclusion 12
References 12

Introduction

Since the beginning of the COVID-19 pandemic, clinicians and patients have witnessed an astounding degree of digital transformation. From the widespread adoption of telehealth to the rapid advancement of voice technologies, nurses are central to this digital evolution. Today's nurses must embrace and understand technical innovations to stay current and effective in delivering care. Nurses also work in partnership with nurse informaticists at the forefront of the implementation of information technology in healthcare. From its inception, the specialty of nursing informatics has been indispensable for its role in technology assessment and adoption (American Nurses Association, 2015). The nurse informaticist's role includes safeguarding patient safety and minimizing the potential for error that technology can trigger. Optimizing the capabilities of technologies and systems to enhance nursing documentation and improve workflow efficiency are among the critical components of the nurse informaticist role (HIMSS, 2020b). As digital transformation continues to accelerate, it is important for all nurses to be knowledgeable of emerging trends and embrace the positive impact while mitigating the risks. This chapter reviews the top informatics trends for the next decade and details their importance for nurses, including key drivers, benefits and challenges for adoption.

Emerging Trends and Nursing's Role

The innovations experienced over the past decade have been instrumental in preparing us for an increasingly digital future in the way healthcare is managed, experienced and delivered. The ultimate promise of digital transformation is to leverage digital capabilities to achieve improved performance and more importantly, improved outcomes (Adler-Milstein, 2021). Future innovations will have significant value for nurses. These advances may enhance a current process to make it more efficient or streamline documentation through improved automation. Improvements in interoperability will enhance the connectivity of systems and allow us to understand and leverage the deep store of data and information (KLAS Research, 2021). These new capabilities will build evidence that increases our knowledge and understanding of which nursing practices lead to improved health outcomes. This digital transformation holds great promise for enabling nursing practice that can leverage innovation to support and enhance the work of nurses. However, nurses must work in partnership with nurse informaticists to build capabilities that make this transformation beneficial to nursing practice. The future of nursing depends on active engagement and transformational leadership to support a culture of clinical inquiry. Innovative leaders will inspire others to cultivate and apply innovation to achieve a sustained impact on clinical practice and outcomes (Ridge, 2021).

Nurses have an infinite number of day-to-day responsibilities including documentation of patient care, administering medications, procuring supplies and communicating with family and clinical team members

(Scott, 2021). Each of these responsibilities takes time away from patients. Innovative technology can alleviate some of this burden by increasing efficiency, streamlining communications or procuring data from smart devices. Decreasing the documentation burden on clinicians and across healthcare settings is an important priority of professional organizations, government agencies and applied informatics efforts (Collins et al., 2018). Capturing data by using cardiac monitors or smart pumps that are interfaced with the electronic health record (EHR) will free up nurses from cumbersome or duplicative tasks, enabling them to use their knowledge and skills to deliver quality patient care. The disruption caused by the pandemic is also creating new opportunities for the adoption of digital health technologies to transform healthcare delivery (Bannon, 2020). Nurse executives from health systems across the country are now relying on a vast array of digital health tools, driven, in part, by their use during the pandemic (Jercich, 2021).

It is imperative that nurses keep up with the pace of innovation and yet stay true to the art and science of providing care (Carroll, 2021). Given the rapid acceleration of technical innovations, nurses practicing in the coming decade will need to be proficient in using emerging technology. Nursing expertise is essential when designing, analyzing and applying data to ensure health equity using digital platforms and other innovative technologies (National Academy of Medicine, 2021). The demand and significance of knowledge generation to improve nursing and healthcare continue to be urgent (Delaney et al., 2021), and now is the time for nurses to embrace and understand informatics trends to fully engage in the digital evolution.

To address the rapid advances in digital health, the Australian Digital Health Agency has developed the National Nursing and Midwifery Digital Health Capability Framework (Australian Digital Health Agency, 2020), for use as a resource to guide individuals, employers and educators in their workforce and professional development planning and delivery. The Framework 'has been created to:

- define the digital health knowledge, skills and attitudes required for professional practice,
- complement existing individual knowledge, skill and attitudinal frameworks and
- provide a solid basis for tailored learning.'

The Framework represents a central theme of safety and quality in healthcare within the digital healthcare environment and consists of five domains which describe capability statements for nurses and midwives progressing from formative to proficient levels. This resource asserts that technology should be understood and used appropriately by nurses and midwives to deliver safe, quality care. This Framework emphasizes the need for nurses to maintain knowledge in relation to digital health innovations and their use, relevant to their practice.

Top Informatics Trends for the Next Decade

As the digital health landscape evolves, innovation continues to progress as well. This section describes the top informatics trends that are essential for nurses to understand and embrace as we move beyond a primary focus on the EHR, until they are assimilated as foundational to healthcare delivery in the next decade (see Figure 1.1).

Personalized Healthcare

Personalized healthcare leverages genomics, bioinformatics and precision health to tailor healthcare to the individual characteristics of each person. The personalized care model embraces patient engagement and emphasizes long-range planning based on a person's predicted response or risk of disease. To encourage patient and consumer engagement, applications are now widely available to monitor personal health or track physiologic data or physical activity.

Our current healthcare system is experienced at retroactively fighting disease, but often deficient in proactively keeping people healthy. Personalized

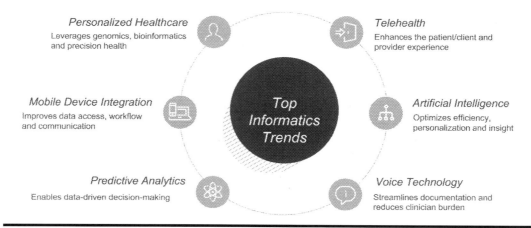

Figure 1.1   Top informatics trends.

healthcare offers a new way of treating patients based on a data-informed understanding of an individual's personal health. According to Hood (2021), 'This is the essence of personalized healthcare—treating each individual according to that person's unique traits.' With the passage into law of the 21st Century Cures Act in 2016, we anticipate that precision health will change the face of healthcare by allowing for personalized disease prevention and treatment (Starkweather et al., 2018).

The research agenda of the National Institute of Nursing Research (NINR) at the National Institutes of Health (NIH) includes a focus on developing personalized strategies to treat individuals with precise interventions and to prevent adverse symptoms of acute and chronic illness across the continuum of care (National Institute of Nursing Research, 2016). This focus area of research, also labeled symptom science, is building evidence-based symptom management strategies assembled on a foundational understanding of the biology of symptoms. By advancing symptom science, NINR promotes the goals of developing and testing new interventions to reduce the disabling effects of symptoms and improve patient health outcomes. The ultimate aim of this field of research is to be able to precisely identify individuals at risk for symptoms and develop targeted strategies to prevent or diminish the severity of symptoms (Dorsey et al., 2019).

As we look ahead toward realizing the opportunity to leverage the benefits of personalized health strategies, potential challenges are considerable. Integrating the necessary information for assessing an individual's predicted response to treatment using today's EHR capabilities will be a daunting task. The system requirements include technologies that can manipulate massive amounts of data integrated into networks of health information (McCormick & Calzone, 2021). Additionally, adequate storage requirements and levels of security, decision support tools, privacy safeguards and big data analytics are each necessary for managing these data to achieve optimal results. However, breaking through these barriers will enable us to realize the ultimate promise of personalized healthcare. To build this new ecosystem, organizations must give individuals ownership and control over their data so that they will have the necessary information to manage their own care (Spence, 2021).

Telehealth

Telehealth is a vehicle for delivering virtual healthcare to provide community-based care and other services for chronic conditions, mental health counseling, in-home patient monitoring and palliative care. Telehealth will enhance the patient/client and provider experience by using a variety of technologies and methods to deliver virtual medical, health and educational services. Growth in the use of telehealth services has enabled access to healthcare that is not limited by time, place or the availability of skilled healthcare professionals. Nursing practice is well-positioned to develop and deliver telehealth services. There is an urgent need for nurses to embrace telehealth services to ensure patients receive the care they need at the optimal place and time (Sensmeier, 2020). And studies have shown that patient satisfaction with virtual visits is comparable to, and in some cases better than, in-person care (Rose et al., 2021).

Telehealth has rapidly become a common delivery method for routine care during the COVID-19 pandemic. Between June 26 through November 6, 2020, over 30% of weekly health center visits occurred via telehealth, according to the Centers for Disease Control and Prevention (CDC) (Demeke et al., 2021). The US Congress temporarily lifted geographic restrictions and enhanced reimbursement so that health centers could expand telehealth services and continue providing care during the pandemic. Sustaining expanded use of telehealth after the pandemic will require continuing the new flexibilities in telehealth services and reimbursement policies. Some providers are signaling a shift to a hybrid care model, which will replace some in-person visits with a combination of both telehealth and in-person visits for services ranging from follow-ups to urgent care (Drees & Dyrda, 2020). As the COVID-19 crisis fades, US healthcare leaders are pushing to preserve the pandemic-fueled expansion of telehealth that has transformed how many Americans visit their providers (Levey, 2021).

The Taskforce on Telehealth Policy was formed to assess early findings under the flexibilities granted by Congress and the Centers for Medicare and Medicaid Services (CMS) during the public health emergency (National Committee for Quality Assurance, 2020). These findings show a positive impact on patient safety from telehealth by preventing care delays, reducing exposure to pathogens and minimizing travel needed for in-person care. Early evidence identified by the Taskforce suggests that the expansion of telehealth has driven a reduction in missed appointments, and the availability of telehealth has not resulted in excess cost or utilization increases, except for behavioral health. To prevent telehealth from adding to the fragmentation and data silos in our healthcare ecosystem, rules and protocols for data sharing and care coordination between telehealth and other care sites should be developed. Safeguards are also needed to prevent fraud, maintain quality and ensure that the shift to virtual care does not leave behind individuals with limited access to technology (Levey, 2021).

Artificial Intelligence

Artificial intelligence (AI) is a collection of technologies that uses complex algorithms and software to emulate human cognition in the analysis, interpretation and understanding of complex healthcare data. AI can enhance the ability for nurses to better grasp the day-to-day patterns and needs of their patients. According to Eric Topol (2019), the promise of AI is to provide a complete, panoramic view of an individual's health information; to improve decision making; to eliminate errors such as misdiagnosis and unnecessary procedures; to assist with ordering and interpreting appropriate tests; and to recommend treatment. Other experts believe that artificial intelligence will transform healthcare through intelligent diagnosis and treatment recommendations, patient communication and care coordination (Davenport & Kalakota, 2019). A recent US Government Accountability Office (GAO) report (2020) highlighted clinical and administrative applications using AI that have shown promise in reducing provider burden and increasing efficiency as shown in Figure 1.2.

One of the most common AI technologies used in healthcare is machine learning—a type of artificial intelligence that enables self-learning from data and then applies that learning without the need for human intervention (Davenport & Kalakota, 2019). Machine learning uses computer algorithms that improve automatically through experience and by the use of data. Rule-based expert systems also use AI technology to provide clinical decision support by constructing a series of rules in a particular knowledge domain. These expert systems require maintenance by human experts

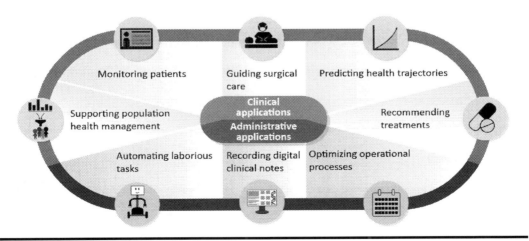

Figure 1.2 Artificial Intelligence clinical and administrative applications.

and knowledge engineers to ensure that they remain current and relevant. Robotics applications leverage AI capabilities including those being used in interventional radiology as well as surgical settings. Advances in cloud computing, big data analytics and artificial intelligence have also led to increased research and development of intelligent surgical robots (Bhandari et al., 2020).

Another promising AI technology is natural language processing (NLP) which is used to help manage and understand large volumes of data (Lareau, 2021). NLP is a useful tool for interpreting and filtering all types of medical text in real time to make the data more useful to clinicians, researchers, payers and other stakeholders at the point of care. Analytics using NLP also allows researchers to gain insights from unstructured text to identify candidates for clinical trials, or more easily assess the efficacy of different treatments. NLP can translate unstructured text into a structured format which can reduce the burden of documentation for clinicians (Juhn & Liu, 2020). Nursing documentation is a valuable source of text-rich clinical information, and NLP offers a sophisticated option that enables the analysis and documentation of EHR data (Douhit et al., 2020).

The Community Health Network in Indiana has begun using AI technology to analyze clinical and social determinants of health data, identifying patients who are overdue for preventative screenings or are experiencing delayed care (Leventhal, 2021). By including social determinants in the analysis, additional barriers to treatment can be identified such as lack of transportation, food insecurity or financial concerns. The hope is that by leveraging these insights, the Community Health Network will be able to better engage with patients to anticipate and address their specific healthcare needs.

The Nursing and Artificial Intelligence Leadership Collaborative (Ronquillo et al., 2021) developed a consensus paper to identify priority areas for action, opportunities and recommendations for the use of AI in nursing. The Collaborative identified the following three priorities that need to be addressed:

- Nurses must understand the relationship between the data they collect and the AI technologies they use.
- Nurses need to be meaningfully involved in all stages of AI, from development to implementation to evaluation.
- There is a substantial untapped and unexplored potential for nursing to contribute to the development of AI technologies for global health and humanitarian efforts.

Given that AI is predicted to transform healthcare, nurses and nurse educators must increase their knowledge and skills to incorporate AI into their practice (Buchanan et al., 2021). AI technologies have the potential to enable nurses to provide more evidence- and data-based personalized care to their patients (Ronquillo et al., 2021). However, AI can also have unintended consequences that result in potential negative impacts including the risk for AI to perpetuate existing human biases into systems. Nurses have a responsibility to advocate for patients to ensure AI is being used safely, ethically and in a manner that positively affects healthcare (Douthit, 2020).

Voice Technology

As digital voice assistants such as Apple's Siri and Amazon's Alexa make inroads in the consumer market, EHR vendors are also incorporating voice technology capabilities into their systems (Drees & Dyrda, 2020). Such ambient listening capabilities enable clinicians to communicate and collaborate completely hands-free, even while performing procedures or physical exams. Communication via ambient listening devices can include making calls, listening to voice messages, responding to events and alerts, or broadcasting to care teams or rapid response teams. The ability to deliver clinical communication in a timely and accurate manner using simple voice commands can increase the efficiency of care team collaboration, reduce the cognitive burden of documentation and improve patient care, safety and experience (Siwicki, 2020).

Secure mobile communication devices can leverage speech recognition capabilities to make documentation easier and less time-consuming. Clinicians are beginning to use speech recognition and NLP technologies for recording digital notes into EHR systems (US Government Accountability Office, 2020). Health systems are evaluating the utility, feasibility and acceptability of speech recognition software to document patient care in an electronic health record (Wolters Kluwer, 2018). Text summarization methods using speech recognition, NLP or other kinds of machine learning can enable documentation support tools to achieve a higher level of automation (US Government Accountability Office, 2020). In a recent survey performed by HIMSS (2020a), one-third of respondents believed that AI-powered speech recognition technology could help reduce documentation burden. Respondents also felt that AI-based documentation solutions made a positive contribution to their work, for example, by improving patient safety, streamlining clinical workflow and simplifying the clinical documentation process.

Predictive Analytics

Predictive analytics is a technology that can be used to predict future outcomes based on historical data using analytics techniques such as statistical modeling and machine learning. The acceleration of digital transformation means more health systems have the technical capabilities to inch closer to benefiting from predictive analytics (Drees & Dyrda, 2020). Some predictive models are in clinical practice today, embedded within EHR software platforms and available in real-time at the point of care (Liu et al., 2019). Today, the use of predictive analytics includes the ability to apply past and current data to reliably forecast trends and behaviors that will occur in the future. These analytic tools yield insights that can help us proactively manage care and patient populations, and keep patients out of the hospital. Predictive analytics can also support specific patient outcomes by personalizing ways to customize treatment based on associated data interrelationships not evident from standard analyses (Bonderud, 2021).

Predictive analytics offers benefits across numerous use cases. By integrating patient records with other health data, providers can detect warning signs of medical events and proactively prevent them, leading to improved patient outcomes (Bonderud, 2021). Predictive tools can also be applied to administrative processes such as medical supply procurement or staffing requirements to help lower overall costs leading to enhanced operations. Accurately scheduling staff to forecasted patient admissions optimizes personnel by matching schedules with patient volume, minimizing cancellations, overtime and last-minute recruitment efforts (Fenush & Barry, 2017). Predictive analytics and the use of a forecasting tool can aid nurse leaders to more accurately match workload to workforce needs and thus, to better support quality patient care delivery.

Advanced computational analysis of healthcare data using predictive analytics can help nurses identify trends using multiple sources of data. For example, predictive analytics can help nurses identify when a patient is experiencing rapid deterioration by sending a warning or risk score based on patient-specific data such as vital signs and lab results in combination with monitoring data from sensors or external devices (Carroll, 2019). By applying predictive models and analyses, nurses can leverage historical, current and simulated future data to identify actionable insights that solve real-world clinical and operational challenges.

Mobile Device Integration

Mobile device integration connects systems and devices to enable seamless data exchange and optimized workflows. This integration helps streamline access to data and can improve the efficiency of business processes. Access to mobile devices such as tablets and pagers enables healthcare staff to securely communicate via email, text, voice and video calling. When used for staff communication, patient education and patient engagement, mobile devices close gaps in communication and improve overall care efficiency. Mobile device integration goes a step further to allow mobile access to EHRs and clinical decision support tools.

Mobile devices are used across nearly every healthcare setting for a variety of purposes. According to a global survey of health IT decision-makers, approximately 90% of healthcare organizations have implemented or are planning to implement some kind of mobile device initiative (Bourne, 2018). Smart versions of common clinical devices such as thermometers, blood pressure cuffs and scales that automatically record readings in the patient record can be used to remotely monitor patients. These apps and devices enable chronic disease patients to manage daily measurements of vital signs such as weight, blood pressure and blood glucose. Readings are visible to patients and this patient-generated data can be transmitted to the physician's office and clinics. Alerts can be generated as appropriate for missing or out-of-range readings.

Mobile device software modules used in conjunction with the EHR or apps that integrate with the EHR to highlight potentially significant changes in patient data (e.g., gain or loss of weight, change in blood chemistry) can also enable clinical decision support. According to a recent survey by the American Medical Association (AMA) (2019), remote care tools are those with the highest likelihood of adoption within the next three years. When asked which digital health tools physicians are most enthusiastic about, remote monitoring tools and telehealth visits are the two that have gained traction since the previous AMA survey in 2016.

Nurses use integrated mobile technology to capture physiological monitoring such as heart rate, sleep patterns and physical activity. In one study using smart sensor technology called *TigerPlace*, data trends were analyzed to detect health changes in elderly, homebound patients (Ward et al., 2020). After one year, the residents with sensors and health alerts showed better health outcomes compared to the control group. In testing over time, the effect of the health alerts was found to be more pronounced where the system was well integrated into the clinical care process and the clinical staff were trained to a high proficiency level.

The trend toward mobile device integration is driving new processes, efficiencies and capabilities. However, to implement mobile tools safely and securely, healthcare organizations must overcome several challenges. If these devices are shared among multiple staff members, they represent a risk for disease transmission, which can be addressed by using anti-microbial device cases, UVC cleaning solutions and thorough cleaning at shift changes (Holloway, 2021). In order to optimize device security, mobile device management solutions offer the ability to deliver devices to users with the necessary software already installed, while ensuring that security configurations meet the organization's needs. These capabilities will allow healthcare organizations to pivot quickly in the face of events such as the COVID-19 pandemic while minimizing the risks of rapid adoption.

Conclusion

Advances in technology and informatics are creating the opportunity to realize a digital health environment that enhances nursing practice and leads to improved health outcomes. Nurses are essential for ensuring that the benefits of this digital transformation are realized and the risks mitigated. By embracing the rapid acceleration of innovative technologies and managing the challenges, nurses will be well equipped to join the digital health evolution of the next decade.

References

Adler-Milstein, J. (2021). From digitization to digital transformation: Policy priorities for closing the gap. *JAMA*, 325(8), pp.717–718 [online]. Available at: https://jamanetwork.com/journals/jama/article-abstract/2776699 (Accessed 7 June 2021).

American Medical Association. (2019). *AMA digital health study, 2019* [online]. Available at: https://www.ama-assn.org/about/research/ama-digital-health-care-2016-2019-study-findings (Accessed 16 July 2021).

American Nurses Association. (2015). *Nursing informatics: Scope and standards of practice*. 2nd ed. [online]. Available at: https://www.nursingworld.org/nurses-books/nursing-informatics-scope-and-standards-of-practice-2nd-ed/ (Accessed 7 June 2021).

Australian Digital Health Agency. (2020). *National nursing and midwifery digital health capability framework*. v1.0, 2020. Sydney, NSW: Australian Government. [online]. Available at: https://www.digitalhealth.gov.au/sites/default/files/2020-11/National_Nursing_and_Midwifery_Digital_Health_Capability_Framework_publication.pdf (Accessed 9 June 2021).

Bannon, M. T. (2020). 8 digital health predictions for 2021. *Forbes.com*, December 23, 2020 [online]. Available at: https://www.forbes.com/sites/marenbannon/2020/12/23/8-digital-health-predictions-for-2021/?sh=1df453434976 (Accessed 7 June 2021).

Bhandari, M., Zeffiro, T., & Reddiboina, M. (2020). Artificial intelligence and robotic surgery: Current perspective and future directions. *Current Opinion in Urology*, 30(1), pp.48–54. https://doi.org/10.1097/MOU.0000000000000692 (Accessed 11 June 2021).

Bonderud, D. (2021). How predictive modeling in healthcare boosts patient care. *HealthTech*, April 16, 2021 [online]. Available at: https://healthtechmagazine.net/article/2021/04/how-predictive-modeling-healthcare-boosts-patient-care-perfcon (Accessed 13 June 2021).

Bourne, V. (2018). *The impact of mobile devices on hospital patient satisfaction* [online]. Available at: https://resources.jamf.com/documents/books/2018-healthcare-survey.pdf (Accessed 18 July 2021).

Buchanan, C., Howitt, M. L., Wilson, R., Booth, R. G., Risling, T., & Bamford, M. (2021). Predicted influences of artificial intelligence on nursing education: Scoping review. *JMIR Nursing*, 4(1), p.e23933 [online]. Available at: https://nursing.jmir.org/2021/1/e23933 (Accessed 11 June 2021).

Carroll, W. M. (2019). The synthesis of nursing knowledge and predictive analytics. *Nursing Management*, 50(3), pp.15–17.

Carroll, W. M. (2021). The future of emerging technologies. In W. M. Carroll, ed., *Emerging technologies for nurses: Implications for practice*. New York: Springer Publishing Company, pp.185–210.

Collins, S., Couture, B., Kang, M. J., Dykes, P., Schnock, K., Knaplund, C., Chang, F., & Cato, K., (2018). Quantifying and visualizing nursing flowsheet documentation burden in acute and critical care. *AMIA Annual Symposium Proceedings*, 2018, pp.348–357 [online]. Available at: https://www.ncbi.nlm.nih.gov/pmc/articles/PMC6371331/ (Accessed 7 June 2021).

Davenport, T., & Kalakota, R. (2019). The potential for artificial intelligence in healthcare. *Future Healthcare Journal*, 2019, 6(2), pp.94–98. https://doi.org/10.7861/futurehosp.6-2-94

Delaney, C. W., Englebright, J., & Clancy, T. (2021). Nursing big data science. *Journal of Nursing Scholarship*, 53(3), pp.259–261.

Demeke, H. B., Merali, S., Marks, S., Pao, L. Z., & Romero, L., Sandhu, P., Clark, H., Clara, A., McDow, K. B., Tindall, E., & Campbell, S. (2021). Trends in use of telehealth among health centers during the COVID-19 pandemic: United States. June 26–November 6, 2020. *Morbidity Mortality Weekly Report*, 70(7), pp.240–244 [online]. Available at: https://www.cdc.gov/mmwr/volumes/70/wr/mm7007a3.htm?s_cid=mm7007a3_w (Accessed 9 June 2021).

Dorsey, S. G., Griffioen, M. A., Renn, C. L., Cashion, A. K., & Colloca, L., Jackson-Cook, C. K., Gill, J., Henderson, W., Kim, H., Joseph, P. V., & Saligan, L. (2019). Working together to advance symptom science in the precision era. *Nursing Research*, 68(2), pp.86–90. https://doi.org/10.1097/NNR.0000000000000339

Douthit, B. J., Hu, X., Richessn, R. L., Kim, H., & Cary, M. P. (2020). How artificial intelligence is transforming the future of nursing. *American Nurse Journal*, 15(9), pp.100–102. Available at: https://www.myamericannurse.com/Digital/Sept_2020_ANJ/#page=103 (Accessed 31 December 2021).

Drees, J., & Dyrda, L. (2020). 10 emerging trends in health IT for 2021. *Becker's Hospital Review*, December 30, 2020 [online]. Available at: https://www.beckershospitalreview.com/healthcare-information-technology/10-emerging-trends-in-health-it-for-2021.html (Accessed 9 June 2021).

Fenush, J., & Barry, R. M. (2017). Predictive analytics empower nurses. *American Nurse Today*, 12(11), pp.26–28.

HIMSS. (2020a). *From overload to burnout: What clinicians think. HIMSS Whitepaper* [online]. Available at: https://www.nuance.com/content/dam/nuance/en_uk/collateral/healthcare/white-paper/wp-from-overload-to-burnout-what-clinicians-think.pdf (Accessed 12 June 2021).

HIMSS. (2020b). *HIMSS nursing informatics workforce survey* [online]. Available at: http://himss.org/ni (Accessed 7 June 2021).

Holloway, C. (2021). How mobile devices are meeting the soaring need for care. *HealthTech*, February 2, 2021 [online] https://healthtechmagazine.net/article/2021/02/how-mobile-devices-are-meeting-soaring-need-care (Accessed 16 July 2021)

Hood, L. (2021). Getting past disease to the science of wellness. *Los Angeles Times*, Sunday, March 21, 2021, A18 [online]. Available at: https://www.latimes.com/opinion/story/2021-03-21/wellness-genome-science-health-chronic-disease (Accessed 9 June 2021).

Jercich, K. (2021). Nursing execs dish on the digital health tools they've found most useful during the pandemic. *Healthcare IT News*, May 12, 2021 [online]. Available at: https://www.healthcareitnews.com/news/nursing-execs-dish-digital-health-tools-theyve-found-most-useful-during-pandemic (Accessed 7 June 2021).

Juhn, Y., & Liu, H. (2020). Artificial intelligence approaches using natural language processing to advance EHR-based clinical research in allergy, asthma, and immunology. *The Journal of Allergy and Clinical Immunology*, 2020 February, 145(2), pp.463–469.

KLAS Research. (2021). *Trends in EMR interoperability. KLAS Research 2021* [online]. Available at: https://chimecentral.org/wp-content/uploads/2021/01/Trends-in-EMR-Interoperability_CHIME_KLAS.pdf (Accessed 8 June 2021).

Lareau, D. (2021). Harnessing healthcare's data explosion with AI-based natural language processing. *Forbes*, June 16, 2021 [online]. Available at: https://www.forbes.com/sites/forbestechcouncil/2021/06/16/harnessing-healthcares-data-explosion-with-ai-based-natural-language-processing/?sh=4d6d1ef35741 (Accessed 15 June 2021).

Leventhal, R. (2021). As patients delay care, one health system turns to AI to identify those at risk. *Healthcare Innovation*, March 17, 2021 [online]. Available at: https://www.hcinnovationgroup.com/analytics-ai/artifical-intelligence-machine-learning/article/21214763/as-patients-delay-care-community-health-network-turns-to-ai-to-identify-those-at-risk (Accessed 17 June 2021).

Levey, N. N. (2021). Covid was a tipping point for telehealth. If some have their way, virtual visits are here to stay. *Kaiser Health News*, June 10, 2021 [online]. Available at: https://khn.org/news/article/covid-was-a-tipping-point-for-telehealth-if-some-have-their-way-virtual-visits-are-here-to-stay/ (Accessed 10 June 2021).

Liu, V. X., Bates, D. W., Wiens, J., & Shah, N. H. (2019). The number needed to benefit: Estimating the value of predictive analytics in healthcare. *JAMIA*, 26(12), pp.1655–1659.

McCormick, K. A., & Calzone, K. A. (2021). Nursing's role in genomics and information technology for precision health. In V. K. Saba, & K. A. McCormick, eds., *Essentials of nursing informatics*. New York: NY McGraw Hill, pp.635–652.

National Academy of Medicine. (2021). *Future of nursing 2020–2030: Charting a path to achieve health equity* [online]. Available at: https://nam.edu/publications/the-future-of-nursing-2020-2030/ (Accessed 26 May 2021).

National Committee for Quality Assurance (2020). *Taskforce on telehealth policy findings and recommendations* [online]. Available at: https://www.ncqa.org/programs/data-and-information-technology/telehealth/taskforce-on-telehealth-policy/taskforce-on-telehealth-policy-ttp-findings-and-recommendations/ (Accessed 9 June 2021).

National Institute of Nursing Research. (2016). *The NINR strategic plan*. Available at: https://www.ninr.nih.gov/sites/files/docs/NINR_StratPlan2016_reduced.pdf (Accessed 9 June 2021).

Ridge, R. A. (2021). Leveraging the nurse scientist role through entrepreneurial innovation. *Nursing Management*, 52(4), pp.32–38.

Ronquillo, C., Pelton, L. M., Pruinelli, L., Chu, C., & Bakken, S., Beduschi, A., Cato, K., Hardiker, N., Junger, A., Michalowski, M., & Nyrup, R. (2021). Artificial intelligence in nursing: Priorities and opportunities from an international invitational think-tank of the Nursing and Artificial Intelligence leadership collaborative. *Journal of Advanced Nursing*, May 18, 2021, pp.1–11 [online]. Available at: https://onlinelibrary.wiley.com/doi/10.1111/jan.14855 (Accessed 11 June 2021).

Rose, S., Hurwitz, H. M., Mercer, M. D., Hizlan, S., Gali, K., Yu, P. C., Franke, C., Martinez, K., Stanton, M., Faiman, M., & Rasmussen, P. (2021). Patient experience in virtual visits hinges on technology and the patient-clinician relationship: A large survey study with open-ended questions. *Journal of Medical Internet Research*, 23(60), p.e18488 [online]. Available at: https://www.jmir.org/2021/6/e18488/ (Accessed 16 July 2021).

Scott, J. (2021). The impact of technology in nursing: Easing day-to-day duties. *HealthTech*, May 12, 2021 [online]. Available at: https://healthtechmagazine.net/article/2021/05/impact-technology-nursing-easing-day-day-duties-perfcon (Accessed 7 June 2021).

Sensmeier, J. (2020). Improving the patient and provider experience through telehealth. *Nursing Management: Safety Solutions*, 51(11), pp.8–15.

Siwicki, B. (2020). Vocera to unveil ambient voice listening tech at HIMSS20. *Healthcare IT News*, February 26, 2020 [online]. Available at: https://www.healthcareitnews.com/news/vocera-unveil-ambient-voice-listening-tech-himss20 (Accessed 12 June 2021).

Spence, P. (2021). Five trends driving the emergence of the personalized health ecosystem. *EY*, April 28, 2020 [online]. Available at: https://www.ey.com/en_us/life-sciences/five-trends-driving-the-emergence-of-the-personalized-health-ecosystem (Accessed 26 July 2021).

Starkweather, A. R., Coleman, B., Mendoza, V. B., Hickey, K. T., Menzies, V., Fu, M. R., Williams, J. K., Prows, C., Wocial, L., O'Keefe, M., & McCormick, K. (2018). Strengthen federal and local policies to advance precision health implementation and nurses' impact on healthcare quality and safety. *Nursing Outlook*, 66, pp.401–406.

Topol, E. (2019). *Deep medicine: How artificial intelligence can make healthcare human again*. New York: New York Hachette Book Group.

U.S. Government Accountability Office. (2020). *Artificial intelligence in health care: Benefits and challenges of technologies to augment patient care*. United States Government Accountability Office, GAO 21–7SP [online]. Available at: https://www.gao.gov/assets/gao-21-7sp.pdf (Accessed 12 June 2021).

Ward, T. M., Skubic, M., Rantz, M., & Vorderstrasse, A. (2020). Human-centered approaches that integrate sensor technology across the lifespan: Opportunities and challenges. *Nursing Outlook*, 68, pp.734–744.

Wolters Kluwer. (2018). The voice of the future? *Health*, January 23, 2018 [online]. Available at: https://www.wolterskluwer.com/en/expert-insights/the-voice-of-the-future (Accessed 18 July 2021).

Chapter 2

Canadian Health Outcomes for Better Information and Care: Making the Value of Nursing Visible through the Use of Standardized Data

Peggy White, Lynn M. Nagle and Kathryn J. Hannah

Contents

Introduction 18
   Nursing in Canada 18
   Value of Nursing Data Standards 19
Canadian Health Outcomes for Better Information and Care
(C-HOBIC) in Canada 20
   Evolution of C-HOBIC 20
   Mapping to ICNP and SNOMED CT 22
   Implementation History of C-HOBIC in Canada 23
      Demonstration Projects 23
      C-HOBIC Transition Synoptic Report 24
      Pilot Project with the Canadian Institute for Health
      Information (CIHI) 24
   Value of Linking the C-HOBIC Dataset with Other National Datasets 26

DOI: 10.4324/9781003281016-2

Lessons Learned..26
    Challenges...26
    Opportunities...27
Where We Are Now?..28
National Nursing Data Standards (NNDS) Initiative 32
    Goals of NNDS..32
Supporting Nursing Practice in the Future..33
Conclusion 34
References 34

Introduction

Nursing in Canada

It is important to recognize that health in Canada is a provincial responsibility not federal. Presently, Canada has more than 439,000 registered nurses, licensed practical nurses, registered psychiatric nurses and nurse practitioners working in a diversity of clinical care settings in every province and territory (CIHI, 2020). As the largest contingent of health professionals, nurses also comprise the largest group of health information system (paper and electronic) users. At the time of this writing, the evolution and use of electronic systems (e.g., electronic health records (EHR)) are varied across the country. As yet, there is little consistency in systems' availability, functionality and design at the regional or provincial levels. In many respects, this variation can be viewed as an opportunity for the nursing profession to ensure that designs include the capability to effectively capture and support the work of nurses. EHRs have introduced the possibility to design standardized approaches to nursing documentation, paving the way for the generation of sharable, comparable data across the continuum of care at every level. However, many healthcare organizations have structured EHRs without considering the inclusion of nursing data standards, such as the Canadian Health Outcomes and Better Information for Care (C-HOBIC). Efforts to broadly advance the adoption of data standards for nursing have been impeded by both the provincial nature of health systems and a lack of appreciation for the value proposition presented by the inclusion of nursing data standards. Perpetuation of unique, organizationally customized EHRs is a missed opportunity for nursing and other health professions, the provincial healthcare systems and Canadians. With information and communications technology (ICT) and digitally connected, health applications transforming the way nurses communicate and document, the integration of data standards is foundational to garner a maximum return for these investments.

The adoption of nursing data standards across Canada has been a three-decade effort. Discussions about minimum nursing datasets and the need for a standardized language to capture nurses' contributions to care delivery first started with the 1992 consensus conference (CNA, 1993) held in Edmonton, Alberta. While there has been progress in achieving consensus on some nursing data standards (e.g., C-HOBIC, LOINC nursing assessment panels), adoption of a comprehensive suite of national nursing data standards is a work in progress.

Value of Nursing Data Standards

For many years, nurse scholars have recognized that the lack of consistency in the information collected by nurses has impeded our capacity to critically and systematically examine those factors that make a difference in the quality of clinical outcomes (Clark & Lang, 1992). Nursing data standards have the potential to make the work of nurses visible; however, there is no easily accessible, concrete evidence that reflects nurses' contributions to the health of Canadians. Moreover, the scientific basis of nursing practice is neither recognized nor appreciated by non-nurses (Sullivan-Marx, 2021). Terminology standards enable structured, codified data that can be stored, aggregated and retrieved for analyses. With these tools, nursing can show the value of their contributions, capture the complexity of nursing practice and build new knowledge.

Additionally, rather than relying on the 'best' available evidence or expertise at hand, nursing practice decisions can be supported by 'practice-based evidence' (Harrington, 2011) (i.e., dynamically generated knowledge derived from standardized clinical documentation). Clinical data standards can also be utilized to align the education of nursing students with the expectations of healthcare organizations. Teaching students to document their practice in accordance with data and practice standards advances this goal.

The COVID-19 pandemic induced a rapid acceleration of virtual care delivery that will likely be sustained in a post-pandemic world, necessitating a heightened level of citizen involvement for the long term. In general, it is evident that citizens are becoming increasingly engaged in the management of their health and being given systems access to contribute health data and information beyond that gathered by clinicians (IPSOS, 2019). Responses to an IPSOS survey (2019) reflected that within 10 years, 77% of Canadians anticipate having access and contributing to their own health records. Additionally, 84% are interested in the ability to access all their health information from one platform, with no difference found across generations (n = 2,005).

The use of comparable, sharable data across clinical care boundaries will also bring consistency to client/family discussions particularly in the face of care transitions from one setting to another.

As an end goal to have nursing data standards used across all care settings, it is important to acknowledge that this requires the synergy of efforts from nursing practice, administration, research, education and health policy. Such widespread use of data standards is foundational to enabling nursing's invaluable contributions to the health of all Canadians, visible and measurable.

Canadian Health Outcomes for Better Information and Care (C-HOBIC) in Canada

Evolution of C-HOBIC

The C-HOBIC program was originally established by the Ontario Ministry of Health and Long-Term Care (OMHLTC) in 1999 as the Nursing and Health Outcomes Project. This initiative was designed to address a shortage of standardized information on patient health outcomes and inadequate information linking patient health outcomes to nursing indicators. In 2004, the project scope was extended beyond nursing to include additional disciplines/interdisciplinary teams. Initially, this extended to pharmacy, physical therapy and occupational therapy in recognition of the interdisciplinary team's contributions to patients' clinical outcomes. With the extension to additional health professionals, the project was renamed Health Outcomes and Better Information for Care (HOBIC).

An expert panel was established to determine which outcomes should be captured and included in databases in Ontario. The process used to identify nurse-sensitive, outcome indicators is well documented elsewhere (Doran, 2003; Hannah et al., 2009). Table 2.1 shows the concepts identified as nurse-sensitive, patient outcomes included in HOBIC and later C-HOBIC (Table 2.1).

The recommended assessment frequency for the HOBIC concepts was on admission and on discharge for all care settings. The one exception was complex, continuing care and long-term care where the HOBIC measures were completed quarterly, or with any significant change in client condition. The Institute for Clinical Evaluative Sciences (ICES, 2021) hosted the resulting database and ensured that it was anonymized and aggregated to make it

Table 2.1 HOBIC Concepts and Measurement Instruments

Concept	Acute Care	Chronic Care	Long-term Care	Home Care
Functional status	interRAI	interRAI	interRAI	interRAI
Continence	interRAI	interRAI	interRAI	interRAI
Therapeutic self-care	Doran et al. (2002)	N/A	N/A	Doran & Sidani tool
Pain—Frequency	interRAI	interRAI	interRAI	interRAI
Pain—Intensity	0–10 numeric	interRAI	interRAI	interRAI
Fatigue	interRAI	interRAI	interRAI	interRAI
Dyspnea	interRAI	interRAI	interRAI	interRAI
Nausea	MOH scale	MOH scale	MOH scale	MOH scale
Falls	interRAI	interRAI	interRAI	interRAI
Pressure ulcers	interRAI	interRAI	interRAI	interRAI

usable by researchers and clinicians for clinical outcomes reports. Each participating site had access to their HOBIC data to utilize in monitoring clinical outcomes. Nurses and managers had the capacity to view the results at the unit or organizational level.

Numerous demonstration projects established the validity and feasibility of collecting these measures. Moreover, the nurses and organizations participating in pilot studies, determined that the collection and monitoring of these measures brought value and support to their clinical practice (Doran et al., 2006). Nurse executives found the information useful in providing insight into care quality. Based on these demonstration projects' success and that of other early adopters, the OMHLTC made a decision to implement the collection of the standardized outcome measures across the province (McGillis Hall et al., 2012; Wodchis et al., 2012; Jeffs et al., 2013; Sun et al., 2014).

Early on, the Canadian Nurses Association (1993) recognized the need for comprehensive, comparable, longitudinal and system-wide health information that focused on the people who are receiving care. Importantly, the Canadian Nurses Association (CNA) highly valued that the HOBIC information could be made available to frontline nurses and clinicians to evaluate their own care quality. As a result, the CNA quickly began to explore opportunities to expand this work across Canada. There was recognition that since

EHRs were to be utilized by nurses and other clinicians, it was important that they contain information of value to clinicians that improved their ability to plan for and evaluate care. Another bonus was that the HOBIC data allowed for sharing clinical information with the interdisciplinary team members.

In 2016, the CNA Board of Directors supported and approved a resolution to advocate for the adoption of C-HOBIC based on the terminology standards of ICNP®, SNOMED CT and LOINC.

Mapping to ICNP and SNOMED CT

The International Classification for Nursing Practice® (ICNP) is the standardized clinical terminology endorsed by the CNA for documenting professional nursing practice in Canada (CNA, 2003, 2016). When C-HOBIC became a national initiative, there was a need to map the C-HOBIC concepts to ICNP®. The result was the C-HOBIC/ICNP® Catalogue published by the International Council of Nurses (ICN), entitled *ICNP Catalogue—Nursing Outcome Indicators* (ICN, 2011). In 2006, Canada Health Infoway (Infoway) approved and adopted Systematized Nomenclature of Medicine—Clinical Terms (SNOMED CT) as the clinical standard to support the EHR and facilitate the building of a pan-Canadian EHR network. Subsequently, the C-HOBIC/ICNP® Catalogue was mapped to SNOMED CT and published by the International Health Terminology Standards Development Organisation (IHTSDO), as the *Technical Report Canadian Health Outcomes for Better Information and Care (C-HOBIC) & SNOMED CT* (IHTSDO, 2013). Thus, nursing data could be included in Canadian EHRs. The approach and methodology for mapping in both cases were similar and are well documented elsewhere (IHTSDO, 2013).

The major deliverable of the mapping activity within the C-HOBIC project was to make it possible for nursing documentation to be included in EHRs as structured, codified data. Further, this work provided an opportunity for Canadian nurses to make substantive contributions to the ongoing development of the standardized clinical terminology for the International Classification for Nursing Practice® (ICNP®) and SNOMED CT.

In 2020, the International Council of Nurses (ICN, 2020) signed an agreement with SNOMED International by which the ICNP is managed, produced, released and distributed by SNOMED International while ICN continues to retain ownership of ICNP and define its content. SNOMED International (formerly International Health Terminology Standards Development Organisation—IHTSDO) incorporated ICNP into its product in the 2021 release and simultaneously continues to make ICNP available as a separate product distributed by SNOMED International from September 2021. Countries that are not SNOMED members and are using ICNP can continue to use ICNP into the future.

Implementation History of C-HOBIC in Canada

Demonstration Projects

In 2006, with funding from Canada Health Infoway (Infoway), CNA partnered with three provinces in Canada to facilitate the inclusion of the C-HOBIC Dataset into their EHRs (Hannah et al., 2009). The collection of these data introduced a systematic, structured collection of patient assessment data, enabling this information to be coded (using standardized clinical terminology), abstracted into jurisdictional EHRs and aggregated to make it available to clinicians across the healthcare systems. And in addition to being formally endorsed by Canada's nursing organizations, the C-HOBIC Dataset won certification as a Canadian Approved Standard in January 2012.

These C-HOBIC demonstration projects focused on increasing clinicians' access to information that was of value to their practice and productivity. A second emphasis was on providing access to information across the care continuum to support continuity and coordination of care for better quality, improved patient satisfaction and effectiveness. Delivering outcome data back to clinicians allowed nurses to know what difference their care made, as well as to evaluate and compare their practice to others. The demonstration projects also contributed to many of Canada's priorities for healthcare renewal at that time including patient safety, collection of outcomes for the home care sector, increased use of information technology and professional accountability. The guiding principles for the demonstration projects were:

- Emphasis on data for which there is empirical evidence that nursing impacts patient care (outcomes).
- Focus on consistent collection of data electronically at the point of care—to provide real-time feedback of information that clinicians can use in planning for and evaluating care.
- Avoid duplication—Integrate C-HOBIC data capture with existing assessments.
- Maximize electronic capture through existing systems—work to build these questions into assessments.

- Provide access to information for nurses, healthcare managers, researchers and ministry planners.
- Work with clinicians regarding the value of these data to their practice.

C-HOBIC Transition Synoptic Report

With funding contributions from Infoway and the Canadian Institute for Health Information (CIHI), the CNA sponsored the development of the C-HOBIC Transition Synoptic Report (TSR). Based on the Rose diagram developed by Florence Nightingale (Nightingale, 1859), the C-HOBIC TSR allowed for a visual comparison of the C-HOBIC clinical data between admission and discharge as shown in Figure 2.1. In addition to showing the improved differences, the visualized comparisons also supported planning for the appropriate care and resources needed to manage ongoing patient care. The TSR summary report displayed normalized admission and discharge scores from the C-HOBIC data to create a 'snapshot' of clinical information (Figure 2.1).

The TSR project occurred in two acute care sites. Initially, the TSR report was to be generated on discharge and shared electronically between sectors to support patient transitions. In Ontario, the C-HOBIC TSR was made available to view and download through a secure web portal. It was available to all healthcare clinicians in one region to support care planning and management as patients transitioned to another care setting. Due to EHR infrastructure limitations in the non-acute care settings, the C-HOBIC TSR was printed on discharge and sent as part of the discharge package. We received strong confirmation that clinicians valued having this information to support care planning. Given the standardization of measures across the continuum, clinicians were able to view a patient's status on admission in relation to activities of daily living (ADL), fatigue and dyspnea and compare it to their discharge status. Subsequently, a primary healthcare provider could then use this information to inform care planning post discharge (C-HOBIC, 2015).

Pilot Project with the Canadian Institute for Health Information (CIHI)

The CIHI mandate includes (1) create and maintain health data and information standards, (2) acquire administrative, financial, statistical and clinical data from across the continuum of care and (3) make these data available for comparability within and across provinces and territories, as well as on

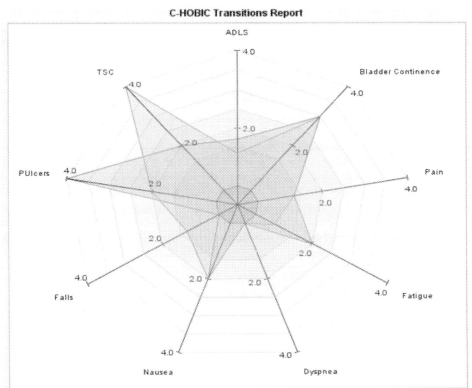

Figure 2.1 C-HOBIC Transition Synoptic Report.

the international stage (CIHI, 2021). In 2013, the CNA and CIHI undertook a pilot project focused on the inclusion of the C-HOBIC dataset in the acute care Discharge Abstract Database (DAD) at CIHI. This joint project's goal was to aggregate standardized, clinical outcomes data from acute care organizations to support outcomes analyses, health system use and performance reporting (CIHI, 2013). The project examined the feasibility, value and utility of including this dataset in the DAD. This was the first time that nursing data was included in the DAD.

Value of Linking the C-HOBIC Dataset with Other National Datasets

Pringle (2010) argued that health services research could be accelerated if databases included clinically relevant information from across all sectors. The use of consistent language and measures provides the capacity to analyze clinical actions and outcomes within and across clinical populations and sectors. When linked with other datasets that are held at CIHI, such as the home care and community care dataset, the consistent capture of standardized clinical outcomes has the potential to support timely research on the quality of care for specific populations and sectors.

Lessons Learned

An evaluation of C-HOBIC demonstration projects was conducted to examine the following:

- Do nurses use C-HOBIC information?
- Are nurses satisfied with C-HOBIC information?
- In what ways has practice changed as a result of C-HOBIC information?

Challenges

For clinicians to be engaged in the EHR, it is key that they can access clinically relevant information at the point of care. This EHR functionality challenges developers to design systems that can be accessed anywhere, such as at the patient's bedside and in the home. This access has to be achieved without multiple log-ons, which often occurs due to a lack of interoperability and integration among clinical systems. As evidenced in the demonstration projects, there is a need to address technical workflow issues that cause barriers and prevent integration with existing data collection systems. While technology aimed at improving patient care coordination has become a priority in healthcare, there is still a lack of evidence on how to ensure success with technology implementations and adoption (McKay & Vanaskie, 2018).

Nurses need to be equipped to integrate technology seamlessly within their workflow. Nurses want better tools to work more safely and efficiently, and that helps them to communicate more effectively with the patient and other healthcare clinicians. More effort needs to be directed to strengthening the processes of information exchange between clinicians across the care continuum and working with clinicians on using clinical data such as C-HOBIC to inform practice.

There is recognition that gaps have existed in what is measured in healthcare and that the focus has been on administrative rather than clinical data (Veillard et al., 2015). With increased pressure on healthcare organizations to improve clinical quality and efficiency, it is important that healthcare organizations realize the benefits of electronic health records by standardizing clinical information (Rhoads & Ferrara, 2012). The C-HOBIC demonstration projects introduced the collection of standardized clinical outcomes at different points in the healthcare continuum—and this accomplishment was a first. Nurses, as with other clinicians, had not had access to real-time, clinical information at the point of care as much of the information was contained in paper-based records. With EHR implementations and the collection of C-HOBIC information, nurses could look at patient status on admission in relation to the C-HOBIC measures of ADLs, symptoms (pain, fatigue, dyspnea, nausea), safety measures (pressure ulcers, falls). All clinicians could now use this information over time to see how a patient was improving and identify needs for further interventions.

Healthcare professionals from the participating provinces cited a lack of understanding of the relationship between patient outcomes and nursing interventions. This lack of connection may be related to the fact that nurses have not had access to outcomes information to be able to see how their practice is impacting the health of the people to whom they provide care. The collection of standardized clinical data at different times throughout the course of care offers the opportunity to support nurses and other clinicians in using outcomes information to identify which practices lead to improved outcomes. As evidenced in this work, ongoing education is needed to support clinicians in seeing the value of collecting standardized clinical data.

Opportunities

Prior to the C-HOBIC project, much of the focus on EHR implementations in Canada had been on laboratory, pharmacy and diagnostics. C-HOBIC changed this by beginning to shift the focus to nurses as end-users. While there is still considerable work to be done in this area, this project provided a start for the inclusion of nursing in discussions about EHRs in Canada. To advance nursing excellence and positive health outcomes, relevant clinical data standards, such as the C-HOBIC dataset, need to be integrated into clinical information systems. Additionally, the data need to be made available to nurses and other clinicians to evaluate outcomes from admission to discharge with the goal of understanding what interventions lead to improved outcomes, as well as supporting transitions of care across the healthcare system.

One of the key learnings from these demonstration projects was that nursing leadership is crucial. Englebright and Caspers (2016) support that nursing leaders need to be effective users of big data technologies to achieve the triple aim of better care, lower cost and greater patient satisfaction. C-HOBIC was successful in organizations where nursing leaders recognized that standardized data are essential for effective, evidence-informed decision-making. These nursing leaders understood the value of balanced scorecard reporting that encompasses financial, patient and staffing measures to support decision-making (e.g., staffing, budgeting, program design, models of care). Standardized data allow nurse leaders to look across the system to better understand the components of operations that drive outcomes. If organizations are measuring the same things in the same way, they can determine where things are working (e.g., new staffing models) and where there are opportunities for improvement (White, 2016).

The assessment of the C-HOBIC information at admission can start the conversation regarding patient issues related to discharge planning. And the assessment of this essential dataset on discharge allows for patients to verbalize their anxieties regarding managing their care at home, when to resume normal activities and what to watch for as danger signs. Ongoing collection of this information at a unit and/or organizational level provides data for monitoring, identifying quality improvement initiatives and information to set and evaluate measurable goals. Assessing these outcomes regularly and comparing unit to unit or organization to organization has the potential to further advance safe quality care. At an aggregate level, this information can be useful to policymakers in examining how well the system is performing in meeting the needs of people within the healthcare system. After all, at the end of the day, that is the ultimate desired outcome.

Where We Are Now?

While there is considerable interest in implementing C-HOBIC within healthcare organizations in Canada, nursing leaders continue to grapple with appreciating the value of standardized clinical data both within their organizations and across the healthcare system. Furthermore, as organizations have implemented new clinical information systems, they have often deferred to vendors and the information within their systems without an analysis of what information nursing should be assessing to inform their practice. Much of this is related to Chief Nurse Executives' lack of understanding of 'what to ask for' as systems are implemented, however, we are seeing stories of interest and success across Canada as shown in these following three case studies.

CASE STUDY 2.1 ALBERTA HEALTH SERVICES CORPORATE APPROACH TO INCLUDING STANDARDS

Debbie Pinter, Executive Director, Provincial Clinical Guidance & Content Management Program, Alberta Health System

Alberta Health Services (AHS) is Canada's first and largest province-wide, fully integrated health system, responsible for delivering health services to nearly 4.4 million people living in Alberta. The implementation of an integrated Clinical Information System (CIS) across primary and ambulatory care, inpatient settings and continuing care is one of the most ambitious healthcare transformation projects in Canada. The CIS will provide nurses with a central access point to patient information, common clinical data standards and evidence-informed clinical guidance at point of care to support decision-making.

The CIS was the incentive for Registered Nurses, Registered Psychiatric Nurses and Licensed Practical Nurses from different care settings and clinical specialties to make provincial decisions in unison. The value of the work is seen through standardized admission, transition and daily care documentation. Common screening tools were implemented with prompts to prevent risk and harm. Reduced burden of documentation was achieved through standardized core and specialty datasets for physical assessment. Evidence-informed care plans customized to patient need with associated teaching materials were endorsed to support family- and patient-centered care. This standardization was done in a short time with inclusion and support from professional associations to ensure the scope of practice for nurses was maximized. Countless hours were spent reviewing metrics to embed into dashboards and reports for evaluation. However, the information provided was less about the improvement of health outcomes and focused more on system usage and adherence to documentation norms. Key challenges were experienced when trying to identify which indicators were the right ones to support quality improvement. This continues to be an ongoing challenge; however, with experience at using in-system CIS reporting tools and increased understanding of what is important to measure, the barriers to establishing a robust analytics and measurement strategy are removed.

In the history of AHS, there has been no other similar effort that has actively supported nurses to lead and drive their own data standardization. Outcomes from this project are strong nursing leadership and governance with mature clinical informatics skills to innovate and make improvements. The heavy lifting of establishing the clinical data standards has been done and the future opportunity is seen with evaluating the effectiveness of standards on care and making refinements as needed. True success will be seen when nurses can use data provided to them for self-reflection of one's practice and to use the data to improve care, health outcomes and patient safety.

CASE STUDY 2.2 VANCOUVER COASTAL HEALTH BUILDS STANDARDS INTO AN EHR

Lorraine Blackburn, Vice President Professional Practice & Chief Clinical Information Officer

Vancouver Coastal Health is a regional health authority within British Columbia, Canada serving 25% of the province's population (1.25 million) providing a wide range of primary, secondary and specialized services. We are currently in the midst of our Clinical and Systems Transformation (CST) project with two partner organizations. The goal is more than the introduction of a common electronic health record: it is transforming care through standardizing clinical processes and utilizing the information and knowledge we can harness from the system to improve care. During the initial build phases of our project, the system's three Chief Nursing Officers collectively advocated for the inclusion of C-HOBIC. They recognized the value of having standardized nurse-sensitive patient outcome data across our three organizations, driving care decisions at the client level and at the broader unit and health system level.

Incorporating C-HOBIC within our EHR was not without its challenges. The key challenge is standardizing the admission and discharge process across three distinct health organizations to consistently capture the

C-HOBIC data elements. Policies and clinical standards were created and implemented, supported by consistent education. In addition, our selected EHR vendor came with pre-built content. In order to prevent duplicity and documentation burden for nurses, we undertook a data mapping exercise during our design sessions to remove unnecessary or repetitive assessment elements for nursing.

We are still on our journey with our foundational EHR implementations but see the promise of integrating these data with other sources to make the impact of nursing care visible and to provide valuable insights into our processes and improvement efforts. Having nurse-sensitive patient outcome data, in addition to the other metrics we monitor, can help us evaluate the impact of care model decisions. Moreover, nurse-sensitive patient outcome data will allow us to focus quality improvement initiatives in areas where outcomes are not meeting established targets. Our next focus will be embedding C-HOBIC language within a standardized discharge process.

CASE STUDY 2.3 HEALTH PRINCE EDWARD ISLAND USING C-HOBIC DATA TO SUPPORT CLINICAL DECISION-MAKING

Marion Dowling, Chief Nursing, Allied Health & Patient Experience, Health Prince Edward Island and Dorothy Dewar, Nurse Research Lead Professional Practice, Quality & Patient Experience, Chief Nursing Office, Health Prince Edward Island

Health PEI is responsible for the delivery of publicly funded health services in Prince Edward Island. The organization operates hospitals, health centers, public long-term care nursing facilities and community-based programs and services. An electronic Clinical Information System has been implemented across all hospitals including order entry, documentation, lab and pharmacy systems. The acute care record is viewable by healthcare clinicians in all other service areas.

Health PEI identified quality improvements toward reporting how nursing care information will be collected and used to measure performance, inform practice improvement and maximize patient outcomes. The improvements were also intended to quantitatively capture the impact of nursing care on patient health outcomes.

> *Leveraging the electronic system and using the standardized C-HOBIC assessment with reportable, validated and reliable measures supported the quality improvements desired by Health PEI. The integration of C-HOBIC assessments provides nurses the ability to monitor patient progress over time, develop treatment and care plans and evaluate patient interventions. C-HOBIC provided nurses information about individual patient needs and problems requiring intervention at admission and prior to discharge. Documenting C-HOBIC in an electronic system provides the ability to report outcome data between admission and discharge at the unit or facility level. Patient data captured over time will identify quality improvement opportunities for these individual units/service areas and the health authority. Reported admission data identifies the percentage of patients admitted to a unit with specific nursing intervention requirements, thus reflecting the intensity of nursing work and the education requirements associated with the unit's patient population.*
>
> **KEY CHALLENGES WITH EHR**
>
> *Within our large hospitals, patient movement among units presented a challenge to manage comparison data when reporting C-HOBIC admission and discharge assessments. Nursing staff complete the admission assessment in one unit and the discharge assessment is completed on a different unit. This results in data gaps when comparing admission and discharge data at the unit level. The C-HOBIC build within our Clinical Information System was new and we did a local build of our content, forms and workflows. When building and presenting data and reports, we learned to consider staff input and engagement. This was key to ensure nurses at the patient's side understood the results and how to use the data. These efforts are ongoing as our implementation began across all hospitals in the beginning of 2020.*

National Nursing Data Standards (NNDS) Initiative

Goals of NNDS

To advance the uptake and clinical data standards in Canada, the National Nursing Data Standards (NNDS) initiative was established by the CNA in 2016 (Canadian Nurses Association, 2016) with a focus on developing short-term objectives and action plans to promote the adoption of national nursing data standards (White, 2016). Beginning in 2016, yearly symposia have been held with nursing and healthcare leaders, vendors, government representatives, and stakeholder organizations (e.g., CIHI, CNA, Infoway, Canadian Patient Safety Institute, Accreditation Canada) from across Canada to discuss the need for and the benefits to be derived from the adoption of national nursing clinical data standards. Funding was provided by CNA, CIHI, Canada Health Infoway and the vendor community. There was recognition that the adoption of national data standards will:

- allow for consistent monitoring of outcomes across the continuum of care, thereby facilitating safe, quality care and the continuity of care;
- enable national, peer-group comparability, providing both macro and micro insights to guide decision-making and inform funding requirements and health human-resource planning; and
- improve population health by enabling individuals to use consistently named, defined and measured clinical outcomes data to understand and manage illness and improve the health of patients.

To advance this national standards work, we have established active Working Groups in the following areas: policy, clinical practice, administration, education and research.

Symposia proceedings (Nagle & White, 2016; Canadian Nurses Association, n.d.b) and information regarding the NNDS Working Groups (Canadian Nurses Association, n.d.a), are available at: https://www.cna-aiic.ca/en/nursing-practice/the-practice-of-nursing/nursing-informatics

Supporting Nursing Practice in the Future

Clinical information systems provide a platform for the generation of new nursing knowledge, or 'clinical intelligence' as described by Harrington (2011). The realm of 'practice-based evidence' suggests that new insights and understandings about the efficacy of nursing care will emerge with the ubiquitous use of online documentation tools by nurses. However, raising the profile of nurses' contributions to health outcomes in all clinical settings will only be realized with the adoption of data standards that transcend boundaries of care (e.g., from primary to acute care, acute care to long-term care). Based on standards, new knowledge can be generated dynamically and made usable with data mining tools. As depicted in Figure 2.2, these data have the potential to inform healthcare policies and nursing decisions that extend from an individual to national level.

Standardized Data – Collected Once, Used for Many Purposes

National
Comparative disease incidence, prevalence, & trends, resource utilization
Data Collected, Abstracted, Aggregated, Analyzed
→ Health Policy
Legislation
Research

Regional/Jurisdictional
Disease incidence & prevalence, outcomes, cost of care, resource utilization
Data Collected, Abstracted, Aggregated, Analyzed
→ Health Policy
Legislation
Health System Performance
Funding
Public Reporting
Research

Organization/Sector
Case volumes, outcomes, cost of care, resource utilization
Data Collected, Abstracted, Aggregated, Analyzed
→ Safety & Quality
Resource Management
Funding
Accreditation
Public Reporting
Research

Individual/CMG
Assessments, interventions, outcomes, provider, hours of care, adverse events, cost of care
→ Safety & Quality
Accountability
Outcomes
Evidence

Nagle & White, 2015

Figure 2.2 C-HOBIC Transitions Report.

Conclusion

The C-HOBIC experience has been a journey of discovery and learning to the benefit of Canadian nursing. The challenges and opportunities have impelled leaders to explore a variety of different strategies to influence the uptake and adoption of nursing data standards. The key learnings to this point underscore the importance of nursing leadership and persistence in conveying the value for nursing practice, the healthcare system at large and for citizens in particular. The realization of nursing data standards in use across all care settings will require the synergy of efforts from all nursing domains and has the potential to make nursing's invaluable contributions to the health of all Canadians, visible and measurable.

References

Canadian Association of Schools of Nursing. (2012). https://www.casn.ca/2014/12/casn-entry-practice-nursing-informatics-competencies/

Canadian Institute for Health Information. (2013). *C-HOBIC information sheet* Available at: https://www.cihi.ca/sites/default/files/document/c-hobic-infosheet-en.pdf (Accessed 25 May 2021).

Canadian Institute for Health Information. (2020). *Nursing in Canada. 2019: A lens on supply and workforce.* Available at: https://www.cihi.ca/sites/default/files/document/nursing-report-2019-en-web.pdf (Accessed 14 May 2021).

Canadian Institute for Health Information. (2021). Canadian Institute for Health Information. Available at: https://www.cihi.ca/en/about-cihi (Accessed 25 May 2021).

Canadian Nurses Association. (1993). Papers from the Nursing Minimum Data Set Conference, October 27-29, 1992, Ottawa: Canadian Nurses Association.

Canadian Nurses Association (2016) Board resolution. Available at: https://hl-prod-ca-oc-download.s3-ca-central-1.amazonaws.com/CNA/2f975e7e-4a40-45ca-863c-5ebf0a138d5e/UploadedImages/documents/Nursing_informatics_joint_position_statement.pdf (Accessed 2 February 2022).

Canadian Nurses Association. (n.d.a). https://www.cna-aiic.ca/en/nursing-practice/the-practice-of-nursing/nursing-informatics

Canadian Nurses Association (n.d.b). *NNDS symposium proceedings.* Available at: https://www.cna-aiic.ca/en/nursing-practice/the-practice-of-nursing/nursing-informatics

C-HOBIC. (2015). Available at: https://www.cna-aiic.ca/-/media/cna/page-content/pdf-en/2015jan_chobic-phase2-final-report.pdf?la=en&hash=F857EFEFDB59BDE71130CAE5BA713DEAE45DC724 (Accessed 25 May 2021).

Clark, J., & Lang, N. (1992). Nursing's next advance: An international classification for nursing practice. *International Journal of Nursing,* 39(4), pp.102–112.

Doran, D. M., ed. (2003). *Nursing-sensitive outcomes: State of the science.* Sudbury, MA: Jones & Bartlett.

Doran, I., Sidani, S., Keatings, M., & Doidge, D. (2002). An empirical test of the nursing role effectiveness model. *Journal of Advance Nursing,* 38(1), pp.29–39.

Doran, D., Harrison, M., Spence-Laschinger, H., Hirdes J, Rukholm, E., Sidani, S., McGillis-Hall, L., & Tourangeau, A. (2006). Nursing sensitive outcomes data collection in acute care and long-term care settings. *Nursing Research,* 55(2S Supplement), pp.S75–S81.

Englebright, J., & Caspers, B. (2016). The role of the chief nurse executive in the big data revolution. *Nurse Leader,* August 2016, pp.280–284. https://doi.org/10.1016/j.mnl.2016.01.001

Hannah, K. J., White, P. A., Nagle, L. M., & Pringle, D. M. (2009). Standardizing nursing information in Canada for inclusion in electronic health records: C-HOBIC. *Journal of the American Medical Informatics Association,* 16, pp.524–530. https://doi.org/10.1197/jamia.M2974.

Harrington, L. (2011). Clinical intelligence. *Journal of Nursing Administration,* 41(12), pp.507–509.

IHTSDO. (2013). *Canadian health outcomes for better information and care (C-HOBIC) & SNOMED CT technical report.*

Institute for Clinical Evaluative Sciences (ICES). Available at: https://www.ices.on.ca/About-ICES/Mission-vision-and-values (Accessed 24 May 2021).

interRAI. Instruments. (2021). Available at https://www.interrai.org/instruments/ (Accessed 24 May 2021).

International Council of Nurses. (2011). *Nursing outcome indicators catalogue.* Available at: icn.ch/what-we-doprojectsehealth-icnptm/about-icnp/icnp-catalogues (Accessed 24 May 24 2021).

International Council of Nurses. (2020). *Press release.* Available at: icn.ch/news/international-council-nurses-and-snomed-sign-ground-breaking-agreement-secure-bright-future (Accessed 24 May 2021).

IPSOS. (2019). Canadians optimistic over the role technology will play in the health care system of the future. *Factum*, August 8, 2020. Retrieved May 18, 2021 from: https://www.ipsos.com/en-ca/news-polls/The-Future-Of-Connected-Health-Care

Jeffs, l., Jiang, D., Wilson, G., Ferris, E., Cardiff, B., Lancetta, M., White, P., & Pringle, D. (2013). Linking HOBIC measures with length of stay and alternate levels of care: Implications for nurse leaders in their efforts to improve patient flow and quality of care. *Nursing Leadership*, 25(4), pp.58–62.

McGillis Hall, L., Wodchis, W. P., Ma, X., & Johnson, S. (2013). Changes in patient health outcomes from admission to discharge in acute care. *Journal of Nursing Care Quality*, Jan–Mar; 28(1), pp.8–16. https://doi.org/10.1097/NCQ.0b013e3182665dab

McKay, C., & Vanaskie, K. (2018). Partnering for success: The role of the nurse leader in health information technology implementation for coordination of care. *Nurse Leader*, 16(6), pp.385–388. https://doi.org/10.1016/j.mnl.2018.07.012

Nagle, L. M., & White, P. (2016). *National nursing data standards symposium proceedings.* Available at: https://www.cna-aiic.ca/-/media/cna/page-content/pdf-en/national-nursing-data-standards-symposium-proceedings-report.pdf?la=en&hash=31EF0680A6F504001CE3203FAA94B008B758CD77 (Accessed 27 May 2021).

Nightingale, F. (1859). *A Contribution to the sanitary history of the british army during the late war with Russia.* London, UK: J. W. Parker.

Pringle, D. M. (2010). Database development: A major need and challenge to accelerate health services research. In C. M. Flood, ed., *Data data everywhere: Access and accountability?* Montreal and Kingston: Queen's Policy Studies Series, McGill-Queen's University Press. The School of Policy Studies, Queen's University at Kingston.

Rhoads, J., & L. Ferrara. (2012). Transforming healthcare through better use of data. *Electronic Healthcare*, 11(1), pp.e25–e31.

Sullivan-Marx, E. (2021). Nurses are scientists too. *Scientific American*, 27 April 2021. Available at: https://www.scientificamerican.com/article/nurses-are-also-scientists/. (Accessed 12 May 2021).

Sun, W., & Doran, D. (2014). Understanding the relationship between therapeutic self-care and adverse events for the geriatric home care clients in Canada. *JAGS*, 62(supp 1), pp.1–7.

Veillard, J., Fekri, O., Dhalla, I., & Klazinga, N. (2015). Measuring outcomes in the Canadian health sector: Driving better value from healthcare. Retrieved 8 April 2021. www.cdhowe.org/ public-policy-research/measuring-outcomes-canadian-health-sector-driving-better-value-healthcare.

White, P. (2016). The case for standardized data in nursing. *Nursing Leadership*, 28(4), pp.29–35.

Wodchis, W. P., McGillis Hall, L., & Quigley, L. (2012). Increasing patient self care to avoid acute care readmissions. In Unpublished data presented at the HOBIC Symposium: Demonstrating Value with HOBIC Data, Toronto, ON.

Chapter 3

Consumer-Generated Whole-Person Health Data: A Structured Approach

Robin Austin, Sripriya Rajamani and Karen A. Monsen

Contents

Consumers and Health Information Technology 40
    Health Literacy, eHealth Literacy and mHealth 40
Standardized, Interoperable Consumer-Generated Health Data 41
Knowledge Representation and Interoperability 41
Whole-Person Health 42
    Development of Simplified Omaha System Terms 46
MyStrengths+MyHealth™ (MSMH) 46
    Research Using MyStrengths+MyHealth App and SOST 48
        Women with Circulation Signs and Symptoms 48
        Older Adults 50
        Clinical Conversations 50
        Exploring Resilience 53
        Expansion of MSMH Using Social Media Studies and
        Community-Engaged Research 53
    International Collaboration 53
Conclusion 54
References 54

DOI: 10.4324/9781003281016-3

Consumers and Health Information Technology

Consumers increasingly depend on health information technology to access, store and use health data (Lai et al., 2017a; Faiola & Holden, 2017). In this chapter, we refer to consumers as individuals who directly interact with the healthcare system either in person and through various digital technologies. Consumer-focused technologies are digital technologies such as mobile health (mHealth) applications (apps) which are increasingly used as a platform by consumers for personal health monitoring and management (Faiola & Holden, 2017; Rowland et al., 2020). MHealth apps refer to digital technology that is accessed via a mobile device such as a smartphone or tablet (Peiris et al., 2018; Rowland et al., 2020). MHealth apps are growing in popularity to collect data on individuals and have been shown to help empower persons with highly complex health needs to self-manage their health (Fox & Duggan, 2013; Fox et al., 2013). The use of mHealth apps often generates similarly diverse and complex data streams, also called consumer-generated health data (CGHD). Studies of consumer-focused technologies including mHealth apps have shown numerous benefits to personal and population health, such as increased access to care, increased control over personal health information, reduced barriers to care and assisted self-management behaviors (Martínez-Pérez et al., 2013; Goyal et al., 2016; Ernsting et al., 2017; Garner et al., 2018; Wildenbos et al., 2019). Given these benefits, scholars assert that CGHD have the potential to transform healthcare and population health (Lai et al., 2017; Hsueh et al., 2017). These benefits will not accrue unless consumers have sufficient health literacy and eHealth literacy to engage meaningfully with mHealth apps.

Health Literacy, eHealth Literacy and mHealth

Health literacy is defined as 'the degree to which an individual has the capacity to obtain, communicate, process, and understand basic health information and services to make appropriate health decisions' (French, Health and Practice, 2014; US Department of Health and Human Services Office of Disease Prevention and Health Promotion, 2020). The importance of addressing health literacy cannot be overstated in the quest to achieve health equity. In the United States, only 12% of adults have proficient health literacy skills (Kutner et al., 2007). Approximately, half of the US adult population has a literacy level below that of the 8th grade, and 4th-grade text is difficult to comprehend for one in five US adults (Cutilli & Bennett, 2009). Further, eHealth literacy is defined as the ability to seek, find, understand and appraise health information from electronic sources and apply the knowledge gained to address or solve a health problem (Norman & Skinner, 2006). Both health literacy and eHealth literacy are needed to achieve the expected and desired goals of mHealth apps to improve personal health.

A majority of mHealth apps are written at a 12th-grade reading level, compared to the average reading level in the United States which is 6th grade (Weiss, 2003; Broderick et al., 2014; Reliability, 2016; Schultz et al., 2017). Scholars suggest that mHealth apps may aid patients in communicating about health with both clinicians and researchers to improve patient self-management and to gain an understanding of factors that support self-management (Jacobs et al., 2003; Green et al., 2012; Baek et al., 2014; Clark et al., 2014). However, simple, plain language validated with consumers is needed as the foundation for mHealth apps to achieve improved communication and desired health behaviors and outcomes.

Standardized, Interoperable Consumer-Generated Health Data

The value of and capacity for exchanging CGHD to support interprofessional and holistic care has yet to be fully realized (Holt et al., 2020; Tiase et al., 2020). It has been shown that when patients are able to contribute to their own health data in a clinical encounter, they are more likely to be engaged in their care, participate in healthcare decision-making and experience improved patient-provider relationships (Hull, 2015; Reading & Merrill, 2018).

However, often CGHD are missing (not recorded), buried (not retrievable) or hidden/invisible (recorded in free text or using customized, non-standard menus) (Lai et al., 2017; Hsueh et al., 2017). Rigorous informatics methods, such as use of a standardized terminology for knowledge representation, may seamlessly integrate CGHD into the broader informatics infrastructure and learning health system through such channels as electronic health record patient portals, personal health records and wearable devices (He et al., 2017).

Knowledge Representation and Interoperability

Data standards refer to the structure and organization of data. Standards are agreed-upon methods for connecting systems together and may pertain to security, data transport, data format or structure or the meanings of codes or terms (Office of National Coordinator, 2020). Data standards support interoperability and information exchange, which is the ability to exchange and share data across platforms. Unstructured data such as free text and other raw data such as images or sensor data are difficult or impossible to model and interpret (Raghupathi & Raghupathi, 2014; Hanna & Stedman, 2021). Conversely, the use of rigorous knowledge representation and interoperability standards and processes to generate data within health information technology is thought to improve direct patient care, population health management and healthcare quality (American Health Information Management Association (AHIMA), 2013).

In order to generate robust and rigorous CGHD, it is essential to use data standards that enable knowledge representation of meaningful health concepts from the consumer's perspective (Mandel et al., 2016). Standardized nursing terminologies (SNT) recognized by the American Nurses Association (Table 3.1) have been developed over several decades to capture a broad range of health diagnoses or problems.

Use of SNTs to capture the consumer perspective has been successful because the terminology's concepts, terms and definitions have been developed using rigorous informatics methods to ensure meaning to interprofessional users, nurses and consumers. Such data enable advanced theory-based and exploratory analyses of relevant clinical questions such as intervention effectiveness, healthcare quality and population health outcomes. These SNT data elements may also be transformed to operationally define and represent more complex concepts such as health literacy (Monsen et al., 2017a; Michalowski et al., 2018; Monsen et al., 2018).

In addition to knowledge representation structures such as SNTs, supportive consumer-friendly technologies and a robust documentation infrastructure are needed to enable data capture. New consumer-facing approaches are needed to capture the consumer voice, support patients to be active participants in their own care and provide tools that can enable active communication to discuss meaningful health concepts (Mirkovic et al., 2016; Monsen et al., 2017b). Conversely, a lack of clinical representation of patient values, health goals and consumer-generated health plans integrated into CGHD can hinder health providers from offering sensitive and individualized self-management support for patients (Rosenbloom, 2016; Woods et al., 2016).

Whole-Person Health

Whole-person health is multidimensional and complex; it is multifaceted and has bio-psycho-social-spiritual elements including strengths, challenges and

Table 3.1 American Nurses Association-Recognized Nursing Terminologies

Terminology	Nursing items from the Nursing Minimum Data Set (NMDS)		
	Nursing problem	Nursing intervention	Nursing outcome
Nursing terminologies			
NANDA International (1992) (NANDA International, 2011)	X		
Nursing Intervention Classification (NIC) (1992) (Butcher et al., n.d.)		X	
Nursing Outcomes Classification (NOC) (1997) (Moorhead et al., 2018)			X
Clinical Care Classification (CCC) (1992) (Saba, 2006)	X	X	X
Perioperative Nursing Data Set (PNDS) (1997) (AORN, 2020)	X	X	X
International Classification for Nursing Practice (ICNP) (2000) (Coenen and Bartz, 2010)	X	X	X
Interdisciplinary Terminologies			
Systematized Nomenclature of Medicine-Clinical Terms (SNOMED-CT) (1999) (SNOMED-CT, 2019)	X	X	
SNOMED-CT Nursing Subset (2017) (National Institute of Health United States National Library of Medicine, n.d.)	X	X	
Logical Observation Identifiers Names and Codes LOINC (2002) (Regenstrief Institute, 2020)	X		X
Omaha System (1992) (Martin, 2005)	X	X	X

needs across environmental, psychosocial, physiological and health-related behaviors domains (Martin, 2005; Sminkey, 2015). Whole-person health may be influenced by determinants of health including health literacy and environmental, political and moral societal factors (Carter et al., 2015; Sterling et al., 2018; Berwick, 2020). There is a need for standardized terminologies to capture and represent all multidimensional aspects of whole-person health as CGHD in mHealth apps (Monsen et al., 2015; Austin et al., 2021a).

The range of personal, social, economic and environmental factors that influence health either positively or negatively are known as *determinants of health*. It is the interrelationships among these factors and one's genetic endowment that determine individual and population health (US Department of Health and Human Services (HHS), 2021). The negative influences on health stem from health inequity, structural racism, low health literacy and health disparities, among others. These related concepts are powerful determinants of health for many populations and individuals (World Health Organization (WHO), 2008; US Department of Health and Human Services (HHS), 2021).

Scholars have attempted to illuminate the complex aspects of the positive aspects of health often described interchangeably as strengths, assets or resilience; both at individual and community levels (Amil et al., 2017; Arevian et al., 2018). A person's strengths have been shown to be protective against negative determinants of health (Lundman et al., 2012; Fuller & Huseth-Zosel, 2020). Resilience is a person's ability to persevere, heal and transform in the face of challenges, setbacks and conflicts; the ability to bounce back when challenged by serious illness and other crises that can arise in life (Caldeira & Timmins, 2016). Strengths, assets and resilience may be operationalized, classified and measured as skills, capacities, actions, talents, potential and gifts of the individual, each family member, the family as a whole, and/or the community (Miles et al., 2006; Rotegaard & Ruland, 2010; Dingley & Roux, 2014).

Whole-person knowledge representation attends to the breadth of health and captures strengths as well as challenges and needs (Monsen et al., 2014; Sminkey, 2015; Austin et al., 2021a). Rigorous knowledge representation science is necessary to derive meaningful information, which can be used to generate whole-person health knowledge. Likewise, this new knowledge can offer insights into clinical practices and improve population health. To provide adequate representation of whole-person health is to answer the ontology question: what are the aspects of whole-person health that exist or can exist and what are the relationships between them?

Using a simple ontology to characterize whole-person health and healthcare has several benefits. First, characterizing all of health and healthcare in a simple ontology creates a knowable information model for information management for clinicians and researchers alike. Second, comprehending the whole leads to the identification of gaps in existing data that may be critical for understanding the whole. The siloes in healthcare research and practice can be diminished by providing shared language to bring clarity regarding the meanings of concepts and relationships as operationalized in clinical decision support, documentation and research (Reed, 1997; Martin, 2005; Matney et al., 2011). One such ontology is a multidisciplinary SNT recognized by the American Nurses Association (2012): the Omaha System (Figure 3.1).

The Omaha System enables a whole-person health assessment that identifies individuals' strengths as well as typical physiological health assessments, including the challenges brought about by experiencing negative social and behavioral determinants of health (Miles et al., 2006; McLeod, 2015; Sminkey, 2015). The Omaha System also enables the representation of a whole-person approach to care, which addresses the needs of the individual as well as treating the disease such as mental health or psychosocial needs and physical symptoms. It seeks to reduce negative impacts of social and behavioral determinants of health and leverage strengths to increase an individual's ability to engage in their own care (Miles et al., 2006; McLeod, 2015; Sminkey, 2015).

The Omaha System exists in the public domain, is embedded within SNOMED-CT and is available through the Unified Medical Language System (UMLS) (Martin, 2005). The Omaha System concepts represent all of health

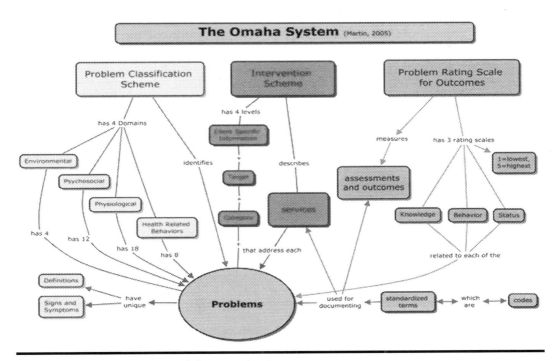

Figure 3.1 Concept map of the Omaha System.

in four domains: environmental, psychosocial, physiological and health-related behaviors (Martin, 2005). An operational definition of whole-person health means understanding all of health across all Omaha System concepts and domains; inclusive of strengths (Problem Rating Scale for Outcomes Status scores), challenges (signs/symptoms of the 42 problem concepts) and needs (intervention category terms) (Martin, 2005; Austin, 2018). It may be used to operationalize many theoretical concepts, including resilience; i.e., the number of strengths for problem concepts having a Status score of 4 [minimal signs/symptoms ('good')] or a 5 [no signs/symptoms ('very good'")] (Austin et al., 2021a; Monsen et al., 2021a).

Development of Simplified Omaha System Terms

The Omaha System was intended for multidisciplinary use since its inception; however, an analysis of the readability of Omaha System terms showed a 16th-grade reading level. MHealth app design guidelines recommend that apps should include plain language, appeal to diverse users and undergo iterative testing and revisions throughout the design process (Broderick et al., 2014). Despite these guidelines, most mHealth apps do not use plain language, or text that is easy to read and understand and that can appeal to a wide range of individuals (Broderick et al., 2014). Plain Language, a federal initiative, recommends use of plain language to enhance writing, particularly health terminology, so it is clear, concise and accessible to all abilities (Plain Language.gov, n.d.; The National Academies Press, 2015; Agency for Healthcare Research and Quality, 2017). Therefore, plain simplified language is needed in mHealth apps to improve accessibility for a broad range of end-users. Consequently, the Omaha System was translated into consumer-facing Simplified Omaha System Terms (SOST) in a multi-method, multi-phase process to accommodate a broad range of potential end-users, while retaining the rigor of standardization, classification and ontological aspects of the Omaha System including the ability to represent whole-person health using community-validated at the 5th-grade reading level (Figure 3.2).

MyStrengths+MyHealth™ (MSMH)

The web-based mobile-enhanced app called MyStrengths+MyHealth (MSMH) was developed to enable consumers to conduct a comprehensive,

Omaha System	MyStrengths+MyHealth
Environmental	**My Living**
Income	Income
Santiation	Cleaning
Residence	Home
NeighborshoodWorkplace safety	Safe at work and home
Psychosocial	**My Mind and Networks**
Communication with community resources	Connecting
Social contact	Socializing
Role change	Role change
Interpersonal relationship	Relationships
Spirituality	Spirituality or faith
Grief	Grief or loss
Mental health	Emotions
Sexuality	Sexuality
Caretaking/parenting	Caretaking
Neglect	Neglect
Abuse	Abuse
Growth and development	Growth and development
Physiological	**My Body**
Hearing	Hearing
Vision	Vision
Speech and language	Communication
Oral health	Oral health
Cognition	Thinking
Pain	Pain
Consciousness	Consciousness
Skin	Skin
Neuro-musculo-skeletal function	Moving
Respiration	Breathing
Circulation	Circulation
Digestion-hydration	Digesting
Bowel function	Bowel function
Urinary function	Kidneys and bladder
Reproductive function	Reproductive health
Pregnancy	Pregnancy
Postpartum	Postpartum
Communicable/infectious condition	Infections
Health-related Behaviors	**My Self-Care**
Nutrition	Nutrition
Sleep and rest patterns	Sleeping
Physical activity	Exercising
Personal care	Personal care
Substance use	Substance use
Family planning	Family planning
Health care supervision	Health care
Medication regimen	Medications

Figure 3.2 Omaha System terms and Simplified Omaha System terms.

whole-person health assessment and generate useful CGHD using SOST (Austin, 2018; Austin et al., 2021a; Monsen et al., 2021a, b). Thus, MSMH retained the rigor of the Omaha System while providing a robust consumer-friendly platform for whole-person health assessments. MSMH is a person-centered comprehensive assessment that enables individuals to self-report strengths, challenges and needs, including social and behavioral determinants of health influences; thus providing a more complete picture of an individual's health and the factors that influence their health. MSMH operationalizes physical health in 18 Physiological Domain concepts along with their signs/symptoms (challenges); and the determinants of health as the concepts and signs/symptoms in Environmental (My Living, N = 4), Psychosocial (My Mind and Networks, N = 12), Physiological (My Body, N = 18) and Health-related Behaviors Domains (My Self-care, N = 8) (Martin, 2005; Monsen et al., 2017b) (Figure 3.3).

Research Using MyStrengths+MyHealth App and SOST

CGHD generated in a number of studies using MyStrengths+MyHealth have enabled exploration of whole-person health of various populations (e.g., women with *Circulation* problems, older adults) using data-driven methods (e.g., data visualization and correlational analysis for pattern detection). Several examples are provided below.

Women with Circulation Signs and Symptoms

De-identified CGHD (n = 383) were utilized to identify women with *Circulation* signs/symptoms (n = 80), who were matched to an equal number of women without *Circulation* signs/symptoms. Visualizing strengths, challenges and needs of both groups using heat maps, patterns were detected and nine hypotheses were generated, of which four were supported. Findings revealed that women with *Circulation* signs/symptoms (compared to women without *Circulation* signs/symptoms) had more strengths, and also more challenges and needs (Figure 3.4); i.e., strengths in *Connecting*; challenges in *Emotions*, *Vision* and *Healthcare*; and needs related to *Info and Guidance* (p = 0.044). Such whole-person health findings have interesting implications and provide an important new perspective for consumers, clinicians and researchers alike.

Consumer-Generated Whole-Person Health Data ■ 49

My Living	My Mind & Networks	My Body		My Self-care
Income	Connecting	Hearing	Breathing	Nutrition
Cleaning	Socializing	Vision	Circulation	Sleeping
Home	Role change	Speech and language	Digestion	Exercising
Safe at home and work	Relationships	Oral health	Bowel function	Personal care
	Spirituality or faith	Thinking	Kidneys or bladder	Substance use
	Emotions	Pain	Reproductive health	Family planning
	Sexuality	Consciousness	Pregnancy	Health care
	Caretaking	Skin	Postpartum	Medications
	Neglect	Moving	Infections	
	Abuse			
	Growth and development			

Figure 3.3 MyStrengths+MyHealth domains and concepts.

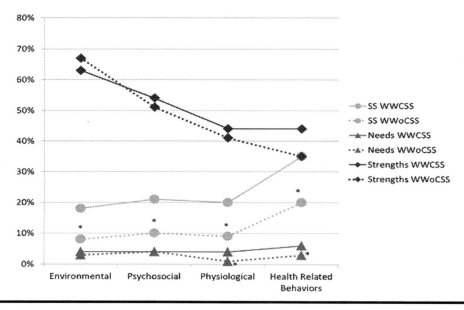

Figure 3.4 Strengths, challenges and needs by domain for women with and without *Circulation* signs/symptoms.

Older Adults

From a sample of de-identified CGHD (N = 345), adults 65 and older were identified (n = 76). Analysis showed that these older adults had more strengths than challenges, and more challenges than needs ($p < 0.001$). Strengths and challenges were correlated ($p < 0.001$), as were challenges and needs ($p < 0.001$). Those that reported a large number of strengths (21–30) had significantly more needs ($p = 0.04$), suggesting possible high patient engagement for this group. These analyses support the need for further research regarding patient engagement and whole-person health to inform the care of older adults (Figure 3.5).

Clinical Conversations

A community-based study testing MSMH data entry and reports illustrated the potential to use MSMH as a platform and common language for providers and patients around SBDH and whole-person health and to begin conversations about ways to leverage strengths to mitigate challenges. The reuse of data in reports and visualizations was well received by community members, suggesting there may be value of SOST data to enhance care planning for older adults and healthcare teams (Monsen et al., 2021) (Figure 3.6).

Consumer-Generated Whole-Person Health Data ■ 51

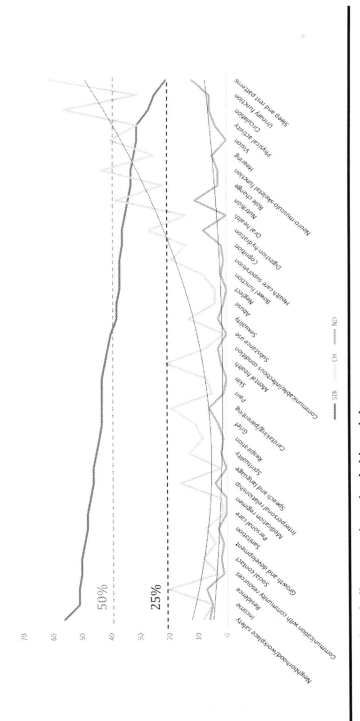

Figure 3.5 Strengths, challenges and needs of older adults.

Domain	Strengths	Challenges	Needs
My Living 25.00% Strengths 5 challenges 5 needs	Strengths: Cleaning	Safe at home and work: violence Home: needs a lot of repairs, no heat or cooling Income: not enough income, too many health care bills	Info / Guidance: Safe at home and work, Home Hands-on Care: Home, Income Care Coordination: Income
My Mind & Networks 25.00% Strengths 6 challenges 6 needs	Strengths: Connecting Relationships Caretaking	Grief or loss: hard to cope with my grief or loss Emotions: very sad, hopeless, fearful, tired Abuse: verbal abuse, others criticize me all the time	Check-ins: Grief or loss, Emotions Info / Guidance: Socializing, Emotions, Abuse Hands-on Care: Emotions
My Body 16.67% Strengths 10 challenges 8 needs	Strengths: Moving Vision Hearing	Digesting: upset stomach, heart burn or reflux Moving: weak muscles, tight muscles, hard to walk Pain: having pain Breathing: hard to breathe, need a breathing machine, cough Circulation: blood pressure is too high or too low	Check-ins: Breathing Info / Guidance: Moving, Pain, Breathing, Circulation Hands-on Care: Digesting, Circulation Care Coordination: Digesting
My Self-Care 25.00% Strengths 11 challenges 13 needs	Strengths: Medications Personal care	Health care: get health care only when I am sick Substance use: take over the counter or prescription drugs more than I should, use alcohol too much Nutrition: over weight, eat too much, unbalanced diet, eating times not on schedule, high blood sugar Sleeping: wake up a lot at night Exercising: lack of exercise, hard to exercise like I need to	Check-ins: Substance use, Nutrition Info / Guidance: Health care, Substance use, Medications, Nutrition, Sleeping, Exercising Hands-on Care: Health care, Medications, Nutrition, Exercising Care Coordination: Nutrition

Figure 3.6 MyStrengths+MyHealth Report example.

Exploring Resilience

To explore resilience in the context of whole-person health and the social determinants of health at the individual and community levels using a combination of three large, standardized nursing datasets, we conducted a retrospective, observational, correlational study of existing de-identified HIPAA-compliant clinical Omaha System data and MSMH data. We operationalized resilience as Omaha System Status scores of 4 or 5 as a discrete strengths measure. There were fewer strengths by problem in the clinical and COVID-19 data compared to the pre-COVID-19 community data. For community, an average of 77% of the sample self-reported a given concept as a strength, ranging from *Sleep and rest patterns* (30%) to *Pregnancy* (99%). For clinical, an average of 68% of the sample had a given concept documented as a strength, from *Grief* (14%) to *Spirituality* (95%). Thus, it was feasible to examine and compare resilience within existing clinical and MSMH data. Visualizing correlations within the data, we identified several patterns indicating strengths and resilience that were consistent with literature related to community *Connecting* for community participants, and with *Sleep and rest patterns* for individuals in the clinical data (Austin et al., 2021c).

Expansion of MSMH Using Social Media Studies and Community-Engaged Research

Virtual outreach was conducted in a study of strengths, challenges and needs in the community during the COVID-19 pandemic using social media messaging via Facebook, Instagram, LinkedIn, Twitter, emails, WhatsApp and ResearchMatch. Despite the pandemic, participants (N = 339) had more strengths (13.6 ± 4.7) than challenges (11.8 ± 6.6) or needs (9.4 ± 8.6), although fewer strengths were found compared to previous studies (Austin et al., 2021b). The most frequently identified strength was *Safe at home and work* (84.3%). In contrast to previous studies, the *Income* concept was never identified as a strength in this study, demonstrating the impact of the pandemic on this important determinant of health.

International Collaboration

MSMH and SOST have been translated into numerous world languages and employed in research projects internationally. An MSMH International

Research Collaboration has been established within the Center for Nursing Informatics at the University of Minnesota to create a global health community to develop and exchange ideas, develop research partnerships and share resources in an effort to build sustainable methods to examine individual and community resilience using a standardized informatics method via MSMH to generate actionable data. This research program aligns with international organizations' efforts to build health resilience through partnerships and collaboration (Amil et al., 2017; USAID, 2021).

Conclusion

Consumer documentation of whole-person health including strengths is feasible using the Omaha System, when simplified and embedded in a consumer-facing app. MyStrengths+MyHealth generated CGHD that was useful to clinicians in having a better understanding of each person's health and priorities, empowering consumers to recognize and use their strengths and aided communities to make decisions about programs. Furthermore, use of the Omaha System within MSMH provides the ability to collect structured mHealth data and enable integration into existing EHRs and PHRs to enable whole-person big data research in health. The rigorous approach used in MSMH development and research should be replicated with other standards, datasets, populations and programs in order to advance the use of CGHD and whole-person health data to transform healthcare.

References

Agency for Healthcare Research and Quality. (2017). *AHRQ health literacy universal precautions toolkit.* Available at: https://www.ahrq.gov/health-literacy/improve/precautions/index.html (Accessed 12 April 2021).

American Health Information Management Association (AHIMA). (2013). *Data standards, data quality & interoperability.* Available at: http://library.ahima.org/doc?oid=107104#.WH_e661abwB

American Nurses Association (2012). *ANA Recognized Terminologies that Support Nursing Practice.* Silver Spring, Maryland: The American Nurses Association, Inc.

Amil, B. et al. (2017). *Strengthening resilience: A priority shared by health 2020 and the sustainable development goals.* Available at: https://onlinelibrary.wiley.com/doi/abs/10.1111/cjag.12228%0A

AORN. (2020). *Perioperative nursing data set (PNDS)*. Available at: https://www.aorn.org/education/individuals/continuing-education/online-courses/introduction-to-pnds (Accessed 16 January 2020).

Arevian, A. C. et al. (2018). Participatory technology development to enhance community resilience. *Ethnicity and Disease*, 28, pp.493–502. https://doi.org/10.18865/ed.28.S2.493

Austin, R. R. (2018). *Picturing patterns in whole-person health: Leveraging visualization techniques with structured consumer-generated mHealth data.* University of Minnesota, School of Nursing. Available at: https://conservancy.umn.edu/handle/11299/202216

Austin, R. R., Monsen, K., & Alexander, S. (2021a). Capturing whole-person health data using mobile applications. *Clinical Nurse Specialist*, 35(1), pp.14–17. https://doi.org/10.1097/nur.0000000000000572

Austin, R. R. et al. (2021b). Assessing whole-person health using mystrengths+myhealth during COVID-19: A virtual community outreach case study. In NI 2020 International Congress, Melbourne.

Austin, R. R. et al. (2021c). Understanding women's cardiovascular health using mystrengths+myhealth: A patient-generated data visualization study of strengths, challenges, and needs differences. *Journal of Nursing Scholarship*, (Cvd), 53(5), pp.634–642. https://doi.org/10.1111/jnu.12674

Baek, R. N., Tanenbaum, M. L., & Gonzalez, J. S. (2014). Diabetes burden and diabetes distress: The buffering effect of social support. *Annals of Behavioral Medicine*, 48(2), pp.145–155. https://doi.org/10.1007/s12160-013-9585-4

Berwick, D. M. (2020). The moral determinants of health. *JAMA: Journal of the American Medical Association*, 324(3), pp.225–226.

Broderick, J. et al. (2014). Designing health literate mobile apps. pp.1–12. Available at: http://www.iom.edu/Global/Perspectives/2014/HealthLiterateApps.aspx

Butcher, H. et al. (n.d.). *Nursing Interventions classifications (NIC)*. 7th ed. St. Louis, MO: Elsevier.

Caldeira, S., & Timmins, F. (2016). Resilience: Synthesis of concept analyses and contribution to nursing classifications. *International Nursing Review*, 63(2), pp.191–199.

Carter, J. et al. (2015). Assessing the whole person: Case managers take a holistic approach to physical and mental health. *Professional Case Management*, 20(3), pp.140–146. https://doi.org/10.1097/NCM.0000000000000087

Clark, N. M. et al. (2014). Heart disease management by women: Does intervention format matter? *Health Education and Behavior*, 41(5), pp.518–527. https://doi.org/10.1177/1090198114547516

Coenen, A., & Bartz, C. (2010). ICNP: Nursing terminology to improve health care worldwide. In *Nursing and informatics for the 21st century: An international look at practice, education, and EHR trends*. 2nd ed. Chicago, IL: HIMSS, pp.207–216.

Cutilli, C. C., & Bennett, I. M. (2009). Understanding the health literacy of America: Results of the national assessment of adult literacy. *Orthopaedic Nursing*, 28(1), pp.27–32. https://doi.org/10.1097/01.NOR.0000345852.22122.d6

Dingley, C., & Roux, G. (2014). The role of inner strength in quality of life and self-management in women survivors of cancer. *Research in Nursing and Health*, 37(1), pp.32–41. https://doi.org/10.1002/nur.21579

Ernsting, C. et al. (2017). Using smartphones and health apps to change and manage health behaviors: A population-based survey. *Journal of Medical Internet Research*, 19(4), pp.1–12. https://doi.org/10.2196/jmir.6838

Faiola, A., & Holden, R. J. (2017). Consumer health informatics: Empowering healthy-living-seekers through mHealth. *Progress in Cardiovascular Diseases*. Elsevier Inc., 59(5), pp.479–486. https://doi.org/10.1016/j.pcad.2016.12.006

Fox, S., & Duggan, M. (2013). *Health online 2013*. Available at: https://www.pewresearch.org/internet/2013/01/15/health-online-2013-2/

Fox, S., Duggan, M., & Purcell, K. (2013). *Family caregivers are wired for health*. Washington, DC: Pew Research Center. Available at: https://www.pewinternet.org/2013/06/20/family-caregivers-are-wired-for-health/

French, M. G., Health, P., & Practice, P. H. (2014). *Health literacy and numeracy*. Washington, DC: National Academies Press.

Fuller, H. R., & Huseth-Zosel, A. (2020). Lessons in resilience: Initial coping among older adults during the COVID-19 pandemic. *The Gerontologist*, 61(1), pp.114–125. https://doi.org/10.1093/geront/gnaa170

Garner, S. L., Sudia, T., & Rachaprolu, S. (2018). Smart phone accessibility and mHealth use in a limited resource setting. *International Journal of Nursing Practice*, 24(1), pp.1–5. https://doi.org/10.1111/ijn.12609

Goyal, S. et al. (2016). Uptake of a consumer-focused mHealth application for the assessment and prevention of heart disease: The <30 days study. *JMIR mHealth and uHealth*, 4(1), p.e32. https://doi.org/10.2196/mhealth.4730

Green, J. K., Rothman, R. L., & Cavanaugh, K. L. (2012). Patient-provider communication in patients with diabetes and depressive symptoms. *Diabetes Research and Clinical Practice*. Elsevier Ireland Ltd, 95(1), pp.e10–e13. https://doi.org/10.1016/j.diabres.2011.09.024

Hanna, K. T., & Stedman, C. (2021). *What is unstructured data? Search business analytics*. Available at: https://searchbusinessanalytics.techtarget.com/definition/unstructured-data (Accessed 10 September 2021).

He, Z. et al. (2017). Enriching consumer health vocabulary through mining a social Q&A site: A similarity-based approach. *Journal Biomedical Informatics*, 69(1), pp.75–85. https://doi.org/10.1016/j.jbi.2017.03.016

Holt, J. M. et al. (2020). Incorporating patient-generated contextual data into care: Clinician perspectives using the Consolidated Framework for Implementation Science. *Healthcare*. Elsevier Inc., 8(1), p.100369. https://doi.org/10.1016/j.hjdsi.2019.100369

Hsueh, P.-Y. et al. (2017). Added value from secondary use of person generated health data in consumer health informatics. *IMIA Yearbook*, 26(1), pp.1–12. https://doi.org/10.15265/IY-2017-009

Hull, S. (2015). Patient-generated health data foundation for personalized collaborative care. *CIN: Computers Informatics Nursing*, 33(5), pp.177–180. https://doi.org/10.1097/CIN.0000000000000159

Jacobs, E. A. et al. (2003). *Language barriers in health care settings: An annotated bibliography of the research literature.* The California Endowment, (August). Available at: https://ncihc.memberclicks.net/assets/documents/cal.endow.bibliography.pdf

Kutner, M. et al. (2007). *Literacy in everyday life: Results from the 2003 national assessment of adult literacy.* NCES 2007–490. National Center for Education Statistics.

Lai, A. et al. (2017a). Present and future trends in consumer health informatics and patient generated health data. *Yearbook of Medical Informatics* 26(1), pp.152–159. https://doi.org/10.1055/s-0037-1606497

Lai, A. M. et al. (2017b). Present and future trends in consumer health informatics and patient-generated health data. *Yearbook of Medical Informatics*, 26(1), pp.152–159. https://doi.org/10.15265/IY-2017-016

Lundman, B. et al. (2012). Inner strength in relation to functional status, disease, living arrangements, and social relationships among people aged 85 years and older. *Geriatric Nursing*, 33(3), pp.167–176. https://doi.org/10.1016/j.gerinurse.2011.11.001

Mandel, J. C. et al. (2016). SMART on FHIR: A standards-based, interoperable apps platform for electronic health records. *Journal of the American Medical Informatics Association*, 23(5), pp.899–908. https://doi.org/10.1093/jamia/ocv189

Martin, K. (2005). *The Omaha system: A key to practice. Documentation and information management.* 2nd ed. Omaha, NE: Health Connections Press.

Martínez-Pérez, B. et al. (2013). Mobile apps in cardiology: Review. *Journal of Medical Internet Research*, 15(7), pp.1–15. https://doi.org/10.2196/mhealth.2737

Matney, S. et al. (2011). Philosophical approaches to the nursing informatics data-information-knowledge-wisdom framework. *Advanced Nursing Science*, 34(1), pp.6–18.

McLeod, T. C. V. (2015). Addressing psychological concerns to practice whole-person health care. *Journal of Athletic Training*, 50(3), pp.229–230. https://doi.org/10.4085/1062-6050-50.3.04

Michalowski, M. et al. (2018). Relationships among interventions and health literacy outcomes for sub-populations: A data-driven approach. *Kontakt*, 20(4), pp.e319–e325. https://doi.org/10.1016/j.kontakt.2018.10.009

Miles, P. et al. (2006). *The wraparound process user's guide: A handbook for families.* Portland, OR: National Wraparound Initiative, Research and Training Center on Family Support and Children's Mental Health, Portland State University.

Mirkovic, J. et al. (2016). Patient insights into the design of technology to support a strengths-based approach to health care. *JMIR Research Protocols*, 5(3), p.e175. https://doi.org/10.2196/resprot.5906

Monsen, K. A. et al. (2014). Seeing the whole person: Feasibility of using the Omaha system to describe strengths of older adults with chronic illness. *Research and Theory for Nursing Practice*, 28(4), pp.299–315. https://doi.org/10.1891/1541-6577.28.4.299

Monsen, K. A. et al. (2015). The gap in big data: Getting to wellbeing, strengths, and a whole person perspective. *Global Advances in Health and Medicine*, 4(3), pp.31–39. https://doi.org/https://doi.org/10.7453/gahmj.2015.040

Monsen, K. A. et al. (2017a). Evaluation of the Omaha System Prototype Icons for Global Health Literacy. *Informatics*, 4(2), p.13. https://doi.org/10.3390/informatics4020013

Monsen, K.A et al. (2017b). Care coordination from a strengths perspective: A practice-based evidence evaluation of evidence-based practice. *An International Journal*, 31(1), pp.39–55. https://doi.org/10.1891/1541-6577.31.1.39

Monsen, K. A. et al. (2017c). Social determinants and health disparities associated with outcomes of women of childbearing age who receive public health nurse home visiting services. *JOGNN: Journal of Obstetric, Gynecologic, and Neonatal Nursing*, 46(2), pp.292–303. https://doi.org/10.1016/j.jogn.2016.10.004

Monsen, K. A. et al. (2018). Use of the Omaha system for ontology-based text mining to discover meaning within CaringBridge social media journals. *Kontakt*, 20(3), pp.e210–e216. https://doi.org/10.1016/j.kontakt.2018.03.002

Monsen, K. A. et al. (2021a) Exploring large community- and clinical-generated health datasets to understand resilience before and during COVID-19 pandemic. *Journal of Nursing Scholarship*, 5(3), pp.262–269. https://doi.org/10.1111/jnu.12634

Monsen, K. A. et al. (2021b). Incorporating a whole-person perspective in consumer-generated data. *CIN: Computers, Informatics, Nursing*, Publish Ah(0), pp.1–9. https://doi.org/10.1097/cin.0000000000000730

Moorhead, S. et al. (2018). *Nursing outcomes classification (NOC): Measurement of health outcomes*. 6th ed. St. Louis, MO: Elsevier.

NANDA-International. (2011). *Nursing diagnoses: Definitions and classification*. 9th ed. New York: Wiley-Blackwell.

National Institute of Health United States National Library of Medicine. (n.d.). *Unified medical language system. Nursing problem list subset of SNOMED CT*. Available at: https://www.nlm.nih.gov/research/umls/Snomed/nursing_problemlist_subset.html.

Norman, C., & Skinner, H. (2006). eHealth literacy: Essential skills for consumer health in a networked world. *Journal of Medical Internet Research*, 8(2), p.e506

Office of National Coordinator. (2020). *Interoperability standards advisory: ONC's resource for industry to reference standards and implementation specifications*. Available at: https://www.healthit.gov/isa/

Peiris, D., Jaime Miranda, J., & Mohr, D. C. (2018). Going beyond killer apps: Building a better mHealth evidence base. *BMJ Global Health*, 3(1), pp.2017–2019. https://doi.org/10.1136/bmjgh-2017-000676

Plain Language.gov. (n.d.). *Plain Language*. Available at: https://www.plainlanguage.gov/ (Accessed 14 April 2021).

Raghupathi, W., & Raghupathi, V. (2014). Big data analytics in healthcare: Promise and potential. *Health Information Science and Systems*, 2(1), p.3. https://doi.org/10.1186/2047-2501-2-3

Reading, M. J., & Merrill, J. A. (2018). Converging and diverging needs between patients and providers who are collecting and using patient-generated health data: An integrative review. *Journal of the American Medical Informatics Association*, 25(6), pp.759–771. https://doi.org/10.1093/jamia/ocy006

Reed, P. (1997). Nursing: The ontology of the discipline. *Nursing Science Quarterly*, 10(2), pp.76–9.

Regenstrief Institute, I. (2020). *LOINC*. Available at: https://loinc.org/ (Accessed 2 February 2020).

Reliability, T. (2016). *HHS Public Access*, 33(4), pp.150–156. https://doi.org/10.1097/CIN.0000000000000146.Testing

Rosenbloom, T. S. (2016). Person-generated health and wellness data for health care. *Journal of the American Medical Informatics Association*, 23(3), pp.438–439. https://doi.org/10.1093/jamia/ocw059

Rotegaard, A. K., & Ruland, C. M. (2010). Patient centeredness in terminologies: coverage of health assets concepts in the International Classification of Nursing Practice. *Journal of Biomedical Informatics*, Elsevier Inc., 43(5), pp.805–811. https://doi.org/10.1016/j.jbi.2010.04.010

Rowland, S. P. et al. (2020). What is the clinical value of mHealth for patients? *NPJ Digital Medicine*, Springer US, 3(1), pp.1–6. https://doi.org/10.1038/s41746-019-0206-x

Saba, V. (2006). *Clinical Care Classification (CCC) System Manual: A guide to nursing documentation*. New York: Springer Publishing Company.

Schultz, P. L. et al. (2017). Evaluating the use of plain language in a cancer clinical trial website/app. *Journal of Cancer Education*, 32(4), pp.707–713. https://doi.org/10.1007/s13187-016-0994-5

Sminkey, P. V. (2015). The "whole-Person" approach : Understanding the connection between physical and mental health. *Professional Case Management*, 20(3), pp.154–155. https://doi.org/10.1097/NCM.0000000000000094

SNOMED CT. (2019). *Content development*. Available at: https://confluence.ihtsdotools.org/display/DOCSTART/9.+Content+Development (Accessed 1 March 2020).

Sterling, S. et al. (2018). Association of behavioral health factors and social determinants of health with high and persistently high healthcare costs. *Preventive Medicine Reports*, Elsevier, 11(May), pp.154–159. https://doi.org/10.1016/j.pmedr.2018.06.017

The National Academies Press. (2015). *Health literacy and consumer-facing technology, health literacy and consumer-facing technology*. https://doi.org/10.17226/21781

Tiase, V. L. et al. (2020). Patient-generated health data and electronic health record integration: a scoping review. *JAMIA Open*, 3(4), pp.619–627. https://doi.org/10.1093/jamiaopen/ooaa052

U.S. Department of Health and Human Services (2020). *Health literacy in healthy people. healthy people 2030*. Washington, DC: U.S. Department of Health and Human Services. Available at: https://health.gov/our-work/healthy-people-2030/about-healthy-people-2030/health-literacy-healthy-people (Accessed 4 November 2020).

U.S. Department of Health and Human Services. (2021). *Healthy people 2030, office of disease prevention and health promotion.* Washington, DC: U.S. Department of Health and Human Services. Available at: https://health.gov/healthypeople (Accessed 18 October 2021)

USAID. (2021). *Blueprint for global health resilience.* Washington, DC.: USAID.

Weiss, B. (2003). *Health literacy: A manual for clinicians.* Chicago, IL: American Medical Association, American Medical Foundation.

Wildenbos, G. A., et al. (2019). Mobile health for older adult patients: Using an aging barriers framework to classify usability problems. *International Journal of Medical Informatics*, Elsevier, 124(September 2018), pp.68–77. https://doi.org/10.1016/j.ijmedinf.2019.01.006

Woods, S. S., Evans, N. C., & Frisbee, K. L. (2016). Integrating patient voices into health information for self-care and patient-clinician partnerships: Veterans Affairs design recommendations for patient-generated data applications. *Journal of the American Medical Informatics Association*, 23(3), pp.491–495. https://doi.org/10.1093/jamia/ocv199

World Health Organization (WHO). (2008). *Commission on social determinants of health. Closing the gap in a generation: Health equity through action on the social determinants of health.* Available at: http://apps.who.int/iris/bitstream/handle/10665/69832/WHO_IER_CSDH_08.1_eng.pdf;jsessionid=F8617EFD2035F2A76713433B2D8ED811?sequence=1 (Accessed 10 September 2021).

Chapter 4

Sensors and the Internet of Things

Thomas R. Clancy

Contents

Introduction 61
The Building Blocks of the IoT 62
    Sensors 62
    Networks 65
    Standards 66
The Information Value Loop 67
The Current State of the IoT and Nursing Practice 69
    Inpatient Nursing 69
    Outpatient Nursing 72
    The Future of the IoT 77
Conclusion 77
References 79

Introduction

A number of technological advances are creating a perfect storm that will result in improved quality of care, lowered costs, increased access to care and better value for healthcare consumers (Clancy, 2020a, b). Exponential improvements in microchip processing speed, digital storage capacity, sensor technology, device miniaturization, software design and wireless networks are creating new opportunities to combine and analyze data. Sensors worn

DOI: 10.4324/9781003281016-4

or implanted in patients, medical devices, cell phones and other technologies can capture and send digital data to clinical repositories where analytics software can support and augment provider decision-making. Taken as individual devices, these advances clearly benefit providers; however, even greater value is achieved if these devices are connected and share data. This is already happening as the ongoing build-out of the Internet, improved interoperability and the adoption of industry standards all contribute to greater connectivity. This emerging ecosystem of connected devices that share data is called the Internet of Things (Merriam-Webster Dictionary, n.d.)

Imagine a world where data is ubiquitous in a healthcare ecosystem comprised of clinical providers, patients, payers, medical device makers, regulatory institutions and so forth. For any healthcare provider, clinical, demographic, environmental and other data would be available in real time for their patients through large, integrated databases. Advanced healthcare analytics software could mine these databases and discover patterns that lead to new knowledge regarding diagnosis and treatment of disease conditions, ways to improve efficiency and reduce cost, prediction of patients at high risk for safety issues, patient empowerment and self-care and population health. The IoT has the potential to achieve this vision and in many healthcare organizations, it already has.

The IoT will also change where care is provided. Historically, diagnosis and treatment of disease conditions were provided where providers and medical equipment were available such as in hospitals and outpatient clinics. However, with data streaming to providers via the IoT, advances in telehealth, self-administered tests and home monitoring equipment will allow patients to remain in their homes for much of their care. This transition from a hospital-centric model to an outpatient model already is and will continue to have a profound impact on nursing practice.

The Building Blocks of the IoT

Sensors

A key component of the IoT is sensors. In their most basic form, sensors capture physical inputs such as motion, temperature or pressure and convert them to an electrical, optical or digital signal (Taylor et al., 2018). These signals can then be transformed by another device into usable information. For example, sensors in digital thermometers sense body heat and transmit this signal to a microchip which converts it to a digital readout. There are many different types of sensors and their use depends on the type of information needed. Table 4.1 presents several different types of sensors and examples in healthcare.

The total number of sensors in the world is growing exponentially. In the year 2010, the estimated number of sensors worldwide was slightly less than 10 billion. By the year 2020, the number of sensors had grown five-fold and is now estimated to be approximately 50 billion (*What is the Internet of Things?*, 2016). Everything from automobiles, medical equipment, mobile devices, home appliances and so forth can utilize sensors that capture and share data with each other. Sensors thus allow data to be communicated from machine to machine and from machine to person. This connectivity allows different types of sensors to collect data from the environment simultaneously and create new, useful information. For instance, motion and light detectors placed in the home of an elderly patient can alert family members if the patient wanders. Force sensors placed in a mattress combined with skin moisture sensors can identify body areas that are prone to tissue damage. Biosensors implanted in a diabetic patient can note changes in blood glucose levels during exercise and send signals to a smartphone where they are combined with data from accelerometers to recommend adjustments in the patient's activity level.

There are a number of reasons for the increased use of sensors today. One reason is the steady decline in the price of sensors. In 2004, the average price of a sensor was US$ 1.30, but by 2018, it had dropped to US$ 0.44, a threefold drop in price (Leonard, 2019). This, in part, is driving medical technology companies to consider implementing new business models that integrate sensor technology in many of their products. A recent poll by Research2Guidance (Taylor et al., 2018, p. 7) found that 51% of medical technology companies today are implementing new business models that focus on connected medical devices.

A second reason for the increased number of sensors today is improvements in processing power. The number of transistors placed on micro-chips continues to grow and this has allowed the speed and amount of data that can be processed through sensors to double approximately every 3 years (Holdowsky et al., 2015, p. 9). As a result of improvements in sensor speed and capacity, patients can now receive data in real time. This is especially critical for patients being monitored remotely with biosensors to detect changes in cardiac ECG rhythm, blood glucose concentration in diabetics, or changes in oxygenation levels in patients with pulmonary disease.

Table 4.1 Types of Sensors and Representative Examples in Healthcare

Type of Sensor	Description	Healthcare Example
Temperature	Temperature sensors measure the continuum of temperature from cold to hot. They can be either contact or non-contact sensors.	A digital thermometer is a contact sensor while a room thermostat is a non-contact sensor.
Force	Force sensors measure the magnitude of pressure applied to an object.	A mattress with force sensors can measure whether or not certain areas of the body are at risk for skin damage.
Flow	Flow sensors measure the rate at which fluid moves through a system.	Intravenous (IV) pumps utilize flow sensors to determine the rate at which fluid flows through IV tubing.
Acoustic	Acoustic sensors measure the level of sound and then convert those signals to digital data.	Digital stethoscopes use acoustic sensors to amplify heart sounds.
Light	Light sensors detect and measure the magnitude of light.	Finger pulse oximeters measure oxygen saturation by passing beams of light through the finger and measuring changes of light absorption in oxygenated or deoxygenated blood.
Velocity and Acceleration	Velocity sensors measure the speed of motion while acceleration sensors measure changes in velocity.	Accelerometers and gyroscope sensors integrated into cell phones allow patients to self-monitor their activity by measuring their walking speed and distance.
Motion	Motion sensors capture the movement of objects.	Motion sensors placed on individuals or in rooms can be useful in preventing patients from wandering or falling.

(Continued)

Table 4.1 (Continued)   Types of Sensors and Representative Examples in Healthcare

Type of Sensor	Description	Healthcare Example
Biosensor	Biosensors detect signs from biologic components such as glucose levels, oxygen saturation, cardiac electric signals and blood pressure.	Biosensors can be implanted to monitor a patient's blood glucose level (diabetes), electrocardiogram (cardiac disease) and oxygenation level (pulmonary disease).
Chemical	Chemical sensors measure the concentration of a chemical within its environment.	Air quality sensors in cell phones can detect high levels of pollution and alert patients with asthma and prevent an asthma attack.

Source: Holdowsky, J., Mahto, M., Raynor, M.E. and Cotteleer, M. (2015). *Inside the Internet of Things*. Deloitte University Press. Available at: https://www2.deloitte.com/us/en/insights/focus/internet-of-things/iot-primer-iot-technologies-applications.html. Accessed on January 10, 2021.

A final reason for the growth in sensors has been the success of technology companies in significantly decreasing sensor size. Advances in devices that combine digital microelectronics and mechanical components or 'MEMS' sensors are rapidly being deployed in a variety of devices. Multiple sensors can be integrated into one device such as a smartphone which today may have ten or more different sensors (Holdowsky et al., 2015, p. 8).

Networks

The second building block of the IoT is the networks that communicate the signals captured by sensors to other devices that store and analyze the data. A network uses a set of common communication protocols to transfer data between devices connected to the network (Computer Networks, 2021). These devices may be computers, cellphones or medical equipment such as IV pumps or physiologic monitors. The interconnections between devices and the network occur through various types of gateways such as hubs, routers or switches. There are two types of networks: wireless and wired. Wireless networks provide remote users the convenience of almost continuous connectivity, especially with mobile devices such as smartphones.

Alternatively, wired networks are more secure and can transmit higher volumes of data. Both types of networks can be further categorized by the area they serve. Personal area networks (PAN), such as Bluetooth, provide connectivity over short distances, for example, between your smartphone and an IV pump to allow you to see the pump's dashboard on your phone. Local area networks (LAN) expand their range beyond PAN's to include an entire hospital through the hospital's Intranet. Wide area networks (WAN) extend connectivity beyond LAN's via interconnected gateways such as routers and hubs. Wi-Fi is an example of a WAN and can capture and send data between a patient's home and the healthcare organization.

Like sensors, improvements in the technology-supporting networks are providing faster data transfer, at lower costs and with less energy requirements. This has accelerated the build-out of both wireless and wired networks and increased the number and diversity of connected devices. As a result, the IoT market is expected to grow from US$ 41 billion in 2017 to US$ 158 billion by 2022 (Taylor et al., 2018, p. 6).

Standards

The third building block of the IoT is standards. Technical standards make it possible for different manufacturers' network components and devices to work together. As different original equipment manufacturer (OEM) devices have developed over time, uniform standards to enable interoperability between them have lagged. As a result, the adoption of the IoT by healthcare organizations has been hampered by a lack of technical interoperability. Today, the ability of patients, providers and payers to access and share clinical, administrative and financial data remains a significant problem (*About the Health IT Certification Program*, 2021).

The US Office of the National Coordinator for Health Information Technology (ONC) has recognized interoperability as a key challenge for the successful use of the IoT. Two important strategies the ONC has implemented to adopt standards and improve access to healthcare data are the Health IT Certification Program and the 21st Century Cures (Cures) Act. The Health IT Certification Criteria require electronic health record (EHR) vendors to meet 62 criteria in eight categories for certification. These categories include clinical processes, care coordination, clinical quality measurements, privacy and security, patient engagement, public health, design and performance, and electronic exchange. The certification also includes criterion for APIs (Application Programming Interface) which support app and mobile-based solutions and allow providers the ability to export data without intervention by their health IT vendor. Medical providers must use a certified EHR to receive incentive payments from both Medicare and Medicaid.

The passage of the Cures Act builds upon the Health IT Certification Program by providing the Department of Health and Human Services (HHS) the authority to address business practices of health IT developers and vendors related to interoperability (*ONC's Cures Act Final Rule*, 2021). These include:

- Establishing a strategy for reducing the regulatory and administrative burden on healthcare providers relating to the use of EHRs.
- Developing or supporting a trusted exchange framework for trust policies and practices and a common agreement for exchange between health information networks nationally.
- Enforcing the statutory provisions that penalize or deter information blocking.
- Promoting patient access to health information in a manner that ensures information is available in a reasonable and convenient form for the patient, without burdening the healthcare provider involved.

There are also many professional standards groups such as the National Institute of Standards and Technology (NIST) and Institute of Electrical and Electronics Engineers (IEEE) that are in the process of developing standards for the IoT (NIST, 2021; IEEE, 2021). However, the challenge of harmonizing the many standards and protocols for the various components of the IoT including connectivity infrastructure, communications, data transmission, security and device management will remain an ongoing challenge into the future.

The Information Value Loop

The IoT makes possible new opportunities to improve health through the idea of ubiquitous computing (Holdowsky et al., 2015). Ubiquitous computing is a state in which machines (computers, devices, equipment) and humans are so interconnected that information flows autonomously and unobtrusively between them. In a ubiquitous computing environment, various sensors described in Table 4.1 may work in combination to autonomously change the lighting and heating in a patient's room, alert you if certain physiologic thresholds are exceeded, predict skin damage if a patient is not repositioned and even document in the patient's EHR. Although ubiquitous computing does not fully exist today, the ongoing build-out of the IoT moves us along a continuum that is ever closer to it.

The benefit to patients and providers of the IoT and ubiquitous computing can be demonstrated through the conceptual framework of the information value loop (Holdowsky et al., 2015). The information value loop (IVL) starts with *creating data* from environmental sensors, as described in Table 4.1. The data are then *communicated* through either wired or wireless networks to a database where they are *aggregated*. The database could be located in a variety of internal (health system clinical repository) or external (commercial Cloud platform) areas. More recently, edge computing or processing the data by the device itself is becoming more commonplace. Regardless of where the data are processed, they are *analyzed* using the health analytics software to create new decision-support information or *augmented intelligence*. Patients and providers can use augmented intelligence to add additional information to the knowledge they already have for decision-making. The final step in the IVL is to *act* by using augmented intelligence to help change the *behavior* of the patient.

To illustrate the healthcare benefits of the IVL, the example of a biosensor embedded in an oral medication is used. There is a corpus of existing knowledge from clinical trials and medical practice that inform providers of the efficacy of any oral medication approved by the Food and Drug Administration (FDA). However, by embedding a biosensor in an oral medication additional, new therapeutic information can be processed and created through the IoT. Biosensors *create* data on whether or not the patient took the medication on time (or at all), the optimal dosage and when the therapeutic effect peaked. These data can be *communicated* via a wireless network to a health system where they are *aggregated* in a database and *analyzed* using health analytics software. This new information is then added to the existing pharmacotherapeutic information and can *augment* a provider's clinical decision-making. For instance, it is now possible to determine if the patient is taking the medication at a time that optimizes its therapeutic effect (especially important for certain kinds of oncology medications). This new information can now be used to change the patient's behavior through technology. For example, a smartphone application could be used to alert the patient when to take the medication to achieve its optimal therapeutic effect. This information is then revised through machine learning systems in the Cloud to improve its accuracy each time the medication is taken (Raylor et al., 2015).

The Current State of the IoT and Nursing Practice

Inpatient Nursing

The integration of the IoT into nursing practice is evolving as sensors, networks and standards evolve and improve. A review of the literature found no randomized, large-scale clinical trials that evaluated the overall impact of the IoT on nursing practice. A 2017 systematic review of the literature, focusing on what applications of the IoT are being utilized in hospitals by nurses, evaluated 5,036 papers on the topic (Mieronkoski et al., 2017). Although most papers were peer-reviewed proceedings of conferences or articles published in technological journals, a total of 265 papers met the criteria for further review. The authors identified four categories of basic nursing care activities where the IoT was being utilized in hospitals. These included comprehensive assessment, periodical clinical reassessment, activities of daily living and care management. Table 4.2. provides some examples of how the IoT is used in hospitals today.

The authors concluded that nursing practice and research regarding the use and benefits of the IoT in acute care is in its infancy. A further review of the literature by the authors, limited to nursing informatics only, revealed just one more article that met inclusion criteria. The majority of nursing informatics articles focused primarily on the integration of nursing information and knowledge with information management technologies.

Although in its infancy, use of the IoT in acute care offers nurses a number of key opportunities. The flow of data in acute care hospitals utilizing early-stage IoT technology can be described in three layers of information management systems that align well with the information value loop. These layers are identified as perception, gateway and the Cloud (Mieronskoski et al., 2017). The perception layer consists of the various devices described in Table 4.2 that nurses use to capture data on vital signs, medications, communications, falls and other nurse-sensitive indicator information. The gateway layer is comprised of the networks and hubs that connect this flow of data to the Cloud layer. The Cloud layer consists of the health system's internal and external data centers where data analysis occurs and where information is routed back to nurses on smartphones, tablets or computers via the hospital's Intranet.

A key responsibility of nursing is monitoring a patient's ongoing condition through periodic assessments and then using critical thinking skills to make treatment decisions. The collection of clinical data from the sensors in the perception layer improves care by advancing the monitoring of patients from

Table 4.2 Examples of How the IoT is Used in Hospitals Today

Category	Area	Description
Comprehensive Assessment	Hand Hygiene	Sensors placed in patient rooms can reinforce hand hygiene to mitigate the transmission of infection. These systems utilize sensors or cameras to monitor healthcare professionals' hand hygiene and provide a reminder if it is missed.
Periodical Clinical Assessment	Vital Signs Monitoring	The use of continuous wireless devices placed on patients to monitor heart rate, blood pressure, respiratory rate, skin temperature, force and electrocardiogram. Multifunctional devices may have sensors located on the skin (EKG electrodes), finger (pulse oximetry), chest (motion detectors for respiration rate), nasal cannula (airflow humidity and respiration rate) or mattress (skin damage).
	Neonatal Monitoring	Wireless sensors placed on a neonate can send signals to a server and alert nurses of sleep apnea, the humidity of oxygen in infant masks and pain detection.
	Medication Management	Radio-frequency identification tags placed on packaging for unit dose medication can be scanned to a pharmacy information system in the Cloud to alert nurses of potential allergic reactions and medication errors.
Activities of Daily Living	Sleep Assessment	Non-invasive wearable sensors that monitor vital signs, motion and skin temperature can also be employed for sleep detection. Using health analytics software to evaluate sensor data, the quality of sleep can be assessed including apnea events.
	Incontinence Management	For patients suffering from incontinence, sensors can alert nurses via a smartphone regarding the amount of moisture in a patient's diaper.

(Continued)

Table 4.2 (Continued)   Examples of How the IoT is Used in Hospitals Today

Category	Area	Description
	Fall Risk Alerts	A combination of cameras, motion detectors and accelerometers placed in a patient room can capture an individual's balance, gait and other physical functions and send the data to analytics software to determine their level of fall risk. These devices can also detect a patient fall and immediately alert a nurse.
Care Management	Prediction Models	The incorporation of real-time streaming of clinical data from sensors with historical data from patients' longitudinal electronic health records provides clinicians the ability to better diagnose, treat and predict disease conditions. These algorithmic models can predict the early onset of sepsis, heart failure, kidney failure and other events. They may also alert nurses of the potential for adverse events such as patient falls, skin damage and hospital-acquired infections.
	Communication	Wireless, hands-free communication devices eliminate the need for nurses to physically search for other nurses on the floor and throughout the hospital. These devices can also be interfaced with patient call systems so that nurses can communicate directly with their patients.

Source: Mieronkoski, R., Azimi, I., Rahmani, A.M., Aantaa, R., Terava, V., Liljeberg, P. and Salantera, S. (2017). The Internet of Things for Basic Nursing Care—A Scoping Review. *International Journal of Nursing Studies*, 69, pp. 78–90.

periodic assessments to continuous, real-time assessments. Advancements in wired and wireless network technology provide near-ubiquitous access to information through the gateway layer. The Cloud layer provides the capacity to store large, complex data sets (also known as 'big data') and utilize analytics software that supports a nurse's decision-making at the bedside. The end result is that the collection and analysis of raw clinical data by nurses to support clinical decision-making can be automated, in real time, through the IoT. This should allow nurses to spend more time providing care at the bedside.

Outpatient Nursing

The same building blocks of the IoT, sensors, networks and standards which provide opportunities to improve care for inpatients are also benefiting outpatients. Historically, the resources needed to care for patients have been centralized in hospitals and clinics. These resources include health professional staff, medical equipment and supplies, treatment rooms and so forth. Centralizing resources in a hospital-centric model has been necessary because medical equipment was not mobile, communication networks such as the Internet were not established and sensors were not technologically advanced enough to accurately monitor patients outside of the hospital. Thus, it was more efficient and cost effective to consolidate resources in one location such as a hospital to care for patients.

The ability to create data from external sensors, communicate those data via networks, aggregate them in centralized databases, analyze the data using analytics software and augment a provider's decision-making through the IoT is rapidly changing how and where care is provided. This is no more evident than in outpatient care where the IoT is evolving toward a ubiquitous computing environment by democratizing information to providers and patients. Specifically, the IoT, in part, is transitioning care from hospitals and clinics to patients in their homes. From telehealth visits with medical providers, to in-home lab tests, to wearable's that monitor vital signs, blood tests, activity and sleep, the IoT is changing where care is provided. Using the same framework in Table 4.2, Table 4.3 presents some examples of technologies that are shifting care from hospitals and clinics into the home.

Tables 4.2 and 4.3 provide examples of individual applications of how nurses are utilizing the IoT today. However, even more value can be gained by integrating these IoT technologies along the entire continuum of care. The Mercy Virtual Care Center (MVCC) located just outside of St Louis, Missouri, provides one example of how this can be done (Mercy Virtual Care Center, 2021). The MVCC is a state-of-the-art 125,000-square-foot building that opened in 2015. Today, the Center delivers virtual services to over 600,000 patients in Arkansas, Kansas, Missouri, North Carolina, Oklahoma, Pennsylvania and South Carolina. The MVCC is staffed with more than 300 clinicians and operates 24 hours per day, 7 days per week. These clinicians, using telehealth equipment, collaborate with hospitals, clinics and patients in their homes to monitor their health along the entire continuum of care. The Center provides virtual ICU (vICU) and hospitalist services to hospitals, telehealth office visits to clinics (including behavioral health) and in-home monitoring by telehealth nurses.

Table 4.3 Examples of How the IoT Is Used in Outpatient Care Today

Category	Area	Description
Comprehensive Assessment	Telehealth Primary Care and Specialist Visits	Patients with limited access to healthcare can schedule a comprehensive clinical assessment with their primary care providers or specialist. Specific telemedicine devices, such as electronic otoscopes, vital sign monitors, EKG monitors, ultrasound devices and so forth are commercially available for a full assessment. Nurses conducting a comprehensive telehealth visit should take a telehealth assessment course prior to conducting a comprehensive visit.
	Virtual Office Visits	Individuals requiring a less comprehensive assessment may access a virtual office visit. Virtual office visits generally begin with a web-based health questionnaire which is reviewed by a nurse practitioner. Based on the scope of practice required, the nurse practitioner follows up with the patient via a chat room. If more comprehensive diagnosis and treatment are needed, the patient is triaged to a physician who follows up with the patient. The 2020 COVID-19 pandemic significantly accelerated the use of virtual office visits.
Periodical Clinical Assessment	Telehealth Home Visits	Telehealth home visits allow nurses to monitor the health status of their patients between their in-home visits. Patients may utilize a number of devices including smartphones, iPads, laptops or personal computers to interact remotely with caregivers. Digital monitoring devices for heart rate, temperature, pulse oximetry, EKG, weight and other vital signs can be interfaced with telehealth devices to provide data remotely to home health nurses.

(Continued)

Table 4.3 (Continued) Examples of How the IoT Is Used in Outpatient Care Today

Category	Area	Description
	Implantable Biosensor Monitoring Devices	A number of biosensors and delivery systems are available to patients to continuously monitor specific measures. Two examples include automated insulin delivery systems which continuously monitor blood glucose and adjust insulin levels, and subcutaneous rhythm monitors which identify dangerous cardiac arrhythmias and defibrillate when necessary. These monitors can be adjusted remotely by clinicians via the IoT.
	Wearable Monitoring Devices	A number of external wearable monitoring devices can be worn by patients for their own self-care. These may include smartwatch heart rhythm monitors, smartphone monitors for sleep, activity, oxygen saturation, skin temperature, stress and so forth. Individuals can upload the information to their own personal health record and make this available to clinicians.
	Point of Care (POC) Diagnostics	A variety of POC diagnostic devices are available to home health nurses and patients for in-home and outpatient clinic use. These may include tests for glucose and cholesterol levels, electrolytes and enzymes, drug abuse, infectious diseases, pregnancy testing, blood gases, cardiac markers, cancer screening and fecal occult blood. Hand-held devices such as portable ultrasound units and digital thermometers for diagnosis of cardiac problems are also available to home health nurses.

(Continued)

Table 4.3 (Continued)   Examples of How the IoT Is Used in Outpatient Care Today

Category	Area	Description
Activities of Daily Living	Patient Safety Monitors	Patients at risk for falls and wandering can be monitored in 'smart' homes with a mix of motion detectors and cameras. Automated thermostats, door locks and lighting can also assist in keeping individuals safely in their homes by alerting family members on their smartphones of real and potential problems.
Care Management	Clinical Decision Support	The integration of streaming data from implanted and wearable sensors, in-home diagnostic testing, patient safety monitors and other sources into a Cloud-based central repository can provide decision support for home health nurses. Nurses can be alerted to potential problems such as sepsis, heart and kidney failure and other disease conditions through prediction models created by data analytic software embedded in longitudinal EHR's.
	Medication Management	A number of commercially available medication management apps and devices are available to patients to assist with medication compliance. These may include apps on smartphones that alert patients when medications are due to devices that parse out medications by day and time. Alerts can be routed to home health nurses or family members if medication doses are missed. Some medications now come with radio frequency identification tags implanted in them which allows providers to track compliance as well as optimize the drug's therapeutic effect.

(Continued)

Table 4.3 (Continued)   Examples of How the IoT Is Used in Outpatient Care Today

Category	Area	Description
	Virtual Personal Assistants	Advancements in automated speech recognition and natural language processing have enabled the development of virtual personal assistants (VPA) or chatbots. A VPA is a software application used to conduct an online conversation in lieu of direct contact with a person. Virtual personal assistants are now employed in a variety of healthcare settings to provide patient access to such activities as health screenings, medical questions, symptom checks, nutrition counseling, exercise advising, cognitive behavioral therapy, self-scheduling and other activities. As VPA's advance in their sophistication they will likely be the first line of phone triage for medical questions from patients.

Source: Clancy, T.R. (2020b). Technology Solutions for Nurse Leaders. *Nursing Administration Quarterly*. 44(4): pp. 300–315. doi: 101097/NAQ.0000000000000439.

Upon discharge from the hospital, MVCC patients are given a 'Health Kit' which includes an iPad, automated blood pressure cuff and a finger pulse oximeter to be used for follow-up monitoring. Nurses, located in individual pods within the MVCC, monitor patients in the different levels of care through multiple computer dashboard screens. The Center has worked closely with their EHR vendor to develop an integrated inpatient and outpatient digital patient record that provides a holistic view of the patient. Data analytics software, interfaced with a centralized database that can accommodate the different sources of streaming data from patients, has enabled analysts to create predictive models for disease conditions such as sepsis. By integrating alerts from these prediction models into the EHR, providers can head off a potential problem before it arises.

Since the opening of the MVCC in 2015, it has demonstrated some impressive clinical and financial outcomes (Mercy Virtual Care Center, 2021). In 2016, patients admitted into the vICU program had 35% lower mortality and 35% fewer hospital days. This resulted in a total decrease of 40,000 fewer ICU days for patients in the vICU program. Client organizations that entered the MVCC's 'Integrated Care Management Program,' which provides virtual chronic disease management, had 22 fewer sick days, a 20% reduction in medical spend and a 15% decrease in hospital admissions. Patients admitted to the Center's, 'vEngagement Program,' which provides home monitoring with Health Kits, reduced costs by 30% and decreased hospital admissions by 50%. The combined-use data analytics for prediction models and virtual care services has reduced the number of sepsis deaths by 60% and reduced the number of false positive alerts for bedside nurses by 90% (https://www.mercyvirtual.net/).

The Future of the IoT

Advances in artificial intelligence, primarily through machine learning, are rapidly creating the next generation of computing platforms. Machine learning is an application of artificial intelligence that utilizes machines (computer hardware and software) to automatically learn from experience without being explicitly programmed. A frequently used method of machine learning in healthcare is deep learning, which uses neural networks to analyze different factors with a structure that is similar to the human neural system (Gavrilova, 2020). These platforms are enabling the automation of once routine tasks, providing sophisticated clinical decision support, and transforming clinical research and drug discovery. Ongoing improvements in sensors, networks and standards are accelerating the adoption of these technologies through the IoT and creating an ecosystem of stakeholders that includes patients, providers, payers, academic centers, life science companies and regulatory agencies. Within this interconnected ecosystem, stakeholders are collaborating to advance the IoT and transform health systems toward new models of care that are of high quality, personalized, easily accessible and cost efficient (Mercy Virtual Care Center, 2021).

Although difficult to predict, a number of themes are positively impacting the future of the IoT, as outlined in Table 4.4.

Conclusion

The combined impact of improvements in sensor technology, the build-out of wired and wireless networks and adoption of regulatory standards are rapidly advancing the use of the IoT by providers, payers and patients.

Table 4.4　Four Themes Driving Future Adoption of the IoT in Healthcare

Number	Theme	Description
1	Improved access to health information is empowering patients to manage their own care.	Those technologies described in Table 4.3 are driving the 'quantified self' movement where AI embedded in wearable devices, personal assistants and apps share data with providers and provide individuals with personalized health information.
2	The trend toward ubiquitous computing created by the IoT is transforming where and how care is provided.	The IoT is transforming the hospital-centric model of care to a patient-centric model as patients, providers, payers, life science companies and academic centers collaborate in a connected ecosystem that encompasses the entire continuum of care. The Mercy Virtual Care Center exemplifies these future models of care.
3	Improvements in sensors, networks and standards are accelerating the volume, velocity, variety and veracity of data collected by health systems and are used to develop AI that improves care and lowers cost.	The life science industry, academic research centers and health systems are using big data and methods from the field of data science to create prediction models for disease conditions, personalized treatment plans using genetic sequencing, and public health policy to better manage population health.
4	The IoT is providing opportunities to lower costs and improve care by automating processes historically performed by humans.	Robots to deliver supplies to nursing units, drones to provide surveillance of disaster sites, RFID tags to monitor medication compliance and motion cameras to safely observe elderly patients in their homes are all examples of how the IoT can automate tasks typically performed by humans. By using Cloud-based AI, device sensors and wireless networks more and more human tasks will be replaced through automation. It is hoped that by eliminating certain tasks, such as nurses having to leave the unit in search of supplies, nurses will be able to spend more time in direct patient care.

Source: Taylor, K. and Hanno, R. (2017). Deloitte Centre for Health Solutions. London. The Future Awakens: Life Sciences and HealthCare Predictions for 2022. Available at: https://www2.deloitte.com/xe/en/insights/industry/dcom/the-future-awakens.html. Accessed on January 6, 2021.

The capacity to collect a variety of data through sensors, stream it at high velocity via wired and wireless networks, store it in large volume databases located in the Cloud, analyze the veracity of the data and ultimately create augmented intelligence using AI methods are all enabled through the IoT. Although healthcare's use of the IoT is in a nascent stage, it is already transforming traditional models of care from hospital-centric to patient-centered care along the entire continuum of care. The MVCC provides a glimpse of that future transformation by demonstrating how nurses play a key role in monitoring and caring for their patients whether in the home, clinic or hospital through ubiquitous computing facilitated by the IoT.

References

About the Health IT Certification Program. (n.d.). *HealthIT.gov website.* Available at: https://www.healthit.gov/topic/certification-ehrs/about-onc-health-it-certification-program/ (Accessed 8 March 2021).

Clancy, T. R. (2020a). Artificial intelligence and nursing. The future is now. *Journal of Nursing Administration*, 50(3), pp.125–127. https://doi.org/10.1097/NNA.0000000000000855.

Clancy, T. R. (2020b). Technology solutions for nurse leaders. *Nursing Administration Quarterly*, 44(4), pp.300–315. https://doi.org/101097/NAQ.0000000000000439.

Computer Networks. (n.d.). *Wikipedia website.* Available at: https://en.wikipedia.org/wiki/Computer_network (Accessed 23 March 2021).

Gavrilova, Y. (2020). Artificial intelligence vs. machine learning vs. deep learning: Essentials. *Artificial Intelligence.* Available at: https://ai.plainenglish.io/artificial-intelligence-vs-machine-learning-vs-deep-learning-whats-the-difference-dccce18efe7f (Accessed 19 May 2021).

Holdowsky, J., Mahto, M., Raynor, M. E., & Cotteleer, M. (2015). *Inside the Internet of Things.* Deloitte University Press. Available at: https://www2.deloitte.com/us/en/insights/focus/internet-of-things/iot-primer-iot-technologies-applications.html (Accessed 10 January 2021).

IEEE: Institute for Electrical and Electronics Engineers. (n.d.). Available at: https://www.ieee.org/ (Accessed 19 April 2021).

Leonard, M. (2019). Declining price of IoT sensors means greater use in manufacturing. *Supply Chain Drive.* Available at: https://www.supplychaindive.com/news/declining-price-iot-sensors-manufacturing/564980/#:~:text=The%20average%20price%20of%20an,connected%20IoT%20devices%20by%202021/ (Accessed 18 January 2021).

Mercy Virtual Care Center Website. (n.d.). Available at: https://www.mercyvirtual.net/ (Accessed 20 February 2021).

Merriam-Webster Dictionary. (n.d.). Available at: https://www.merriam-webster.com/dictionary/Internet%20of%20Things (Accessed 5 March 2021).

Mieronkoski, R., Azimi, I., Rahmani, A. M., Aantaa, R., Terava, V., Liljeberg, P., & Salantera, S. (2017). The Internet of Things for basic nursing care: A scoping review. *International Journal of Nursing Studies*, 69, pp.78–90.

NIST: National Institute of Standards and Technology Website. (n.d.). Available at: https://www.nist.gov/ (Accessed 14 April 2021).

ONC's 21st Century Cures Final Rule. (n.d.). HealthIT.gov website. Available at: https://www.healthit.gov/curesrule/ (Accessed 10 March 2021).

Raylor, M., & Cotteleer, M. (2015). *The more things change: Value creation, value capture, and the Internet of Things.* Available at: https://www2.deloitte.com/insights/us/en/deloitte-review/issue-17/value-creation-value-capture-internet-of-things.html (Accessed 19 April 2021).

Taylor, K., Sanghera, A., Steedman, M., & Thaxter, M. (2018). *Medtech and the Internet of medical things: How connected medical devices are transforming health care.* London: The Creative Studio at Deloitte. Available at: https://www2.deloitte.com/global/en/pages/life-sciences-and-healthcare/articles/medtech-internet-of-medical-things.html/ (Accessed 16 April 2021).

What is the Internet of Things? (2016). *The mesh-net website.* Available at: https://www.mesh-net.co.uk/what-is-the-internet-of-things-iot/ (Accessed 24 February 2021).

Chapter 5

Applied Data Science

Lisiane Pruinelli and Maxim Topaz

Contents

Introduction 81
Applied Data Science Framework 83
    Machine Learning Data Science Applications 84
Regression and Clustering to Address Highly Heterogeneous Populations......84
Propensity Score Matching to Model Health Trajectories 86
   Extracting Meaning from Millions of Nursing Notes Using
   Natural Language Processing 87
Using Nursing Notes to Identify Patients at Risk 87
Open-Access Nursing Sensitive Software to Implement Natural
Language Processing 88
Identifying Symptom Information in Clinical Notes 88
Effect of Data Biases in Applied Data Science 90
Model Transferability and Adoption 91
Conclusion 92
References 92

Introduction

The widespread implementation of electronic health records (EHR) and the creation of national and international healthcare data repositories, from both EHRs and additional electronic systems (e.g., geolocation, social welfare), are increasingly enabling access to large healthcare datasets. Combining datasets from multiple organizations, such as the current National COVID Cohort

Collaborative (N3C) (National Center for Advancing Translational Sciences, 2021), results in very large datasets (up to tens of millions of patients) that can be used to address population health and inform clinical research. Although the term 'big data' has been used and is a well-accepted concept in the healthcare field, moving beyond big data to discuss data science applications is needed.

Over the years, more components have been added to the definition of big data; however, the basic components include '*Volume, Velocity, Variety, Veracity, and Value*' (Topaz & Pruinelli, 2017). *Volume* refers to how large the data are, as in the number of terabytes or gigabytes. If data in storage represent terabytes (one trillion gigabytes), then we can assume it embodies a large volume of data. For reference, a typical laptop contains about 4 gigabytes of random-access memory (RAM), or storage volume. *Velocity* is the speed at which data can be accessed. *Variety* describes one of the biggest challenges of big data in healthcare. Data can be unstructured or structured, and range from text to video to message formats. Organizing the data in a meaningful way is not a simple task, especially if the data are also changing rapidly.

Variability is different from variety. For example, a coffee shop may offer six different blends of coffee, but if you get the same blend every day and it tastes different each day, that is described as variability. The same holds true for data; if the meaning is constantly changing, it can have a substantial impact on the data homogenization. *Veracity* refers to making sure the data are accurate, which requires processes to keep bad data from accumulating in systems. The simplest example of lack of veracity is data that enter a database as inaccurate information. For example, blood pressure containing negative values is clearly not accurate. This is the classic 'garbage in, garbage out' challenge. *Value* is the ultimate goal. After addressing volume, velocity, variety, variability and veracity—which takes a great deal of time, effort and resources—the potential value that can be extracted from the data and used for research and/or clinical applications must be assured.

Data science has a broader definition, including all of the processes needed to extract meaning from big data for a specific knowledge domain. Data science is defined as the 'field with a broad scope, encompassing approaches for generation, characterization, management, storage, analysis, visualization, integration and use of large, heterogeneous datasets that have relevance to population health' (NIH, 2020).

As suggested previously, a diverse range of stakeholders now have access to large healthcare datasets that have the potential to derive better clinical decision-making, improve care quality, advance research and improve patient experience. However, healthcare datasets are challenging to work with and as such, big data science techniques have to consider poor data quality, lack of healthcare data standardization, issues of patient data privacy and security and the sheer complexity of the data. A better understanding of data science concepts and skillsets is needed to move this discipline forward, including concepts and resources available to conduct real-world analytics projects that have the potential to improve health outcomes. Although several conceptual frameworks have been used and adapted from other fields to support data science, only a few are focused on healthcare data and those frameworks are not widely adopted nor are they readily available to stakeholders, including researchers, clinicians and the general public.

Applied Data Science Framework

Several initiatives have embraced the understanding that healthcare is in a continuum of evolution and learning. In the United States, the Learning Health System approach posits that 'science, informatics, incentives, and culture are aligned for continuous improvement and innovation' (Foley & Vale, 2017, p. 1). Such a healthcare system would have the potential to learn from each patient and the development of best practices could greatly improve the safety, effectiveness and reduce the cost of healthcare.

To address the lack of a focused healthcare data science framework, an Applied Healthcare Data Science Roadmap (Pruinelli et al., 2020) was developed with the goal of educating healthcare leaders on the use of data science principles and tools to inform decision-making, thus, supporting research and approaches in clinical practice that will improve healthcare for all. This step-by-step roadmap (Figure 5.1) was developed and tested in several real-world scenarios to evaluate whether the roadmap could explain a life-cycle process needed to conduct a healthcare project from beginning to end. The roadmap includes descriptions of each of the life-cycle processes and their explanation as applied to healthcare data scenarios (Pruinelli et al., 2020).

This chapter introduces big data, data science and concepts and their application to healthcare while reinforcing expected outcomes on the use of such an approach for population health, quality improvement and clinical decision-making. Frameworks to support such approaches and exemplars of applied nursing data science are described, such as the use of machine learning, natural language processing and informatics implications for symptom science.

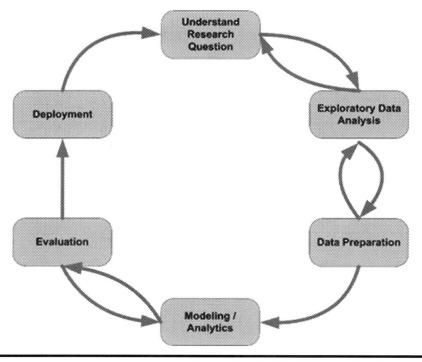

Figure 5.1 Applied Healthcare Data Science Roadmap. © Pruinelli et al., 2020.

Machine Learning Data Science Applications

Machine learning refers to a set of computational algorithms and statistical models that can learn patterns from data. Machine learning algorithms can be trained in a supervised (need of known labels, i.e., the outcome is known), unsupervised (no need of known labels) or semi-supervised (use both known and unknown labels) manner. Machine learning techniques may include, but are not limited to regression, data mining, clustering, classification, association and decision trees, among others. A good summary of machine learning in healthcare can be found elsewhere (Beam & Kohane, 2018) and further in this book. This section provides several examples of the application of machine learning in healthcare.

Regression and Clustering to Address Highly Heterogeneous Populations

In a liver transplantation study, a machine learning method was used to address heterogeneous and high-dimensional population characteristics and to identify characteristics predictive of post-transplant patient mortality

(Pruinelli et al., 2016, 2018a). A logistic regression model was developed to reduce the high dimensionality of the data. Using multiple patient problems, regression was used to extract the high priority problems categorized by organ system, and summarize them into risk scores; thus, having one single score with different weights for each organ system. These risk scores, along with sociodemographic characteristics in a hierarchical clustering algorithm, were used to show how clusters of patients' characteristics are predictive of mortality post-liver transplant.

Figure 5.2 is an example of the resulting clustering, demonstrating identified clusters. The darker the greyscale, the higher the severity score for a particular organ system. In the same study, the clusters' membership was extracted using another regression approach, a penalized Lasso regression (Tibshirani, 1996, 1997). This data science example shows the potential of using different machine learning techniques to analyze high-dimensional clinical data and develop personalized strategies, while accounting for multiple factors that, when combined, may explain population outcomes.

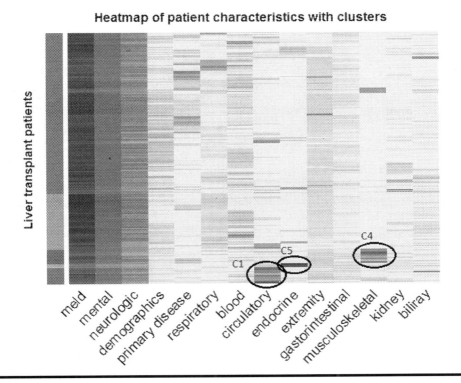

Figure 5.2 Meaningful patients characteristics by organ system. ©Pruinelli et al., 2018a.

Propensity Score Matching to Model Health Trajectories

Using sepsis as an example, Pruinelli et al. (2018) developed a machine learning model to estimate the effect of delay in implementing the 3-hour Surviving Sepsis Guideline on mortality of patients with severe sepsis and septic shock. Using sequential propensity score matching and bootstrapping to compensate for differences in health status at every 5-minute delay, time t was incorporated to analyze the impact of interventions on outcomes. These findings have significantly impacted sepsis evidence-based guidelines and quality metrics (Farrell & Casserly, 2018; Rhee et al., 2018). Figure 5.3 illustrates the results of this application, where the trajectory of serum lactate levels and the number of minutes after the diagnosis of sepsis is suspected are shown. Figure 5.3 also highlights at what point the treatment delay has a statistically significant impact on mortality.

In these examples, machine learning applications have been used to develop, validate and demonstrate the possibility of not only using healthcare data for quality improvement and research, but also the potential for transferability of the application across healthcare systems. It is believed that the modeling approach, in which a machine learning model is learned from large cohorts (i.e., nationwide) and is externally validated, produces a transferable model, allowing patients at smaller healthcare systems to also benefit from precise care; thus, contributing to the Learning Health System (Kim et al., 2019; Pruinelli et al., 2021).

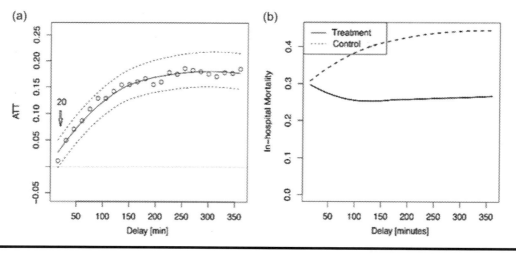

Figure 5.3   Effect of delay of lactate collection on sepsis mortality. ©Pruinelli et al., 2018b.

Extracting Meaning from Millions of Nursing Notes Using Natural Language Processing

Natural language processing refers to a set of data science techniques focused on extracting meaning from narrative data. In healthcare, it is estimated that these narrative data constitute around 80% of all available data, hence techniques to process these data at scale are critical (Sheikhalishahi et al., 2019). Healthcare narrative data include information presented in EHRs, such as a variety of types of clinical notes (e.g., nursing and physician notes, discharge summaries, emergency department assessments, primary or specialty care consults, etc.) and semi-structured notes (e.g., laboratory findings or imaging results).

In addition, there are other narrative data sources that are healthcare-related, including an exponentially growing number of research articles that are available both electronically and via multiple varieties of social media data, just to name a few. Natural language processing techniques are helping to extract meaning from these increasingly expanding terabytes of data. In this section, several practical and nursing-relevant examples of data science projects focused on natural language processing are presented.

Using Nursing Notes to Identify Patients at Risk

Home healthcare represents a large healthcare setting wherein nurses are frequently charged with managing direct care for multiple patients. In the United States alone, home healthcare settings serve more than 10 million patients annually (*FastStats - Home Health Care*, 2016). Recent evidence indicates that up to one in five home healthcare patients are hospitalized or visit an emergency department during their home healthcare stay (Ma et al., 2018; Wang et al., 2019). Early identification of patients at risk for poor outcomes, such as hospitalization, can help to reduce negative outcomes. However, implementing risk identification in healthcare is challenging due to the large number of clinical data that are being continuously documented in EHRs.

In a recent study of nursing notes, Topaz et al. (2020b) applied natural language processing to identify patients at risk. Specifically, the study used a large database of home healthcare visit notes (n = 727,676) containing documentation by clinicians for 112,237 home healthcare patients of the largest nonprofit home healthcare agency in the United States. The study applied several natural language processing and machine learning algorithms (e.g., Naïve Bayes, decision tree, random forest) to predict patient risk for hospitalization or emergency department visit using the content of clinical notes.

Machine learning performance is typically measured by an algorithm's ability to make correct predictions about the outcome of the study. Algorithms implemented in this study achieved good predictive performance in identifying patients at risk. Specifically, the algorithm's performance metrics were: precision = 0.83 (the number of true positives out of the total number of predicted positives); recall = 0.81 (the number of true positives out of the actual number of positives); F score = 0.82 (the weighted harmonic mean of the precision and recall); and area under the precision–recall curve = 0.76 (a single scalar value that measures the overall performance of a binary classifier).

Table 5.1 presents the risk factor categories as identified in the study. These risk factor categories were extracted based on the language nurses use to describe concerning signs and symptoms.

Open-Access Nursing Sensitive Software to Implement Natural Language Processing

Implementation of natural language processing often requires extensive expertise and knowledge of programming languages. However, recently, several software tools emerged that can enable clinicians less familiar with natural language processing to implement these methods at scale. One such application is NimbleMiner, an open-source free natural language processing software available at https://github.com/mtopaz/NimbleMiner. In essence, the software enables its users to implement all stages of natural language processing in a user-friendly and interactive manner.

NimbleMiner was designed by a nurse and implemented in more than a dozen of studies that processed nursing data (Topaz et al., 2019). Detailed description of the software and its use is available online (Topaz et al., 2019) and a list of studies where NimbleMiner was applied can be found here: https://www.ncbi.nlm.nih.gov/sites/myncbi/maxim.topaz.1/collections/59137650/public/. Several examples below highlight studies that used NimbleMiner.

Identifying Symptom Information in Clinical Notes

Symptom information is a key concept in nursing. Large-scale symptom research can be implemented by analyzing data collected in EHRs on

Table 5.1 Home Healthcare Risk Factor Categories and Examples

Clinical factors	Coordination/ communication	Service use	Social/ environmental factors	Temporal	Device/ equipment	Other
Dehydrated	d/c*	to er*	shopping	in am	catheter	goals met
Vomited	with ns*	no skilled	lives alone	started on	diaper	negotiate
Nausea	md called	to hospital	in apt	today vn*	with cane	all goals
Wound care	c[are] planning	skilled nursing	income	last night	Foley [catheter]	final
Incision	plan discussed	outpatient	pt* lives with	this am	rollator	no further
Kidney	pt* in agreement	no further skilled	private insurance	today for	in chair	experienced
Cleansed	c[are] plan	hospitalized for	children	when he	with rollator	large
Worsening	supplies ordered	surgery	spouse	at pm	rolling walker	render
Unsteady gait	vn* called	physical therapy	child	next week	device	yo* female
hx* falls	vn* unable to	pharmacy	house	tomorrow	wheel chair	pt* was

*Abbreviations: hx - history; d/c- discharge; ns - nursing service; pt - patient; vn - visiting nurse; er - emergency room; yo - years old millions of patients. However, most symptom information is documented in free-text clinical notes. Natural language processing can be applied to identify symptoms and enable further research and identify clinical implications.

One recent study implemented NimbleMiner to identify symptom information in inpatient clinical notes (Koleck et al., 2021). Specifically, the study focused on five diverse symptom concepts: constipation, depressed mood, disturbed sleep, fatigue and palpitations. The study's natural language processing system achieved excellent performance in symptom identification. This validated natural language processing algorithm is being applied to a large dataset of inpatient clinical notes to identify symptom clusters. For example, the ongoing study will explore which symptoms are reported together, such as fatigue and shortness of breath among patients with heart failure.

In another study, NimbleMiner was used to identify common neuropsychiatric symptoms of Alzheimer's disease using 2.6 million home healthcare clinical notes (Topaz et al., 2020a). The study found that neuropsychiatric symptoms were documented for 40% of home healthcare patients. Further exploration of symptom clusters revealed such common combinations as impaired memory, anxiety and/or depressed mood. About a third of home healthcare patients without a formal diagnosis of Alzheimer's disease had documented symptoms. This finding indicates that these patients might be at a higher risk for being diagnosed with Alzheimer's disease in the future and thus might require additional cognitive and behavioral assessments.

Effect of Data Biases in Applied Data Science

Data generated by humans and collected by computerized systems are prone to existing societal biases. For example, a recent study by the United States National Institute of Standards and Technology (NIST) found that machine learning-based facial recognition systems falsely identified Asian or black faces 10–100 times more than white faces (Hanacek, 2019). This result was in part because Asian or black faces were not as available in the data that were used to train the facial recognition systems, hence system performance for these groups of individuals was suboptimal.

Healthcare data are also likely affected by diverse types of biases that can have a significant impact on applied data science projects. For example, in the United States, racial bias was found to affect treatment prioritization algorithms. In a recent study, Obermeyer et al. (2019) found that a widely used algorithm assigned black patients a lower level of risk compared to white patients. The reason for this bias was due to the fact that risk algorithm was trained to predict healthcare cost rather than the severity of illness. However, black patients in the United States often experience unequal access to care compared to white patients which results in less money spent on black patients compared to white patients. The resulting algorithm underestimated black patients' risk about two times lower than the risk of white patients, given the same severity of illness. With careful examination of racial biases, the algorithm could be improved by changing the outcome from cost to illness severity.

Similar to the previous example, healthcare data might include racial and other types of biases. Hence, when developing applied data science-based machine learning models or natural language processing algorithms, there is a constant need to examine biases and eliminate their effect on clinical practice. As outlined in a recent report by the Nursing and Artificial Intelligence Leadership (NAIL) Collaborative (Ronquillo et al., 2021), nurses and other clinicians have an ethical obligation to carefully examine and report potential algorithm biases. In addition, to avoid biases affecting algorithms in the first place, clinicians must be engaged in all stages, from algorithm development through implementation.

Model Transferability and Adoption

Data science projects can be developed in one healthcare system (or using one healthcare system dataset), and yet be transferable to another healthcare system. This model transferability, or how well a model generalizes to the patients in another healthcare system, measures the validity of such models and their ability to be transferable across institutions, datasets and populations. A highly transferable model could be adopted by several healthcare systems at the same time, yet render the same results for accuracy and effectiveness (Kim et al., 2019; Chin et al., 2021). Model transferability is an important applied data science consideration, given current challenges, such as the lack of consistent use of standards, lack of interoperable systems (i.e., systems that easily exchange health information), isolated healthcare datasets and/or repositories, and the small single-center data made available to develop and test data science such models. The ultimate goal is to develop and train models in one set of data, which can be a split of a major dataset or an entire single dataset, and then test and/or validate the model in an unseen and/or external (another center) dataset. This process would enable investigators to validate a model's results in different populations, allowing for models to be replicated and then transferable to an entire population.

Many studies have shown that machine learning models, when developed and trained on a large amount of healthcare data, are transferable to small health systems with the same accuracy. Such transferability is viewed as a result of the modeling approach, in which a model is learned from a large, primarily national cohort and is externally validated. This approach produces a transferable model, allowing patients at smaller healthcare systems to benefit from broader research (Kim et al., 2019; Pruinelli et al., 2021). These results and the goal of building more accurate models and transferability would greatly benefit small health systems where there may be a lack of data science skills and resources, as well as in situations where datasets are not large or for cases with a lack of reliable data for research.

Conclusion

This chapter defines data science and provides several examples of how data science can be applied in the field of nursing. In these examples, data science techniques such as machine learning and natural language processing, and their use are described. Several concepts are important to consider when applying data science, for example, avoiding biases and exploring a model's transferability as the concept of a model's transferability is becoming even more important as healthcare data are made increasingly available from multiple sources and/or from multi-centers. Further, this chapter showed several examples of data science applications toward better models of care; thus, showing the potential of using this type of a data-driven approach to address critical clinical questions, both from a patient and system perspective. With the use of such a data science approach, nurse leaders have the roadmap needed to use real-world data to inform research, teaching and quality improvement and to achieve better patient outcomes.

References

Beam, A. L., & Kohane, I. S. (2018). Big data and machine learning in health care. *JAMA: Journal of the American Medical Association*, American Medical Association, 319(13), pp.1317–1318. https://doi/org/10.1001/jama.2017.18391

Chin, Y. P. H. et al. (2021). Assessing the international transferability of a machine learning model for detecting medication error in the general internal medicine clinic: Multicenter preliminary validation study. *JMIR Medical Informatics*, JMIR Publications Inc., 9(1), p.e23454. https://doi.org/10.2196/23454

Farrell, C., & Casserly, B. (2018). Sepsis, the earlier the better, 3- to 1-hour bundle. *Journal of Emergency and Critical Care Medicine*, AME Publishing Company, 2, pp.85–85. https://doi.org/10.21037/jeccm.2018.10.05

FastStats - Home Health Care. (2016). *CDC/National Center for Health Care Statistics*. Available at: https://www.cdc.gov/nchs/fastats/home-health-care.htm (Accessed 10 June 2021).

Foley, T. J., & Vale, L. (2017). What role for learning health systems in quality improvement within healthcare providers? *Learning Health Systems*, John Wiley and Sons Inc., 1(4), p.e10025. https://doi.org/10.1002/lrh2.10025

Hanacek, N. (2019). *NIST study evaluates effects of race, age, sex on face recognition software | NIST. National Institute of Standards and Technology (NIST)*. Available at: https://www.nist.gov/news-events/news/2019/12/nist-study-evaluates-effects-race-age-sex-face-recognition-software (Accessed 7 June 2021).

Kim, E. et al. (2019). Towards more accessible precision medicine: Building a more transferable machine learning model to support prognostic decisions for micro- and macrovascular complications of type 2 diabetes mellitus. *Journal of Medical Systems*, 43, pp.1–12.

Koleck, T. A. et al. (2021). Identifying symptom information in clinical notes using natural language processing. *Nursing Research*, Lippincott Williams and Wilkins, 70(3), pp.173–183. https://doi.org/10.1097/NNR.0000000000000488

Ma, C. et al. (2018). The prevalence, reasons, and risk factors for hospital readmissions among home health care patients: A systematic review. *Home Health Care Management & Practice*, SAGE Publications Inc., 30(2), pp.83–92. https://doi.org/10.1177/1084822317741622

National Center for Advancing Translational Sciences. (2021). *National COVID Cohort Collaborative (N3C) | National Center for Advancing Translational Sciences. NIH*. Available at: https://ncats.nih.gov/n3c (Accessed 20 May 2021).

NIH. (2020). *Data science blog | Data science at NIH*. Available at: https://datascience.nih.gov/blog/author/164 (Accessed 9 November 2018).

Obermeyer, Z. et al. (2019). Dissecting racial bias in an algorithm used to manage the health of populations. *Science*, American Association for the Advancement of Science, 366(6464), pp.447–453. https://doi.org/10.1126/science.aax2342

Pruinelli, L. et al. (2016). Clustering the whole-person health data to predict liver transplant survival. Available at: http://europepmc.org/abstract/med/27332227.

Pruinelli, L. et al. (2018a). A holistic clustering methodology for liver transplantation survival. *Nursing Research*, 67(4), p.1. https://doi.org/10.1097/NNR.0000000000000289

Pruinelli, L. et al. (2018b). Delay within the 3-hour surviving sepsis campaign guideline on mortality for patients with severe sepsis and septic shock*. *Critical Care Medicine*, 46(4), pp.500–505. https://doi.org/10.1097/CCM.0000000000002949

Pruinelli, L. et al. (2020). An applied healthcare data science roadmap for nursing leaders: A workshop development, conceptualization, and application. *CIN: Computers Informatics Nursing*. Lippincott Williams and Wilkins, 38(10), pp.484–489. https://doi.org/10.1097/CIN.0000000000000607

Pruinelli, L., Zhou, J., Stai, B., Schold, J., Pruett, T., Ma, S., & Simon, G. (2021). A likelihood- based convolution approach to estimate major health events in longitudinal health records data: An external validation study. *JAMIA*, 28(9), pp.1885–1891. https://doi.org/10.1093/jamia/ocab087

Rhee, C. et al. (2018). Compliance with the national SEP-1 quality measure and association with sepsis outcomes: A multicenter retrospective cohort study. *Critical Care Medicine*, Lippincott Williams and Wilkins, 46(10), pp.1585–1591. https://doi.org/10.1097/CCM.0000000000003261

Ronquillo, C. E. et al. (2021). Artificial intelligence in nursing: Priorities and opportunities from an international invitational think-tank of the Nursing and Artificial Intelligence Leadership Collaborative. *Journal of Advanced Nursing*, John Wiley & Sons, Ltd, 77(9), pp.3707–3717. https://doi.org/10.1111/jan.14855

Sheikhalishahi, S. et al. (2019). Natural language processing of clinical notes on chronic diseases: Systematic review. *JMIR Medical Informatics*, JMIR Publications Inc., 7(2), p.e12239. https://doi.org/10.2196/12239

Tibshirani, R. (1996). Regression shrinkage and selection via the Lasso. *Journal of the Royal Statistical Society*, 58(1), pp.267–288.

Tibshirani, R. (1997). The lasso method for variable selection in the Cox model. *Statistics in Medicine*, Department of Preventive Medicine and Biostatistics, University of Toronto, Ontario, Canada., 16(4), pp.385–395. https://doi.org/10.1002/(SICI)1097-0258(19970228)16:4<385::AID-SIM380>3.0.CO;2-3 [pii]

Topaz, M., & Pruinelli, L. (2017). Big data and nursing: Implications for the future, *Studies in Health Technology and Informatics*, 232, pp.165–171. Available at: http://www.ncbi.nlm.nih.gov/pubmed/28106594 (Accessed 6 February 2017).

Topaz, M. et al. (2019). NimbleMiner: An open-source nursing-sensitive natural language processing system based on word embedding. *CIN: Computers Informatics Nursing*, Lippincott Williams and Wilkins, 37(11), pp.583–590. https://doi.org/ 10.1097/CIN.0000000000000557

Topaz, M. et al. (2020a). Free-text documentation of dementia symptoms in home healthcare: A natural language processing study. *Gerontology and Geriatric Medicine*, SAGE Publications, 6, p.233372142095986. https://doi.org/10.1177/2333721420959861

Topaz, M. et al. (2020b). Home healthcare clinical notes predict patient hospitalization and emergency department visits. *Nursing Research*. Lippincott Williams and Wilkins, 69(6), pp.448–454. https://doi.org/10.1097/NNR.0000000000000470

Wang, J. et al. (2019). Inverse dose-response relationship between home health care services and rehospitalization in older adults. *Journal of the American Medical Directors Association*, Elsevier Inc., 20(6), pp.736–742. https://doi.org/10.1016/j.jamda.2018.10.021

Chapter 6

Understanding the Foundations of Artificial Intelligence: Data, Math and Machine Learning

Tracie Risling

Contents

Introduction 96
Data, Statistics and Algorithms...97
Machine Learning 100
    Deep Learning and Neural Networks..101
    Machine Learning Models 103
    Supervised Learning 103
    Unsupervised Learning...103
    Reinforcement Learning 103
Artificial Intelligence 105
    AI Application...106
    Ethics..107
Into the Future...108
Conclusion 109
References 110

DOI: 10.4324/9781003281016-6

Introduction

The application of artificial intelligence (AI) is accelerating in healthcare systems around the world, including in many other areas of our work, home and daily lives (Davenport & Kalakota, 2019). The pervasiveness of this technology, along with the potential for it to be a catalyst for unprecedented transformation in health and care delivery, means that all nurses include AI as a priority in their ongoing learning and professional development. This includes nurses in practice and those still enrolled in formal education programs.

While depictions of AI in popular culture create a sense that this is a new or futuristic technology, the concept of AI has been around for decades. AI was first introduced in the 1950s by John McCarthy at Stanford University (Robert, 2019; Yin et al., 2021). McCarthy coined the phrase to refer 'to a branch of computer science wherein algorithms are developed to emulate human cognitive functions, such as learning, reasoning, and problem solving.' It is [now] a broadly encompassing term that includes, but is not limited to, machine learning (ML), deep learning (DL), natural language processing (NLP), and computer vision (CV) (Yin et al., 2021). AI is a complex and interdisciplinary pursuit requiring contribution from computer and data scientists, as well as critical social science contributions from fields such as philosophy, psychology, linguistics and many others (Meskó & Görög, 2020).

In healthcare, informatics, public health and ethics specialists are critical partners in the advancement of AI technology as a means to enhance health and care delivery. As the largest global healthcare workforce, nurses must also be better prepared to assume active roles in the design and integration of AI health technologies (AIHTs) into healthcare systems (Buchanan et al., 2020). This includes moving beyond unfounded concerns of robots 'taking over' much of the role of nurses (Robert, 2019). A more informed use of nursing time and professional development would be the pursuit of an improved understanding of the potential usefulness of embodied AI or social robots, in addition to the host of other AI-enabled technologies that can support the advancement of the profession and compassionate care in an increasingly digitally complex health landscape (Booth et al., 2021).

There are key building blocks that should be put in place to advance understanding of the complexities of AI. This chapter introduces several of these beginning with a look at the essential driver of this technology, data. Moving from the exploration of data, additional foundational information on machine learning will be detailed to support a more in-depth discussion of AI. With these key components described an examination of how these tools are advancing AIHTs will conclude the chapter. Recommendations for what nurses need to do to ensure our profession is positioned to be an active participant in a future that in many respects is already here, are shared.

Data, Statistics and Algorithms

Healthcare has always relied on data for both individual care and system change. The advancement of digital health and implementation of tools such as electronic health records (EHRs) has created a very data-rich industry (Sensmeier, 2017). Think about your own education or practice. Beginning on a typical work or school day, how long does it take before you are consuming or creating data essential to your role as a clinician, nurse, student, researcher, teacher or administrator? Nursing has a long history of recognizing the importance of data and using it to generate new knowledge and/or theories. The nursing theory development of the 1950s–1960s changed both practice and education and was heavily influenced by the collection, categorization and analysis of data. For example, the work of psychiatric nurse Hildegard Peplau used observation, interviews and other data sources. Peplau worked to identify classifications and patterns and used these to develop interventions that ultimately led to the internationally recognized model of Interpersonal Relations in Nursing (Sitzman & Eichelberger Wright, 2017). Today, nurses are among the largest creators and contributors of data in health systems (Ronquillo et al., 2021). However, while nursing students are comprehensively taught the importance and legal requirements of documentation, there is significantly less understanding among students and practicing nurses about the relationship of the clinical data they generate and the ongoing evolution of AIHTs (Ronquillo et al., 2021). Enhanced understanding of the importance of nursing data is essential to the future advancement of the profession and must be supported by immediate curricular and ongoing professional learning opportunities to help nurses transition from existing competencies in data literacy to more in-depth data science skills (Risling, 2017; Booth et al., 2021).

When we are examining data as a driver of AI, we need to move beyond a discipline-specific focus on health data to a review of mathematics in general. Mathematics is the essential foundation for ML, and the larger field of data science. Data are organized and manipulated through algorithms, mathematical modeling and other statistical tools in aspects of ML and other AI applications. Many nursing programs, if not undergraduate, then graduate study, require a course in basic statistics. Nurses are taught to understand the importance of statistics and research to be able to evaluate emerging study that contributes to the ongoing evolution of evidence-informed practice for the profession. We can add to this understanding by further clarifying key differences between statistics and machine learning, prior to moving on to review the concept of algorithms.

In health science, statistics are typically used to understand or infer an outcome from the examination of a certain population or set of variables often through probability models (Bzdok et al., 2018). While ML employs some of the same methods from these statistical processes, it tends to be used for 'prediction by using general purpose learning algorithms to find patterns in often rich and unwieldy data' (Bzdok et al., 2018). As data have increasingly morphed into 'big data' (see Chapter 5) over the last decade, the use of classic statistical approaches has become more challenging, for example, in large population studies, and the opportunities for the meaningful application of machine learning in analysis more frequent. The rapid expansion of ML and AI has also likely fueled the overuse of these new methods, many of which have larger socioeconomic costs, in comparison to traditional statistical approaches. In many cases, traditional statistical approaches are often still sufficient for a significant amount of health research (Vollmer et al., 2019).

Both statistics and ML use algorithms to accomplish the work of inference and/or prediction. As stated by Robert (2019),

> In the field of AI, algorithms are automated instructions that tell a computer what to do. The instructions are mathematically driven and can be as simple as 'if X, then Y' actions or encompass complex mathematical layers of instructions to execute a task or find an answer to a problem.

Essentially, algorithms are the building blocks of AI used by data scientists and computer programmers to advance machine learning (Robert, 2019). So, we begin with data, and those data can then be manipulated by algorithms, either with more hands-on classic statistical tools/programs or increasingly through automated and learned processes by computers in a wide range of ML and AI applications. While this evolution is producing a host of clinical advances, there are still significant challenges in translating this technology into consistent and widespread use in real-life clinical practice (Yin et al., 2021).

One of the obstacles to the advancement of AI in healthcare concerns technical challenges with algorithms including issues of generalizability and bias further complicated by a 'lack of algorithm transparency' (Yin et al., 2021). Nurses should understand the important function of the data they generate in current and future applications of AI and, perhaps even more importantly, the barriers that may prevent nursing data from being utilized or represented in ML or AI data sets. A continued national focus on data standards and use is critical for the advancement of AI that represents nursing work and priorities (Risling & Low, 2019). Nurses are also well-positioned to help resolve other issues related to the uptake and sustained use of AI applications. A recent systematic review noted data sharing and privacy, regulatory challenge, the rapid evolution of healthcare practice and fiscal constraints as additional significant barriers (Yin et al., 2021). Ongoing concerns with disruption to existing clinical workflow, interoperability between healthcare providers and systems, potential environmental impact and lack of patient involvement and access to their own data should be added to the list of nursing concerns with how data are currently being operationalized in ML and AI applications.

Finally, as the use of algorithms continues to be advanced in other aspects of our lives and our data are used to predict behavior and/or encourage certain outcomes, purchasing for example, nurses need to take on a leadership role in further defining what should be labeled as health data. ML is allowing large social media data sets to be examined, for example, with analysis of these data predicting certain health-related outcomes or health service usage (Correia et al., 2020).

Healthcare practitioners have been using institutional data, from EHRs and other internal sources in conjunction with ML for population and public health predictions for many years, primarily to anticipate future disease burden or to evaluate the impact of policy or programming (Morgenstern et al., 2020). However, many of the data sets used for much of this work have tended to be smaller, not of a size considered to be 'big data.' The use of social media as a supplemental or even primary data source for similar predictions has been steadily increasing in recent years as a means to address this data issue. In their work on mining social media data for health, Correia et al. (2020) noted the value of Twitter and Instagram posts in signaling the spread of diseases such as the flu, and providing 'warning signals of drug interaction issues, and depression.' A similar review also identified

Twitter as a tool for early outbreak warning for several types of flu and other diseases like syphilis, tuberculosis and Ebola (Gupta & Katarya, 2020). Another group of researchers in the United States used machine learning to examine changes in language in social media posting as a possible predictor of emergency department visits (Guntuku et al., 2020). The team did find a significant change in the language used in Facebook posts leading up to emergency department visits or inpatient admission (Guntuku et al., 2020). Ultimately, the researchers noted that this type of work could aid in the development of new interventions that could be employed with patients earlier, hopefully avoiding a trip to the hospital (Guntuku et al., 2020). When used in combination with other data sources, such as internet searches, or physical environmental data for example, social media analytics may also support improved interventions for disaster management, the spread of misinformation, and a host of widespread mental health diagnoses such as anxiety and depression (Correia et al., 2020).

There are challenges with the use of these data including both sample and algorithmic biases, noise or irrelevant posts that infiltrate the data set, and overall data validity and confidence (Correia et al., 2020; Gupta & Katarya, 2020). However, as the number of social media users increases on a global scale each year, the utility of social media as a data source for predictive analytics continues to improve with many possible applications still to explore. Nurses are particularly interested in the use of these data as a way to enrich existing 'representations of the social determinants of health' (Morgenstern et al., 2020). Certainly, we should be aware of the value of expanding our professional view of what is considered health data.

Machine Learning

With a reinforced understanding of the relationship between data, statistics and algorithms, we can begin a more in-depth examination of ML. Machine learning, a subset of AI, includes many different types and approaches. An underlying commonality is that algorithms are used 'to derive knowledge from data and interpret that data without being explicitly programmed' (Robert, 2019; Buchanan et al., 2020). We will review the most common types of ML and look at the current use of this technology in healthcare. The use of ML is much more pervasive in our daily lives than many people may realize. For several years, data scientists and technology developers have worked to deliver the message that ML is everywhere (Nirmal, 2017).

In the mobile phone applications we use, the media content we stream, the internet searches we run, the voice assistant requests we speak, our digital data are being collected and ML is being used to find patterns and leverage opportunities to use the information (Hao, 2018; Nirmal, 2017). While at times this analysis is done for our benefit, more often it is used to profit those who provide those services. *MIT Technology Review* author Karen Hao (2021) equates this process to leaving 'a trail of digital breadcrumbs,' noting that these data feeds ML algorithms and benefits companies such as Google who makes billions of dollars each year of targeted ad revenue (Hao, 2021).

Similar to AI, the concept of ML is not new. Some of the elements of ML, such as neural networks, have been in and out of use for decades with well-established application in healthcare research and use (Davenport & Kalakota, 2019). In this section, we will examine the concepts of deep learning including neural networks, and supervised, unsupervised and reinforcement learning.

Deep Learning and Neural Networks

One of the keys to understanding ML and AI is recognizing how they relate to one another. Figure 6.1 demonstrates this relationship and incorporates deep learning as a subset of machine learning. Deep learning is considered an advanced form of ML employing the use of neural networks to give 'machines an enhanced ability to find – and amplify even the smallest patterns' (Hao, 2018). In these processes, data move across a multitude of networked algorithmic nodes with each 'firing' the next, which some have noted loosely parallels the connectivity of neurons in a human brain (Robert, 2019).

Deep learning is a common feature of complex prediction or categorization applications in healthcare (Buchanan et al., 2020) wherein there can be thousands or even millions of components in the model. Recognizing and identifying potential cancer risks in radiology images is a commonly used example (Davenport & Kalakota, 2019). This type of deep learning is already having a profound impact on healthcare and nursing practice. For example, researchers at Duke University used deep learning to create Sepsis Watch (Douthit et al., 2020). Trained using millions of patient data inputs, this ML application assesses patient sepsis risk by monitoring findings and, when needed, automatically activating the hospital's rapid response team as well as guiding them through the first hours of intervention (Douthit et al., 2020).

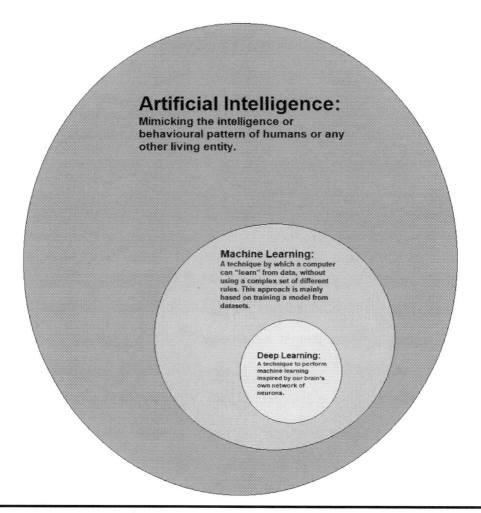

Figure 6.1 Understanding the relationship between artificial intelligence and machine learning.

Because of their ability to handle this volume of complex data and processing demand, deep learning neural networks are also commonly used in the advancement of natural language processing or NLP (Davenport & Kalakota, 2019). NLP is a subfield of AI focused on the exploration of human language and includes 'applications such as speech recognition, text analysis, translation and other goals related to language' (Davenport & Kalakota, 2019). The use of NLP has many potential benefits for the advancement of nursing presence in AI applications, primarily through the processing of open text nursing notes (Douthit et al., 2020). This technology may also be used to streamline future nursing practice through improved voice recognition and transcribing which may have several valuable uses in practice, education and research. NLP is an essential element of conversational AI both in text and social robotic applications and should be further explored as a driver of trust and sustained use of these tools. However, it is also critically important for nurses to be aware of the potential cost of the advancement of deep learning and NLP, not only fiscally, but environmentally. Recent examinations have revealed that the processing required to train and operationalize NLP models is significant, with one large model producing the equivalent carbon dioxide emissions of 125 round-trip flights from New York to Beijing (Dhar, 2020). Using the comprehensive and holistic view of human health that is the cornerstone of nursing, the profession has much to offer in seeking solutions to the advancement of AI that respects all social determinants of health including environmental concerns.

Machine Learning Models

Both traditional and deep or neural network-driven ML can be constructed using a variety of models. Three of the most common models are supervised, unsupervised and reinforcement learning.

Supervised Learning

In this subtype of ML, the learning is explicitly guided by labels applied to the data (Hao, 2018; Meskó & Görög, 2020). This is the most commonly used training model, and the learning algorithm is clearly defined along with the expected outcome (Meskó & Görög, 2020). Once the algorithm knows what it is looking for, it simply continues to return results based on that pattern.

Unsupervised Learning

In unsupervised learning, the 'teacher' is essentially out of the room. The data are not labeled or categorized in any pre-determined way and the machine is given the task of searching for groupings or patterns (Hao, 2018; Meskó & Görög, 2020). While certain rules may be set, the algorithm is left to learn on its own with no outcome-based modifications (Meskó & Görög, 2020).

Reinforcement Learning

The newest of the three ML model types is reinforcement learning. In these applications, learning is done primarily by trial and error, with reward as a key driver (Hao, 2018). Pet-owners may recognize this approach from long-held training principles using food or other positive reinforcement as a way to rapidly shape animal behavior. Here the 'teacher' takes on more of a 'coach' role by watching a series of actions and then encouraging the adoption of those behaviors that are part of a winning strategy (Meskó & Görög, 2020). This approach was very useful in having a computer learn to beat any human player in online two-person games, by simply having it play millions of games against itself to learn from winning outcomes. However, the potential 'losses' when human patient lives are at stake creates additional challenges when the model is applied in healthcare (Meskó & Görög, 2020).

Overall, it is important to remember that any ML model is only as good as the data that drives it. The long-standing computer science principle of 'garbage in, garbage out' most definitely applies to these complex models. Nursing input in the design, implementation and evaluation of ML applications is highly recommended as a means to improve the quality and, perhaps even more importantly, the accuracy of these technologies (Douthit et al., 2020).

In summary, machine learning is an essential subset to the larger overarching concept of artificial intelligence. Machine learning has different model types and applications within healthcare. While the clinical benefits of this technology are emerging, there are human and environmental costs that must be considered in the balanced advancement of these tools, especially in process-heavy deep learning or NLP application.

If you are interested in taking the next step in developing your understanding of machine learning, exploring the commonly used programming languages is a worthwhile investment. Those engaged in advanced statistical work may already be familiar with R, 'a programming language that is primarily used for data manipulation, statistical analyses, and creating graphics' (Wright et al., 2019). Like R, Python is another open-source programming language, typically more heavily favored by computer scientists as an all-purpose tool. While there are many other programming languages in use in ML and AI development, either of these basic tools is a good start, especially if you want to pursue coding. There are also large online communities associated with each of these languages, and more nurses are beginning to explore programming as part of their professional development. Data boot camps and other certificate courses are plentiful offering a wide range of options both in terms of cost and time commitment. While there is likely not a need for all nurses to become proficient ML programmers, there is a distinct advantage for the profession to have nurses experienced in this area as the rapid evolution and integration of this technology continues.

Artificial Intelligence

By examining the building blocks of the complex AI entity, you will now have a better understanding of the critical importance of data and machine learning in the advancement of AI. As previously stated, AI is not a new or futuristic goal, it is a concept that was introduced in the 1950s and has been an active focus of scientists across a broad scope of disciplines ever since. When McCarthy first introduced the concept of AI he defined it as a 'branch of computer science wherein algorithms are developed to emulate human cognitive functions, such as learning, reasoning, and problem solving' (Yin et al., 2021). The definition of AI has been subject to much revision and debate in the decades since it was first introduced, with some suggesting there is no single universally agreed-upon definition (Alami et al., 2020; Douthit et al., 2020). When the Registered Nurses Association of Ontario and AMS Healthcare (2020) explored AI and compassionate care they used the following definition 'a collection of techniques used to teach computers to simulate human learning, reasoning, communication and decision making' (p. 41).

Despite a decades-long grounding, the concept of AI is still the subject of much speculation especially in terms of future-casting how the technology might continue to advance and what potential consequences that could have for humanity. The continuum of possible AI development is typically summarized into levels or types of AI. First, levels of AI are well detailed in a book by philosopher Nick Bostrom called *Superintelligence* (Meskó & Görög, 2020). Bostrum offered the classifications of Artificial Narrow Intelligence (ANI), Artificial General Intelligence (AGI) and Artificial Superintelligence (ASI) (Meskó & Görög, 2020). As the name suggests, ANI is AI that has a very narrow or specific focus. The famous IBM supercomputer Watson is an example of this type of AI. Essentially, a specific algorithm or set of algorithms enables a computer to outperform a human at a defined task through the use of ANI (Meskó & Görög, 2020). This is the level that has been achieved in the development of AI to date. Reaching AGI would require computers to perform at the equivalence of a human being's comprehension and cognitive abilities (Meskó & Görög, 2020). Last is the concept of ASI or the point at which a computer would perform not just with the cognitive capacity of one human being, but with all of humanity combined (Meskó & Görög, 2020). This is a level of development, also referred to as singularity, when technological development and advancement outpaces that of humans, no longer requiring human intervention or programming in order to continue to evolve. There are those that believe that if this would occur, it would be a potential end for the human race. As we have yet to achieve AGI, the possibility of ASI remains, for now, a future topic of data science discussion.

AI has also been classified in terms of four types labeled reactive machines, limited memory, theory of mind and self-awareness (Hintze, 2016). We may have reached the halfway point on this classification hierarchy with some examples of reactive machines and limited memory AI development (Hintze, 2016). Reactive machines have no capacity to create memories or retain past experiences; the computer must act directly on the data before it (Hintze, 2016). Limited memory AI stores past data or learning and is demonstrated in many of the types of ML as previously discussed. This ability is critical for more complex automation and machine-driven learning, for example, in the technology that is advancing self-driving cars (Hintze, 2016).

Achieving theory of the mind would require computers to be able to harness, process and engage with the full range of human emotion and thought—a type of AI that has not yet been achieved (Hintze, 2016). Self-awareness is the singularity level in this continuum where computers would surpass humans as well as achieve independence. It is important that nurses understand where current AI development is and where it may go. There are significant ethical issues that must be addressed as this technology progresses, and nurses are well-positioned to add value to these ongoing debates. Understanding the difference between AI speculation and reality is also important, especially when questions about robot nurses arise.

AI Application

While a fully autonomous robot nurse is not a likely immediate development, there is a rapid expansion of ML and AI use in healthcare, including in nursing practice and research. There is also an important distinction to be made regarding what can be demonstrated in the laboratory setting, or even in a small pilot test, and what can be scaled and sustainable across healthcare systems. The realities of AI development in real-life clinical applications were summarized by Yin et al. (2021) in a systematic review that examines clinician and patient outcomes and cost. These authors identified that studies with a proof-of-concept or other theoretical work are dominating the literature, and further noted that the quality of the research evaluating AI in clinical application needs improvement (Yin et al., 2021). Additional controlled clinical trials and other robust experimentation designs are needed, especially if the potential value of AI is to be determined (Yin et al., 2021). While some AI applications demonstrated the capacity for effective decision support, it was also noted that when it comes to patient outcomes, AI use without corresponding interventions may not be enough to drive improvement (Yin et al., 2021). It will be important for nurses to continue to be engaged in the design, deployment and evaluation of AI in healthcare in order to maximize achieving positive outcomes (Risling & Low, 2019; Robert, 2019; Ronquillo et al., 2021).

Nurse-led research and publications related to AI are increasing (Ronquillo et al., 2021). This essential work must be continued and expanded. Recent reviews have noted the uptake of ML or AI in nursing clinical decision support, including mental health triage, risk prediction, virtual healthcare assistant chatbots, socially assistive robots and other tools meant to 'streamline workflow processes and improve the accuracy and efficiency of care provided in diverse clinical settings' (Sensmeier, 2017; Buchanan et al., 2020). ML and AI are also proving useful in the improvement of nursing administrative tasks such as scheduling of both nurses and patients, predicted bed needs and availability and other human resource-related processes (Buchanan et al., 2020).

Embodied AI, or the use of robotics, is going to become an important part of the evolving nursing profession, especially with the number of applications in this area to support older adults. There is emerging global work related to the use of socially assistive, humanoid and mobility robots in long-term care and other settings (Buchanan et al., 2020). AI-powered machines can provide social engagement and assistance with many activities of daily living for patients, and can also support nurses with some of the physically demanding work they may encounter (Buchanan et al., 2020). However, it is important to remember that AI is not just integrated into robots, it exists in many computer-drive systems and applications. There are quality of care, safety and ethical considerations to be addressed as AI becomes further integrated into healthcare. And as nurses play an active role in this development, we must be aware of the many potential applications of this technology that are not as readily visible as a robot.

Ethics

As AI continues to transform healthcare, it creates the need for nurses and other practitioners to examine their professional policies and regulations

(Buchanan et al., 2020; Booth et al., 2021). Given the pace of AI development, it may be challenging for nursing associations to keep pace with the necessary changes in competencies and ethical guidelines. Further, there are existing ethical concerns around bias and equity that must be urgently addressed. As noted previously, AI systems are driven by data. Consequently, if the data being used to train algorithms are biased, then the outcomes will be as well (Robert, 2019). Healthcare systems continue to be challenged by systematic racism (Williams & Rucker, 2000; Phillips-beck et al., 2020) and it is important to recognize that the data being generated in these systems are subject to these long-standing biases. It is feasible that ML or AI applications could support nursing efforts to identify and address this issue. For example, NLP or other tools may be especially useful in allowing a more comprehensive accounting and integration of data across the full continuum of the social determinants of health.

There are also ethical concerns in relation to the visibility of the learning that goes on in ML or AI applications. Especially in the case of complex deep learning that is employing the use of neural networks, the pace of the decision-making being performed by the machine is not always discernable, even to the programmer. A good question for nurses to ask is if the AI system has the capacity to explain how its results have been achieved (Robert, 2019). Explainable systems will be essential in advancing AI that is trusted by practitioners and patients (Robert, 2019). Nursing has much to learn about AI, but also much to offer in guiding the ethical integration of AI into healthcare (Risling, 2018). Grounded by a strong professional foundation in social justice, critical thinking and the individual application of evidence-informed care, nurses are a force for the thoughtful enhancement of our health systems using ML and AI.

Into the Future

So, what does the AI future hold for nursing and beyond? Today, there are few certainties other than knowing that the ongoing advancement of this technology will continue. The timing of future breakthroughs is less certain, but we are far enough into this evolution that there is an urgent need for nurses in all areas of practice to become more informed about how ML and AI might change our health systems. It is imperative that nurses act quickly to position the profession for leadership in this new age (Booth et al., 2021; Ronquillo et al., 2021). Nursing practice is already being influenced by ML and AI, and these changes are likely to accelerate in the years ahead.

By incorporating aspects of data and computer science into nursing education and ongoing professional development, we will strengthen our disciplinary influence on the adoption of AI, and perhaps even more importantly, lead efforts to demonstrate how this technology can amplify nursing practice and care. The concept of intelligence amplification (IA) is something that nurses can use as a means to demonstrate their value in pursuit of what is referred to as multiplicity, or the opportunity for machine and human collaboration (Goldberg, 2019). Goldberg champions the development of skills such as intuition, empathy and creativity as valuable tools for the advancement of ML and AI, noting that multiplicity requires this type of diversity (Goldberg, 2019). If nursing can embrace AI as a means to assist a professional evolution rather than working against the technology based on unfounded fears of robot replacement, there is unprecedented opportunity in the years ahead.

Embracing the value of multiplicity and IA is also a strong foundation for the pursuit of more opportunities for nurses to be engaged in the collaborative or co-design of AI integration in healthcare. This priority was highlighted in the work of an international think tank, the Nursing and Artificial Intelligence Leadership Collaborative (Ronquillo et al., 2021). The Collaborative noted that it is much more common for nurses to be used as end-users of technology rather than as collaborators in its development and integration (Ronquillo et al., 2021). In the interdisciplinary efforts it will take to ensure AI assists healthcare in becoming more equitable and efficient in the delivery of patient- and family-centered care, nurses can make an essential and unique contribution. This international Collaborative recommended that nurses improve their understanding of the relationship between the data they collect and the current and future use of AI; advocate for increased participation in AI co-design processes; and join the emerging global movement on AI for good by establishing a formal focus on AI for good nursing (AI4GN) (Ronquillo et al., 2021).

Conclusion

Quality, safe, compassionate care delivered across a multitude of settings is the focus of nursing education, administration, research and practice efforts. Nursing is built on the provision of compassionate care facilitated by the development of meaningful trusting relationships. Consistently, one of the most relied upon and trusted professions in the world, nursing is in the midst of an important professional reckoning. We must invest in developing the necessary knowledge and skills to propel nursing into the future. It will take a united and committed effort in a world forever changed by the recent global events that have accelerated technology agendas in many countries. AI is a part of our nursing future and for many a present reality. What nursing can accomplish by harnessing the potential of this technology is not yet known but we must act now before we are relegated to the sidelines of this unstoppable shift in the future of healthcare.

References

Alami, H., Lehoux, P., Auclair, Y., de Guise, M., Gagnon, M. P., Shaw, J., Roy, D., Fleet, R., Ahmed, M. A. A., & Fortin, J. P. (2020). Artificial intelligence and health technology assessment: Anticipating a new level of complexity. *Journal of Medical Internet Research*, 22(7), p.e17707.

Booth, R. G., Strudwick, G., McBride, S., O'Connor, S., & Solano López, A. L. (2021). How the nursing profession should adapt for a digital future. *BMJ*, 373, p.n1190.

Buchanan, C., Howitt, M. L., Wilson, R., Booth, R. G., Risling, T., & Bamford, M. (2020). Predicted influences of artificial intelligence on the domains of nursing: Scoping review. *JMIR Nursing*, 3(1), p.e23939.

Bzdok, D., Altman, N., & Krzywinski, M. (2018). Statistics versus machine learning. *Nature Methods*, 15(4), pp.233–234.

Correia, R. B., Wood, I. B., Bollen, J., & Rocha, L. M. (2020). Mining social media data for biomedical signals and health-related behavior. *Annual Review of Biomedical Data Science*, 3(1), pp.433–458.

Davenport, T., & Kalakota, R. (2019). The potential for artificial intelligence in healthcare. *Future Healthcare Journal*, 6(2), pp.94–98. https://doi.org/10.7861/futurehosp.6-2-94

Dhar, P. (2020). The carbon impact of artificial intelligence. *Nature Machine Intelligence*, 2(8), pp.423–425.

Douthit, B., Richesson, R., Kim, H., & Cary, M. (2020). How artificial intelligence is transforming the future of nursing. *American Nurse Journal* [online]. Available at: https://www.myamericannurse.com/how-artificial-intelligence-is-transforming-the-future-of-nursing/ (Accessed 9 September 2021).

Goldberg, K. (2019). Robots and the return to collaborative intelligence. *Nature Machine Intelligence*, 1, pp.2–4.

Guntuku, S. C., Schwartz, H. A., Kashyap, A., Gaulton, J. S., Stokes, D. C., Asch, D. A., Ungar, L. H., & Merchant, R. M. (2020). Variability in language used on social media prior to hospital visits. *Scientific Reports*, 10, p.4346.

Gupta, A., & Katarya, R. (2020). Social media based surveillance systems for healthcare using machine learning: A systematic review. *Journal of Biomedical Informatics*, 108. https://doi.org/10.1016/j.jbi.2020.103500

Hao, K. (2018). What is machine learning? *MIT Technology Review* [online]. Available at: https://www.technologyreview.com/2018/11/17/103781/what-is-machine-learning-we-drew-you-another-flowchart/ (Accessed 9 September 2021).

Hao, K. (2021). How to poison the data that Big Tech uses to surveil you. *MIT Technology Review* [online]. Available at: https://www.technologyreview.com/2021/03/05/1020376/resist-big-tech-surveillance-data/ (Accessed 14 September 2021).

Hintze, A. (2016). Understanding the four types of AI, from reactive robots to self-aware beings. *The Conversation* [online]. Available at: https://theconversation.com/understanding-the-four-types-of-ai-from-reactive-robots-to-self-aware-beings-67616 (Accessed 9 September 2021).

Meskó, B., & Görög, M. (2020). A short guide for medical professionals in the era of artificial intelligence. *NPJ Digital Medicine*, 3, p.126. https://doi.org/10.1038/s41746-020-00333-z

Morgenstern, J. D., Buajitti, E., O'Neill, M., Piggott, T., Goel, V., Fridman, D., Kornas, K., & Rosella, L. C. (2020). Predicting population health with machine learning: A scoping review. *BMJ Open*, 10(10), p.e037860.

Nirmal, D. (2017). Machine learning is everywhere: Preparing for the future. *Datanami* [online]. Available at: https://www.datanami.com/2017/07/03/machine-learning-everywhere-preparing-future/ (Accessed 9 September 2021).

Phillips-beck, W., Eni, R., Lavoie, J. G., Kinew, K. A., Achan, G. K., & Katz, A. (2020). Confronting racism within the Canadian healthcare system: Systemic exclusion of first nations from quality and consistent care. *International Journal of Environmental Research and Public Health*, 17(22), p.8343.

Registered Nursing Association of Ontario, & AMS Healthcare (2020). Nursing and compassionate care in the age of artificial intelligence: Engaging the emerging future. [online]. Available at: https://rnao.ca/sites/rnao-ca/files/RNAO-AMS_Report-Nursing_and_Compassionate_Care_in_the_Age_of_AI_Final_For_Media_Release_10.21.2020.pdf (Accessed 9 September 2021).

Risling, T. (2017). Educating the nurses of 2025: Technology trends of the next decade. *Nurse Education in Practice*, 22, pp.89–92.

Risling, T. (2018). Why AI needs nursing. [online]. Available at: https://policyoptions.irpp.org/magazines/february-2018/why-ai-needs-nursing/ (Accessed 9 September 2021).

Risling, T. L., & Low, C. (2019). Advocating for safe, quality and just care: What nursing leaders need to know about artificial intelligence in healthcare delivery. *Nursing Leadership*, 32(2), pp.31–45.

Robert, N. (2019). How artificial intelligence is changing nursing. *Nursing Management*, 50(9), pp.30–39.

Ronquillo, C. E., Peltonen, L., Pruinelli, L., Chu, C. H., Bakken, S., Beduschi, A., Cato, K., Hardiker, N., Junger, A., Michalowski, M., Nyrup, R., Rahimi, S., Reed, D. N., Salakoski, T., Salanterä, S., Walton, N., Weber, P., Wiegand, T., & Topaz,

M. (2021). Artificial intelligence in nursing: Priorities and opportunities from an international invitational think-tank of the nursing and artificial intelligence leadership collaborative. *Journal of Advanced Nursing*, 13(5), p.e14857.

Sensmeier, J. (2017). Harnessing the power of artificial intelligence. *Nursing Management*, 48(11), pp.14–19.

Sitzman, K., & Eichelberger Wright, L. (2017). *Understanding the work of nurse theorists*. 3rd ed. Burlington, MA: Jones & Bartlett Learning.

Vollmer, S., Mateen, B. A., Bohner, G., Kiraly, F. J., Ghani, R., Jonsson P., Cumbers, S., Jonas, A., McAllister, K. S. L., Myles, P., Grainger, D., Birse, M., Branson, R., Moons, K. G. M., Collins, G. S., Ioannidis, J. P. A., Holmes, C., & Hemingway, H. (2019). Machine learning and artificial intelligence research for patient benefit: 20 critical questions on transparency, replicability, ethics, and effectiveness. *BMJ*, 368, p.l6927.

Williams, D. R., & Rucker, T. D. (2000). Understanding and addressing racial disparities in health care. *Health Care Financing Review*, 21(4), pp.75–90.

Wright, M. L., Higgins, M., Taylor, J. Y., & Hertzberg, V. S. (2019). Nursing research in the 21st century: R you ready?. *Biological Research for Nursing*, 21(1), pp.114–120. https://doi.org/10.1177/1099800418810514

Yin, J., Ngiam, K. Y., & Teo, H. H. (2021). Role of artificial intelligence applications in real-life clinical practice: Systematic review. *Journal of Medical Internet Research*, 23(4), p.e25759.

Chapter 7

Artificial Intelligence for Nursing and Healthcare: Potentials and Cautions

Martin Michalowski and Jung In Park

Contents

Introduction	114
Robotics	114
Applications	115
Cautions	116
Machine Learning	116
Applications	117
Cautions	118
Mobile Technology	119
Applications	119
Cautions	120
Virtual Reality/Augmented Reality	121
Applications	122
Cautions	123
Conclusion	123
References	124

Introduction

Artificial Intelligence (AI) has been transformative for many public and private industries, and we are currently observing an AI-led revolution in healthcare. AI is a fundamental paradigm shift in healthcare that is already affecting nurses in their everyday work, and its impact will be even more pronounced in the future. AI is embedded in nurses' daily lives as algorithms, smart systems, and in their education. Even though AI applications in healthcare date back to the late 1970s, technological advances in robotics and computing and the right social climate have created ideal conditions to take full advantage of what AI can contribute to improving the provision of care. Yet healthcare constitutes a complex system that presents many challenges to AI's adoption. Ethics, the ability to explain and justify models' results, education of patients and providers, inherent biases, and social equity are some of the non-technical issues that need to be addressed for AI solutions to be safely integrated into care delivery. In this chapter, we introduce four key sub-areas of AI (Robotics, Machine Learning, Mobile Technology, and Virtual and Augmented Reality), describe their applications to nursing, and discuss cautions that need to be considered in their implementation.

Robotics

Robotics is considered as the combination of hardware and software to design robots. These robots act as physical agents that take actions to manipulate the physical world. As a form of artificial intelligence, they are machines that show behavior that we would consider intelligent by perceiving their environments and performing actions to attain some goals. To do so, they are typically equipped with effectors such as legs, wheels, joints and grippers to assert a physical force on the environment in which they operate, and with sensors (cameras, lasers, gyroscopes, etc.) to observe their environment.

Robots can be broadly categorized into three types: manipulators, mobile and mobile manipulators. Manipulators are anchored to a space and use effectors to perform actions in their environment. A common example of manipulator robots is industrial robots such as those used in automotive assembly lines (Unhelkar et al., 2018). Mobile robots move around their environment using legs or wheels. Examples of these include food delivery robots, unmanned ground vehicles and planetary rovers (Rubio et al., 2019).

The last category of robots, mobile manipulators, combine mobility with manipulation. Humanoid robots are mobile manipulators that mimic the human torso. They can apply their effectors further afield than anchored manipulators can, but their task is made harder because they don't have the rigidity that the anchor provides (Siegwart et al., 2011).

Applications

With respect to the three types of robots described above, the most common in nursing are mobile and mobile manipulators. We briefly discuss these here from an application perspective, as nursing mainly uses robotics for assistive purposes in nursing homes and for at-home, patient care. Assistive robots are used for mobility aid, serving and feeding assistance, carriers and monitoring. They are deployed to help the elderly and the disabled in their daily lives and to monitor subjects such as dementia patients. Mobility aids help these patients move around their environment and include devices that improve visual recognition for visually impaired patients (Lacey & Dawson-Howe, 1998), 'smart' devices such as canes and walkers that detect objects and guide users around them (Spenko et al., 2006) and body support or exoskeleton robots that help subjects walk or stand (Chugo et al., 2008). Serving and feeding assistants range from those that deliver food (Matsukuma et al., 2000) to robots that support upper extremity motion used in eating and drinking (Lu et al., 2009).

Immobility is a common problem in the elder population and carrier robots assist both the nurse and the patient in transferring from one location to another. These robots perform specific tasks to lift and place patients in new locations, reducing the physical exertion of the nurse and providing needed mobility for immobile patients (Ding et al., 2014). Smart beds, which accommodate many different positions, are examples of non-mobile applications of robotics to help in moving immobile patients (Li et al., 2013). Finally, monitoring in the form of telepresence robots helps nurses and caregivers monitor patients by providing audio and visual feedback (Vaughn et al., 2015). Some telepresence robots are designed as humanoids and carry out a range of tasks in the absence of a caregiver (Görer et al., 2017) while others are stationary and collect data that are used to generate alerts and reminders for both caregivers and patients (Wang et al., 2011).

Assistive robots in nursing are geared toward more than just physical assistance. Social assistive robots improve psychological comfort and emotional well-being through their presence and interaction with patients. They manifest in many forms, from humanoids (Whelan et al., 2017) to pet animals (Šabanović & Chang, 2016), and are classified as companion robots. They provide both social and cognitive stimulation to improve patients' well-being.

More broadly, robotics in nursing is an opportunity and benefit for nurses and patients when robots are integrated into the services provided. These benefits include providing assistance as described above, eliminating human error when precision and repetition is required, reducing risk and recovery associated with surgery, reducing hospital stays and creating targeted and personalized treatments.

Cautions

There is a stigma attached to robotics that suggests humans and human work will eventually be replaced by robots. This is a misguided perception often based on a misunderstanding of the role that robotics play in society, and in nursing specifically. Rather than considering the use of robots in nursing as a binary choice of robots or nurses, the nursing profession should consider the opportunities that these robots create. Conversely, robot developers should also remember that robots are meant to augment, not replace, the work performed by human nurses. Therefore, it is imperative that robot applications in nursing should be designed to work with nurses and complement their common sense and reasoning abilities.

Additionally, robots need to be programmed to understand emotions to resonate with humans. Input is needed from people working with the robots and those involved in patient care to ensure that the use of robotics in nursing addresses needs and doesn't create more work for the nurse. Without nursing input, robotics may be seen as a detriment to nursing care and views of a dark future where nurses are entirely replaced by autonomous robots will be falsely reinforced (Broadbent et al., 2016).

Machine Learning

Machine learning (ML), broadly defined, is the study of computer algorithms that improve automatically through experience and using data (Jordan & Mitchell, 2015). In the context of agents, ML enables an agent to learn how to improve its performance on future tasks by making observations about the environment it operates in. Different learning problems exist in ML, but the typical learning problem addresses how to learn a function to predict output for new inputs given a collection of previously observed input/output data pairs (Mohri et al., 2018). ML is important for the design of intelligent systems because it allows the systems to adapt over time to unforeseen changes in their environment. Furthermore, ML can be used to determine solutions to problems that are unknown to system designers (Mohri et al., 2018).

ML takes one of three forms: unsupervised, reinforcement and supervised learning (Sathya et al., 2013; Sugiyama, 2015). Unsupervised learning extracts patterns from input data without any explicit feedback. The most common unsupervised learning task is clustering. Reinforcement learning uses rewards or punishments to update (learn) a model over time. Supervised learning is provided input/output data pairs and learns a function (model) to map the inputs to outputs. While these three forms are distinct, it is not uncommon to use combinations of them for learning tasks. For example, semi-supervised learning uses a small set of labeled input/output data pairs to enhance its ability to learn a function from a large collection of unlabeled pairs.

Applications

ML has several innovative applications in healthcare and nursing (Beam & Kohane, 2018). One of the ML applications in healthcare is the prediction of diseases, such as diabetes, to identify patients at risk in the initial stages so that early interventions can be provided (Escobar et al., 2016; Kavakiotis et al., 2017). A growing number of studies apply the ML approach to find the predictors or risk factors for adverse events, such as hospital readmissions within 30 days of discharge (Min et al., 2019; Park et al., 2021). Preventive care is also possible using ML. One example in nursing would be automated, smart sensor-based detection of activities to enable behavioral modifications (Jansen et al., 2017; Rosen et al., 2018).

Personalized care is another ML application, examples include: predicting patient health outcomes based on individual characteristics from medical histories, clinical notes and other electronic health records (Ashfaq et al., 2019); finding personalized drug combinations (Banda et al., 2016); and generating treatment options tailored to a patient's needs (Pawlyn and Davies, 2019). ML is also applied to identify and diagnose diseases that are hard to detect, such as genetic diseases (Lopez et al., 2018). Medical imaging diagnosis is another application of ML in healthcare that is enabled by deep learning and computer vision advancement (Ardila et al., 2019). This imaging application is possible through the collection of many biomarkers and through advanced technologies (Ardila et al., 2019).

ML is also used to advance clinical decision-support tools (Shortliffe & Sepúlveda, 2018). It is difficult for providers to deliver optimal care given time constraints and uncertainty. However, ML-based clinical decision-support tools can compare the effectiveness of multiple treatment options and make recommendations in real time (Meyer et al., 2018). Real-time monitoring is another application of ML in healthcare (Nashif et al., 2018). With the wide adoption of the Internet of Things (IoT) for patients, from fitness bands to heart-rate monitoring cuffs, a vast amount of live-patient, health data can be collected, allowing for nursing assistance and early detection of abnormal patterns. ML enables real-time analysis with these patient-generated data and delivers faster diagnoses and decision-making.

Another significant application of ML in healthcare is outbreak prediction. With the extensive data collected from multiple sources, ML can monitor and predict epidemic outbreaks. During the COVID-19 pandemic, predicting the outbreaks and consequent surges was critical for effective management and efficient resource allocation. ML played an essential role in many COVID-19-related studies for prediction and real-time reporting (Liu et al., 2020).

Cautions

There are some risks and concerns with ML applications in healthcare that have the potential for negative impacts. One of the concerns about ML applications derives from the variety of its data sources. Training ML applications requires vast amounts of data from multiple sources such as EHRs, insurance claims or wearable sensors. However, these data are often fragmented in their contents and formats because they come from different providers, systems or institutions (Chen et al., 2019). As a result, it can be difficult to track continuity of care and see the big picture of the patient's information. The quality of this fragmented data is also problematic: the quality is often compromised due to inconsistent or missing data, so the performance of the ML applications is impaired (Gudivada et al., 2017).

Another concern is that bias and inequality in healthcare may be exacerbated by ML applications. ML-derived models learn from training data, which can uncritically incorporate or magnify embedded biases and inequalities from the database. Sometimes, even a decent, accurate database contains underlying systemic biases or disparities (Mehrabi et al., 2021). In this case, ML applications that are only beneficial to a specific population may be developed and implemented.

Patient privacy and data security are also concerning (Papernot, 2016). Breached, sensitive-patient data can be used to discriminate against people with vulnerable conditions if used by employers or insurers. Also, ML-based models can predict private information and identify potentially vulnerable groups of patients who do not wish to reveal medical conditions. These concerns and risks of ML-based applications in healthcare and nursing should be addressed before implementing such tools in the actual setting.

Mobile Technology

Mobile technology is a technology developed for cellular communication (Sheng et al., 2005). The technology is meant to travel with the user, typically consisting of portable two-way communications devices, computing devices and the networking technology that connects them. Current mobile technology is typified by internet-enabled devices like smartphones, tablets, smartwatches and other wearable devices that provide real-time monitoring.

In healthcare, mobile technology is referred to as mHealth. The World Health Organization defines mHealth as 'medical and public health practice supported by mobile devices' (World Health Organization, 2011). mHealth combines the use of telecommunication with multimedia technologies within increasingly mobile and wireless healthcare delivery systems. It often refers to consumer healthcare technologies, such as Web-based information resources, telephone messaging (short message service (SMS), multimedia messaging service (MMS)), remote monitoring of patients, telehealth and telerobotics, among others. mHealth provides the technology to increase access to healthcare and health-related information, improve the ability to diagnose and track diseases, and expand access to medical education and training.

Applications

Innovations in mHealth are reshaping disease prevention practices and management through changes in health behavior, better access to health information, and effective communication among patients and healthcare providers. The real-time data collected by mHealth technologies, integrated with other health information, such as electronic health records or genomics, enable personalized care and intervention (Li et al., 2020). Wearable fitness devices are popular for tracking daily activities and sleep habits and for sharing information on social media to get support (Dowdell et al., 2011). With these combined data, healthcare providers can analyze and predict adverse events and suggest the best interventions based on individual characteristics to improve health outcomes.

mHealth applications are also used to enhance the self-monitoring of health behaviors and to obtain live feedback remotely from healthcare providers. Examples include a diabetes prevention program using mHealth self-monitoring and self-reported exercise (MacPherson et al., 2019); self-monitoring for weight loss using personal digital assistants (PDA) and daily, tailored feedback (Burke et al., 2012); and mobile, phone-based, video messages about diabetes for self-monitoring blood glucose levels (Bell et al., 2012).

Another mHealth application is a mobile, symptom-reporting system (Weaver et al., 2007) that allows nurses to monitor and receive alerts associated with abnormal signals or patient feedback. This real-time interaction using wireless devices also enables effective communication between healthcare providers and patients (Kidd, 2011; O'Connor et al., 2009; Wu et al., 2011).

mHealth applications have changed the methods of delivering preventive care and interventions, as well. mHealth technologies are especially helpful in primary care settings where chronic disease management and lifestyle interventions are essential for better health outcomes and reducing health costs (Bauer et al., 2014; Samples et al., 2014). Examples include pairing mHealth technology with tailored activity prescriptions for the prevention of lifestyle-related chronic disease risk (Knight et al., 2014), and the use of telehealth kiosks to monitor and manage blood pressure in community-based senior citizen centers (Resnick et al., 2012).

Sometimes, mobile apps are also recommended by healthcare providers for patient education to provide guidance for wellness with visual tools. mHealth technologies, such as smartphone apps, tablet PCs, wearable watches and e-textbooks are also used in nursing education to prepare a new generation of nurses who are familiar with the internet and advanced technologies (Dowdell et al., 2011).

Cautions

Although it is exciting to think about what mHealth can offer, there are challenges and cautions with mHealth applications (apps). An important concern with mHealth is ensuring health information security and patient privacy. Health systems and individual providers who use mHealth to transmit health information must comply with the Health Insurance Portability and Accountability Act (HIPAA) (United States, 2004) regulations to protect the privacy and security of health information.

The issue of mobile app quality has risen because so many mHealth apps are available on the market, but there is a lack of scientific validation of their efficacy. It is difficult to evaluate and determine which apps provide accurate information and which are most effective for patients and healthcare providers. Therefore, nurses and other healthcare providers should partner with interdisciplinary teams when developing and implementing mHealth apps to assess their reliability and provide guidance (Samples et al., 2014). Moreover, there is a challenge in terms of the quality of the data collected from mHealth devices (Mengesha et al., 2018). To obtain accurate predictions and real-time feedback, it is critical to avoid invalid, irrelevant data that may derive from inappropriate use of mHealth applications, such as fitness trackers. Another challenge relates to usability and interoperability issues in different settings (Saripalle et al., 2019). For general and wide use, mHealth apps should be interoperable with various interfaces and operating systems and retrieving data from mHealth apps should be easy and secure. Also, these apps should be usable for patients or consumers with different levels of familiarity with technology, regardless of age.

Virtual Reality/Augmented Reality

Virtual reality (VR) is defined as

> the computer-generated simulation of a three-dimensional image or environment that can be interacted with in a seemingly real or physical way by a person using special electronic equipment, such as a helmet with a screen inside or gloves fitted with sensors.
>
> **(Oxford/Lexico, n.d., a)**

The illusion of 'being there' (referred to as telepresence) is affected by motion sensors that pick up a user's movements and adjust the view on the screen accordingly. Thus, a user can tour a simulated suite of rooms, experiencing changing viewpoints and perspectives that are convincingly related to his own head turnings and steps. As a simulated experience, VR can be like or completely different from the real world.

On the other hand, augmented reality (AR) is a technology that 'superimposes computer-generated perceptual information on a user's view of the real world, providing a composite view' (Oxford/Lexico, n.d., b). This perceptual information can be additive to the natural environment, or it can mask the natural environment. In this way, AR alters one's ongoing perception of a real-world environment, whereas VR completely replaces the user's real-world environment with a simulated one.

Applications

VR is typically used for simulation in nursing education (Bayram & Caliskan, 2020). The integration of theory and practice drives nurses' development of the skills needed for their professional life. The ability to repeat interventions in real clinical settings is limited by the availability of these settings. Furthermore, the likelihood of errors when first learning new interventions reduces the skills development possible in the real world. Simulated clinical settings provide a solution to the availability problem and reduce the potential harm to patients (Jenson & Forsythm, 2012). VR-based simulations are a popular technology deployed in nursing education that provide access to modern tools and develop the necessary practical and critical nursing skills. VR-based applications can be used to teach nurses a broad range of skills from patient identification to communication, and to reduce potential patient harm by reducing surgical errors and increasing hygiene awareness (Cant & Cooper, 2010).

VR provides both high- and low-fidelity simulations. High-fidelity simulations are image-based, interactive patient simulations that use haptic systems (those simulating touch, vibrations, sensations) to immerse the nurse in clinical settings that they will encounter in practice. These high-fidelity simulations can also include computerized virtual patients replicating human anatomy and physiology (Lane et al., 2001). Low-fidelity simulations are three-dimensional organ models, human cadavers, animal models and simulated patients. Organ models help nurses apply procedures to different organs of the body while simulated patients are used to help them develop communication skills and to teach them how to perform physical examinations (Ziv et al., 2000).

AR applications in nursing are like those of VR, and typically focus on clinical settings and education. AR is deployed using devices such as a smart glass, smart watch, a head- or helmet-mounted display, and a smartphone or tablet. Examples of deployed AR hardware devices include the Microsoft

HoloLens (Frost et al., 2017), Google Glasses (Byrne & Senk, 2017), Apple Watch (Grünerbl et al., 2015) and various handheld devices built using platforms developed by Apple, Microsoft, Arduino and others.

AR devices overlay information onto the current environment, complimenting a nurse's view with context-dependent information when carrying out a clinical task or learning and applying interventions. AR technology has the potential advantages of being a hands-free approach to easily retrieving information about individual patients resulting in the reduction in their anxiety (Fumagalli et al., 2017), saving time for the nurse (Gonzalez et al., 2014) and increased accuracy of documentation (Wüller et al., 2018).

Cautions

While there are many benefits to using VR simulations, such as allowing students to apply theory into practice in safe and realistic environments without the fear of making mistakes and harming patients, these simulations are not straightforward to implement. They typically require interdisciplinary collaboration, in addition to the time and money needed to both design realistic clinical situations and to train instructors on how to use them for education. Finally, there are physical consequences from prolonged VR use such as dizziness, headaches and pain when moving the eyes (Penumudi et al., 2020). Causes of these physical ailments are being studied and solutions developed as the technology matures.

Similarly, while AR applications to nursing provide information at the point of care and training opportunities, they require attention on the AR device. This diversion may negatively impact the patient being treated as the nurse's focuses is taken away from the patient. Further, complicating the use of AR is the challenge of communicating with patients while processing information provided by the AR device itself (Wüller et al., 2019). The required attention can also result in missed patient cues or missed information provided by the AR device when the nurse is focused on the patient. AR-based solutions need to consider the context in which they will be used and how the diverted nurse's attention won't negatively impact the patient encounter.

Conclusion

In the age of AI, new technologies and products will be increasingly involved in the healthcare field. The healthcare field will continue to embrace many approaches of AI, such as ML, robotics, AR/VR and mobile, which will permanently change the nature of nursing practice and the role of nurses. As leading professionals in healthcare, nurses and nursing scholars will need to be prepared with the necessary skillsets for new technologies and be aware of their use cases, risks and cautions. Also, it is important for nurses to participate in the development and implementation of technology to ensure that it meets patient safety and quality care standards. Nurses will need to learn how to deploy AI tools into clinical practice for evidence-based care. In particular, ethical considerations should be central, and privacy concerns should be resolved prior to implementing new AI tools in clinical applications. It will also be imperative to train nursing experts in AI and informatics, who will be equipped with both clinical and technological knowledge, because those nurses are essential in a digital world in which patients and providers can exchange feedback in real time, and new devices are constantly reshaping healthcare delivery.

References

Ardila, D., Kiraly, A. P., Bharadwaj, S., Choi, B., Reicher, J. J., Peng, L., Tse, D., Etemadi, M., Ye, W., Corrado, G., & Naidich, D. P. (2019). End-to-end lung cancer screening with three-dimensional deep learning on low-dose chest computed tomography. *Nature Medicine*, 25(6), pp.954–961.

Ashfaq, A., Sant'Anna, A., Lingman, M., & Nowaczyk, S. (2019). Readmission prediction using deep learning on electronic health records. *Journal of Biomedical Informatics*, 97, p.103256.

Banda, J. M., Callahan, A., Winnenburg, R., Strasberg, H. R., Cami, H., Reis, B. Y., Vilar, S., Hripcsak, G., Dumontier, M., & Shah, N.H. (2016). Feasibility of prioritizing drug–drug-event associations found in electronic health records. *Drug Safety*, 39, pp.45–57. https://doi.org/10.1007/s40264-015-0352-2

Bauer, A. M., Rue, T., Keppel, G. A., Cole, A. M., Baldwin, L. M., & Katon, W. (2014). Use of mobile health (mHealth) tools by primary care patients in the WWAMI region Practice and Research Network (WPRN). *Journal of the American Board of Family Medicine*, 27(6), pp.780–788.

Bayram, S. B., & Caliskan, N. (2020). *The use of virtual reality simulations in nursing education, and patient safety* [Online First], IntechOpen. https://doi.org/10.5772/intechopen.94108. Available at: https://www.intechopen.com/online-first/73839

Beam, A. L., & Kohane, I. S. (2018). Big data and machine learning in health care. *JAMA*, 319(13), pp.1317–1318.

Bell, A. M., Fonda, S. J., Walker, M. S., Schmidt, V., & Vigersky, R. A. (2012). Mobile phone-based video messages for diabetes self-care support. *Journal of Diabetes Science and Technology*, 6(2), pp.310–319.

Broadbent, E., Kerse, N., Peri, K., Robinson, H., Jayawardena, C., Kuo, T., & Jawalkar, P. (2016). Benefits and problems of health-care robots in aged care settings: A comparison trial. *Australasian Journal on Ageing*, 35(1), pp.23–29.

Burke, L. E., Styn, M. A., Sereika, S. M., Conroy, M. B., Ye L., Glanz, K., Sevick, M. A., & Ewing, L. J. (2012 Jul 1). Using mHealth technology to enhance self-monitoring for weight loss: A randomized trial. *American Journal of Preventive Medicine*, 43(1), pp.20–26.

Byrne, P. J., & Senk P. A. (2017). Google glass in nursing education: Accessing knowledge at the point of care. *CIN: Computers. Informatics. Nursing*, 35(3), pp.117–20.

Cant, R. P., & Cooper, S. J. (2010). Simulation based learning in nurse education: Systematic review. *Journal of Advanced Nursing*, 66(1), pp.3–15.

Chen, I. Y., Szolovits, P., & Ghassemi, M. (2019). Can AI help reduce disparities in general medical and mental health care? *AMA Journal of Ethics*, 21(2), pp.167–179.

Chugo, D., Matsuoka, W., Jia, S., Takase, K., & Asama, H. (2008). Standing assistance system for rehabilitation walker. In C. Laugier, & R. Siegwart, eds., Field and Service Robotics: Results of the 6th International Conference. Berlin, Heidelberg: Springer, pp.541–550.

Ding, J., Lim, Y.-J., Solano, M., Shadle, K., Park, C., Lin, C., & Hu, J. (2014). Giving patients a lift-the robotic nursing assistant (RoNA). Paper presented at the 2014 IEEE International Conference on Technologies for Practical Robot Applications (TePRA), Boston, MA.

Dowdell, E. B., Burgess, A. W., & Flores, J. R. (2011). Online social networking patterns among adolescents, young adults, and sexual offenders. *AJN. American Journal of Nursing*. 111(7), pp.28–36.

Escobar, G. J., Turk, B. J., Ragins, A., Ha, J., Hoberman, B., LeVine, S. M., Ballesca, M. A., Liu, V., & Kipnis, P. (2016). Piloting electronic medical record–based early detection of inpatient deterioration in community hospitals. *Journal of Hospital Medicine*, 11(Supplement 1), pp.S18–S24.

Frost, J., Delaney, L., & Fitzgerald, R. (2017). University of Canberra implementing augmented reality into nursing education. *Australian Nursing and Midwifery Journal*, 25(5), p.30.

Fumagalli, S., Torricelli, G., Massi, M., Calvani, S., Boni, S., Roberts, A. T., Accarigi, E., Manetti, S., & Marchionni, N. (2017). Effects of a new device to guide venous puncture in elderly critically ill patients: results of a pilot randomized study. *Aging Clinical and Experimental Research*, 29(2), pp.335–339.

Gonzalez, F. C., Villegas, O. O., Ramirez, D. E., Sanchez, V. G., & Dominguez, H. O. (2014). Smart multi-level tool for remote patient monitoring based on a wireless sensor network and mobile augmented reality. *Sensors*, 14(9), pp.17212–34.

Görer, B., Salah, A. A., & Akın, H. L. (2017). An autonomous robotic exercise tutor for elderly people. *Autonomous Robots*, 41(3), pp.657–678.

Grünerbl, Aa, Pirkl, G., Weal, M., Gobbi, M., & Lukowicz, P. (2015). Monitoring and enhancing nurse emergency training with wearable devices. In Adjunct Proceedings of the 2015 ACM International Joint Conference on Pervasive and Ubiquitous Computing and Proceedings of the 2015 ACM International Symposium on Wearable Computers. Osaka, Japan: ACM, pp.1261–1267.

Gudivada, V., Apon, A. & Ding, J. (2017). Data quality considerations for big data and machine learning: Going beyond data cleaning and transformations. *International Journal of Advanced Research in Computer Science and Software Engineering*, 10(1), pp.1–20.

Jansen, C. P., Diegelmann, M., Schnabel, E. L., Wahl, H. W., & Hauer, K. (2017). Life-space and movement behavior in nursing home residents: results of a new sensor-based assessment and associated factors. *BMC Geriatrics*, 17(1), pp.1–9.

Jenson, C. E., & Forsyth, D. M. (2012). Virtual reality simulation: Using three-dimensional technology to teach nursing students. *CIN: Computers, Informatics, Nursing*, 30(6), pp.312–318.

Jordan, M. I., & Mitchell, T. M., (2015). Machine learning: Trends, perspectives, and prospects. *Science*, 349(6245), pp.255–260.

Kavakiotis, I., Tsave, O., Salifoglou, A., Maglaveras, N., Vlahavas, I., & Chouvarda, I. (2017). Machine learning and data mining methods in diabetes research. *Computational and Structural Biotechnology Journal*, 15, pp.104–116.

Kidd, R. (2011). Benefits of mobile working for community nurse prescribers. *Nursing Standard*, 25(42), pp.56–60. https://doi.org/10.7748/ns2011.06.25.42.56.c8584

Knight, E., Stuckey, M. I., & Petrella, R. J. (2014). Health promotion through primary care: Enhancing self-management with activity prescription and mHealth. *Physician and Sports Medicine*, 42(3), pp.90–99.

Lacey, G., & Dawson-Howe, K. M. (1998). The application of robotics to a mobility aid for the elderly blind. *Robotics and Autonomous Systems*, 23(4), pp.245–252.

Lane, J. L., Slavin S., & Ziv A. (2001). Simulation in medical education: A review. *Simulation & Gaming*, 32(3), pp.297–314.

Li, F., Zhang, C., Liu, H., Gao, L., Ye, J., & Xin, D. (2013). Design of a new multifunctional wheelchair-bed. Paper presented at the World Congress on Medical Physics and Biomedical Engineering, Beijing, China.

Li, J., Hodgson, N., Lyons, M. M., Chen, K. C., Yu, F., & Gooneratne, N. S. (2020). A personalized behavioral intervention implementing mHealth technologies for older adults: A pilot feasibility study. *Geriatric Nursing*, 41(3), pp.313–319.

Liu, Z., Ciais, P., Deng, Z., Lei, R., Davis, S. J., Feng, S., Zheng, B., Cui, D., Dou, X., Zhu, B., & Guo, R. (2020). Near-real-time monitoring of global CO_2 emissions reveals the effects of the COVID-19 pandemic. *Nature Communications*, 11(1), pp.1–12.

Lopez, C., Tucker, S., Salameh, T., & Tucker, C. (2018). An unsupervised machine learning method for discovering patient clusters based on genetic signatures. *Journal of Biomedical Informatics*, 85, pp.30–39.

Lu, G., Tao, B., Liu, J., Chen, F., Shi, J., & Zhang, Z. (2009). Introduction to the development of a robotic manipulator for nursing robot. In M. Xie, Y. Xiong, C. Xiong, H. Liu & Z. Hu, eds., *Intelligent robotics and applications*. Berlin, Heidelberg: Springer, pp.1085–1096.

MacPherson, M. M., Merry, K. J., Locke, S. R., & Jung, M. E. (2019). Effects of Mobile Health prompts on self-monitoring and exercise behaviors following a diabetes prevention program: Secondary analysis from a randomized controlled trial. *JMIR mHealth and uHealth*, 7(9), p.e12956.

Matsukuma, K., Yamazaki, M., Kanda, S., & Maruyama, T. (2000). An autonomous mobile robot for carrying food trays to the aged and disabled. *Advanced Robotics*, 14(5), pp.385–388.

Mehrabi, N., Morstatter, F., Saxena, N., Lerman, K., & Galstyan, A. (2021). A survey on bias and fairness in machine learning. *ACM Computing Surveys (CSUR)*, 54(6), pp.1–35.

Mengesha, W., Steege, R., Kea, A. Z., Theobald, S., & Datiko, D. G. (2018). Can mHealth improve timeliness and quality of health data collected and used by health extension workers in rural Southern Ethiopia? *Journal of Public Health*, 40(suppl_2), pp.ii74–ii86.

Meyer, A., Zverinski, D., Pfahringer, B., Kempfert, J., Kuehne, T., Sündermann, S. H., Stamm, C., Hofmann, T., Falk, V., & Eickhoff, C. (2018). Machine learning for real-time prediction of complications in critical care: a retrospective study. *Lancet Respiratory Medicine*, 6(12), pp.905–914.

Min, X., Yu, B., & Wang, F. (2019). Predictive modeling of the hospital readmission risk from patients' claims data using machine learning: a case study on COPD. *Scientific Reports*, 9(1), pp.1–10.

Mohri, M., Rostamizadeh, A., & Talwalkar, A. (2018). *Foundations of Machine Learning*. Cambridge, MA: MIT Press.

Nashif, S., Raihan, M. R., Islam, M. R., & Imam, M. H. (2018). Heart disease detection by using machine learning algorithms and a real-time cardiovascular health monitoring system. *World Journal of Engineering and Technology*, 6(4), pp.854–873.

O'Connor, C., Friedrich, J. O., Scales, D. C., & Adhikari, N. K. (2009). The use of wireless e-mail to improve healthcare team communication. *Journal of the American Medical Informatics Association*, 16(5), pp.705–713.

Oxford/Lexico. (n.d.). *US dictionary* [online]. Available at: https://www.lexico.com/en/definition/virtual_reality (a) and https://www.lexico.com/definition/augmented_reality (b) (Accessed 1 September 2021).

Papernot, N., McDaniel, P., Sinha, A., & Wellman, M. (2016). Towards the science of security and privacy in machine learning. *arXiv:1611.03814*.

Park, J. I., Kim, D., Lee, J. A., Zheng, K., & Amin, A. (2021). Personalized Risk Prediction for 30-Day Readmissions With venous thromboembolism using machine learning. *Journal of Nursing Scholarship*, 53(3), pp.278–287.

Pawlyn, C., & Davies, F. E. (2019). Toward personalized treatment in multiple myeloma based on molecular characteristics. *Blood Advances*, 133(7), pp.660–675.

Penumudi, S. A., Kuppam, V. A., Kim, J. H., & Hwang, J. (2020). The effects of target location on musculoskeletal load, task performance, and subjective discomfort during Virtual Reality interactions. *Applied Ergonomics*, 84, p.103010.

Resnick, H. E., Ilagan, P. R., Kaylor, M. B., Mehling, D., & Alwan, M. (2012). TEAhM: Technologies for enhancing access to health management: A pilot study of community-based telehealth. *Telemedicine and e-Health*, 18(3), pp.166–174.

Rosen, M. A., Dietz, A. S., Lee, N., Wang, I. J., Markowitz, J., Wyskiel, R. M., Yang, T., Priebe, C. E., Sapirstein, A., Gurses, A. P., & Pronovost, P. J. (2018). Sensor-based measurement of critical care nursing workload: Unobtrusive measures of nursing activity complement traditional task and patient level indicators of workload to predict perceived exertion. *PloS one*, 13(10), p.e0204819.

Rubio, F., Valero, F., & Llopis-Albert, C. (2019) A review of mobile robots: Concepts, methods, theoretical framework, and applications. *International Journal of Advanced Robotic Systems*, March-April 2019, pp.1–22. https://doi.org/10.1177/1729881419839596

Šabanović, S., & Chang, W.-L. (2016). Socializing robots: Constructing robotic sociality in the design and use of the assistive robot PARO. *AI & Society*, 31(4), pp.537–551.

Samples, C., Ni, Z., & Shaw, R. J. (2014). Nursing and mHealth. *International Journal of Nursing Sciences*, 1(4), pp.330–333.

Saripalle, R., Runyan, C., & Russell, M. (2019). Using HL7 FHIR to achieve interoperability in patient health record. *Journal of Biomed Informatics*, 94, p.103188.

Sathya, R., & Abraham, A. (2013). Comparison of supervised and unsupervised learning algorithms for pattern classification. *International Journal of Advanced Research in Artificial Intelligence*, 2(2), pp.34–38.

Sheng, H., Nah, F. F. H., & Siau, K. (2005). Strategic implications of mobile technology: A case study using value-focused thinking. *Journal of Strategic Information Systems*, 14(3), pp.269–290.

Shortliffe, E. H., & Sepúlveda, M. J. (2018). Clinical decision support in the era of artificial intelligence. *JAMA*, 320(21), pp.2199–2200.

Siegwart, R., Nourbakhsh, I. R., & Scaramuzza, D. (2011). *Introduction to Autonomous Mobile Robots*. 2nd. ed. Cambridge, MA: MIT Press.

Spenko, M., Yu, H., & Dubowsky, S. (2006). Robotic personal aids for mobility and monitoring for the elderly. *IEEE Transactions on Neural Systems and Rehabilitation Engineering*, 14(3), pp.344–351.

Sugiyama, M. (2015). *Statistical Reinforcement Learning: Modern Machine Learning Approaches*. Boca Raton, FL: CRC Press.

Unhelkar, V., Dörr, S., Bubeck, A., Lasota, P. A., Perez, J., Siu, H., Boerkoel, J. C., Tyroller, Q., Bix, J., Bartscher, S., & Shah, J. (2018). Introducing mobile robots to moving-floor assembly lines design, evaluation and deployment. *IEEE Robotics & Automation Magazine* 25(2), pp.72–81.

United States. (2004). *The health insurance portability and accountability act (HIPAA)*. Washington, DC: U.S. Dept. of Labor, Employee Benefits Security Administration. http://purl.fdlp.gov/GPO/gpo10291

Vaughn, J., Shaw, R. J., & Molloy, M. A. (2015). A telehealth case study: The use of telepresence robot for delivering integrated clinical care. *Journal of the American Psychiatric Nurses Association*, 21(6), pp.431–432.

Wang, T., Zhang, H., Ma, X., Zhu, Y., Zhou, Z., & Qian, B. (2011). A home nursing robot system. In D. Zeng, ed., *Future intelligent information systems*. Berlin, Germany: Springer, pp.317–324.

Weaver, A., Young, A. M., Rowntree, J., Townsend, N., Pearson, S., Smith, J., Gibson, O., Cobern, W., Larsen, M., & Tarassenko, L. (2007). Application of mobile phone technology for managing chemotherapy-associated side-effects. *Annals of Oncology*, 18(11), pp.1887–1892.

Whelan, S., Kouroupetroglou, C., Santorelli, A., Raciti, M., Barrett, E., & Casey, D. (2017). Investigating the effect of social robot embodiment. *Studies in Health Technology and Informatics*, 242, pp.523–526.

World Health Organization. (2011). *mHealth: New horizons for health through mobile technologies* [online]. GSMA mHA Global Health Summit, June 17, 2011. Available at: https://www.who.int/ehealth/mhealth_summit.pdf (Accessed 31 December 2021).

Wu, R., Rossos, P., Quan, S., Reeves, S., Lo, V., Wong, B., & Morra, D. (2011). An evaluation of the use of smartphones to communicate between clinicians: a mixed-methods study. *Journal of Medical Internet Research*, 13(3), p.e59.

Wüller, H., Behrens, J., Klinker, K., Wiesche, M., Krcmar, H., & Remmers, H. (2018). Smart glasses in nursing – situation change and further usages exemplified on a wound care application. *Studies in Health Technology and Informatics*, 253, pp.191–5.

Wüller, H., Behrens, J., Garthaus, M., Marquard, S., & Remmers, H. (2019). A scoping review of augmented reality in nursing. *BMC Nursing*, 18, p.19.

Ziv, A., Small S. D., & Wolpe, P. R. (2000). Patient safety and simulation-based medical education. *Medical Teacher*, 22(5), pp.489–495.

Chapter 8

Artificial Intelligence-Based Model for Monitoring Pressure Ulcer Changes in Bedridden Patients: A Case Study from Taiwan

Usman Iqbal, Chun-Kung (Rock) Hsu and Yu-Chuan (Jack) Li

Contents

Introduction	132
Pressure Ulcer Status in Taiwan and Globally	132
Current Pressure Ulcer Prevention Standard of Care	133
Virtual Care Model for Pressure Ulcers	133
Innovative Model Development	135
Pressure Ulcer Measurement Standard Settings	136
Pressure Ulcer Photo-Taking Method	137
Camera Monitoring Set Up 24/7 Video Surveillance Process	137
Infrared Image Capturing System 24/7 Surveillance	138
Pressure Ulcer Classification	139
Algorithm Development	141
Implementation Results	142
Expected Impact on Earlier Medicine Approach	143
Conclusion	143
References	143

DOI: 10.4324/9781003281016-8

Introduction

In Taiwan, the focus on health information technology continues to be an increasing priority with initiatives for documenting healthcare data records advancing from the simple use of a flash drive to the adoption of the *Health Cloud* (Li et al., 2017). Moreover, there is an increased understanding that health information ultimately belongs to the patient. Stakeholders are advancing initiatives to empower patients with their own information to make decisions for their health improvement. This case study was made possible because of the availability of large databases of well-structured, quality healthcare data which were also made available to the patients (Braithwaite et al., 2018). This large volume of healthcare data provided an opportunity for stakeholders and researchers to use big data science and advanced methods based on artificial intelligence (AI) to improve healthcare quality by *AI for Earlier Medicine* (Iqbal et al., 2020).

Taiwan has advanced technology initiatives to mitigate the healthcare challenges with an increasing elderly population aged 65 years and older. This number has doubled from 7% in 1993 to 14% in 2018 with an increased life expectancy over the last 50 years for both genders to 77.5 and 84 years (Chen & Fu, 2020). Approximately 55.5% of the elderly population in Taiwan live with their children, and it has been observed that there is an increased demand for long-term care—projected to increase from 577,457 residents in 2017 to 771,431 in 2026 (Klassen et al., 2018). Given this situation, there is an increasing need to use technology to advance care methods, specifically nursing care, where resource management for long-term care is a challenge (Wu et al., 2021). For example, pressure ulcers are a potential risk for long-term care bedridden patients. This potential risk can increase the burden for healthcare utilization, and also increase the risk of complications and infections when pressure ulcers worsen (Fu Shaw et al., 2014). As the elderly population already exceeded 14% of the general population in 2018, Taiwan will enter a 'super-aged society' by 2025 and the number of bedridden patients will likely increase as the population ages.

Pressure Ulcer Status in Taiwan and Globally

The Ministry of Health and Welfare (Ministry of Health and Welfare Taiwan, 2013) estimated up to 33% of long-term bedridden patients develop pressure ulcers, and the mortality rate by pressure ulcer complications is four times higher compared to the general hospitalized patients. Although there are more nursing institutions added each year as the population's age increases, there is still a shortage of healthcare workforce (Lin et al., 2013). Pressure ulcers are frequent complications of bedridden patients, occurring in as many as 60% of patients with quadriplegia. There are currently 100,190 long-term care beds in Taiwan (62,724 beds in 1,098 nursing homes and 37,466 beds in 528 nursing institutions), and there are more than 600,000 individuals in Taiwan who are in need of nursing care. Currently, Taiwan's nurse-to-patient ratio is nearly 1:13, which is more than twice the optimal ratio of 1:6, bringing a vast burden to healthcare staff and affecting the well-being of patients (see Figure 8.1) (Ministry of Health and Welfare Taiwan, 2011; Aiken et al., 2014).

Pressure ulcers are also prevalent in patients in other countries, including the United States. According to the United States Agency for Healthcare Research and Quality (AHRQ), there are approximately 2.5 million pressure ulcer patients in the United States each year, resulting in US$ 9.1–11.6 billion in medical costs (Agency for Healthcare Research and Quality, 2014). According to Padula and Delarmente (2019), pressure ulcer costs in the United States recently increased to US$ 26.8 billion a year. The European Pressure Ulcer Advisory Panel (EPUAP) identified pressure ulcer costs annually between US$ 362 million and US$ 2.8 billion in the Netherlands, and up to £750 million in the United Kingdom (Haesler, 2014).

Current Pressure Ulcer Prevention Standard of Care

The current standard care procedure to prevent pressure ulcers is to reposition the patient once every two hours. Changing the position of the patient avoids pressure building up on one specific area of the body. Although changing the body position can effectively prevent pressure ulcers, the process of changing the body position every two hours day and night is a significant burden with respect to staff time and financial resources. Some studies have shown that while changing the body position every two hours can prevent pressure ulcers, it also disturbs rest for elderly patients (Mervis & Phillips, 2019). Furthermore, the frequency of repositioning each patient may vary based on an individual's condition.

Virtual Care Model for Pressure Ulcers

In this case study, an algorithm is applied to determine individual patient needs based on a medical informatics approach using medical records and

134 ■ *Nursing and Informatics for the 21st Century*

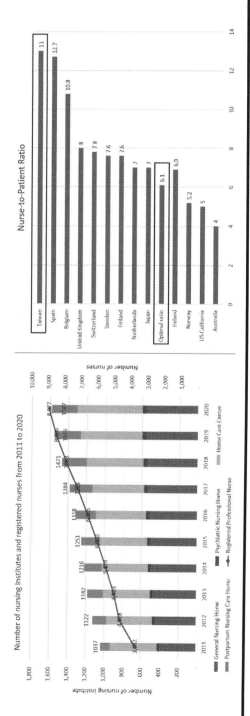

Figure 8.1 Increase in nursing homes and nurse-to-patient ratio.

lab tests that help to facilitate decision making to find the most suitable turning frequency for patients and, thus, reduce the burden on nursing care (Fergus et al., 2018; Islam et al., 2021; Zahia et al., 2020).

Based on the aforementioned demand in healthcare, Taiwan developed this case study titled, 'AI Smart Camera: Developing Deep Learning Prediction Model on Pressure Ulcer Changes in Long-Term Bedridden Patients.' This case study aims to assess the individual needs of patients with a diagnosis of pressure ulcers related to changing their positions, using artificial intelligence to interpret the images of position changes; determine the most suitable frequency for turning patients to improve the pressure ulcers in long-term bedridden patients; and reduce the risk of complications. We aim to determine that this care model achieved a balance between the well-being of patients and the allocation of medical resources, thereby reducing the burden on the clinical staff, specifically nurses.

Innovative Model Development

The innovative pressure ulcer AI-based prediction model was developed by taking into consideration the *Activity-based Pressure Injury Prediction (APIP)* model which is a combination of sequential patient images and electronic health record data which inform a personalized pressure ulcer prediction algorithm. Researchers trained the AI algorithms with large amounts of clinical data to evaluate the need of patients related to changing their position, improving the conditions of pressure ulcers in long-term bedridden patients, thus reducing the chance of complications and the burden on caregivers (Li & Mathews, 2017).

In this case study, a camera was designed for the hospital's inpatient ward, and the setting of the camera angle adjusted the data collection to maintain patient privacy. The camera resolution is suitable for protecting the patients' privacy while detecting the patients' condition (see Figure 8.2).

Through recording the patients' pressure ulcer daily movements and care conditions (images and videos data) over a long period of time, and combining information such as diagnosis, medication and test results (coded data), the results are used as input for deep learning. The evaluation by healthcare professionals/nursing staff of pressure ulcer wound status (better, worse, unchanged) is used as output data, and the daily changes of the patients' wounds are calculated and evaluated through image analysis based on the three primary shades of grey, as shown in Figure 8.3 (Papazoglou et al., 2010).

136 ■ *Nursing and Informatics for the 21st Century*

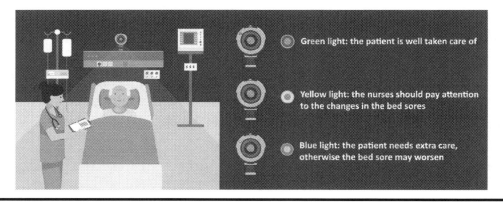

Figure 8.2 Personalized AI-based camera for pressure ulcer monitoring.

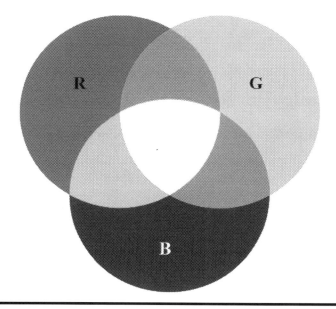

Figure 8.3 RGB primary colors for image analysis and wound assessment.

In addition, the output of the previous day serves as the input for the next day. The algorithm construction uses a convolutional neural network (CNN) to process image data, recurrent neural network (RNN) and the long short-term memory model (LSTM) to process time-series data. The resulting analysis was compared for end-to-end feature extraction, as shown in Figure 8.4 below.

Pressure Ulcer Measurement Standard Settings

In order to control the image quality, the picture content, angle and frame were designed based on the *Triangle of Wound Assessment Made Easy* reference guidelines (Dowsett et al., 2015). Considering that some wounds will have

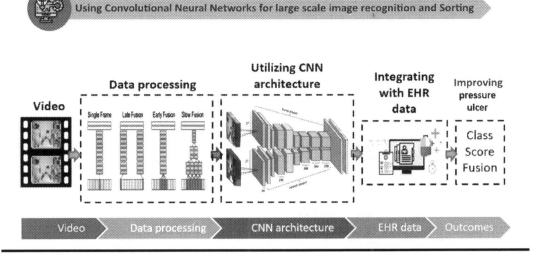

Figure 8.4 AI-based algorithm training using Convolutional Neural Network method.

less than 4 cm of surrounding skin around the ulcer (such as those around the heel), after discussion with experts, the surrounding skin of the pressure sore was defined as 2 cm from the wound margin. This was defined in order to include sufficient surface of the wound and surrounding skin for observation.

Pressure Ulcer Photo-Taking Method

The surrounding skin of the pressure ulcer was included for evaluation. The same ruler frame was used throughout the process to evaluate whether the wound was enlarged or reduced. In order to ensure consistency of photo quality for data analysis, the requirements for capturing images were discussed with the nursing staff, including how to add the frame scale, how to place the labels, including the coverage of the skin around the wound, and minimizing the shadow in the frame, as shown in Figure 8.5. After communicating and coordinating with the nursing staff, the noise of photo-taking was reduced and the consistency of the photo quality was maintained.

Camera Monitoring Set Up 24/7 Video Surveillance Process

The camera setup was placed above the patient's bed on the room ceiling to ensure the subject was fully within the camera range. The AI model can detect and record whether the subject is moving, whether the nurse is

138 ■ *Nursing and Informatics for the 21st Century*

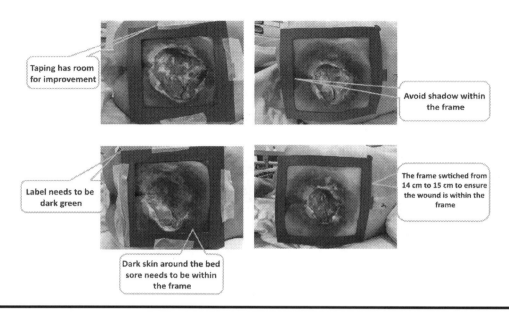

Figure 8.5 The photo-taking process method and execution.

assisting in turning the patient and changing the dressing, or the subject is moving by themselves (see Figure 8.6).

Infrared Image Capturing System 24/7 Surveillance

AIPHAS Inc. provided a complete system structure including a set of independent internal networks in the hospital containing the host server and several wireless sharing devices in the ward that were connected through a wired network. The thermal imaging data collected from the subject through the Alpha-Eye Thermal Imaging Device is sent to the host server for storage and optical image AI analysis. The host server opens the webserver at the time of data collection so that nurses can directly upload the photos of the subjects to the server storage through the wireless network. The photos that are taken with a mobile phone and IoT devices, such as the optical image IP camera, can also be uploaded to the server via wireless networks (see Figure 8.7). This was the ideal method of execution so the system did not negatively impact the hospital's network.

Three infrared cameras were installed directly above the patient's bed for continuous 24-hour monitoring. An estimate of 18,000 pictures of data were collected per hour, and the image resolution was 32×24 pixels (see Figures 8.8 and 8.9). WIFI was used to transmit data, and if the connection was disconnected due to signal interference, it automatically reconnected within 30 seconds.

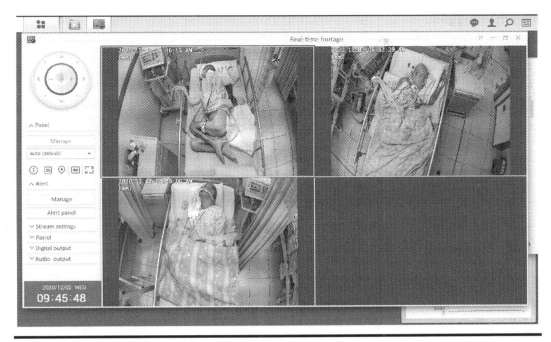

Figure 8.6 The bedridden subjects position monitoring and 24/7 surveillance.

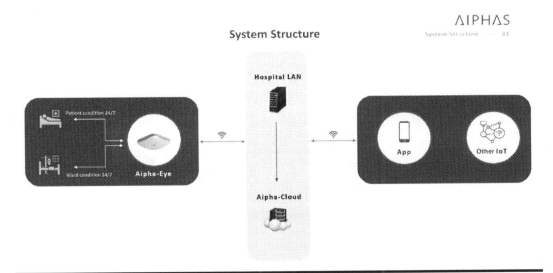

Figure 8.7 System structure of infrared camera for pressure ulcer monitoring.

Pressure Ulcer Classification

The daily images of pressure ulcers were paired, and photos were taken with the large frame to include 2 cm of surrounding skin. These photos were divided into 24-hour, 48-hour and 72-hour blocks to be able to observe the small changes of the pressure ulcer. Three classifications were used to

140 ■ *Nursing and Informatics for the 21st Century*

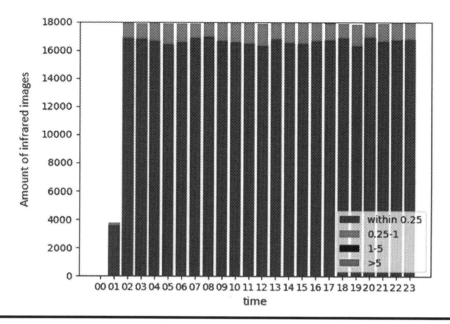

Figure 8.8 Number of infrared pictures collected each hour and transmission time.

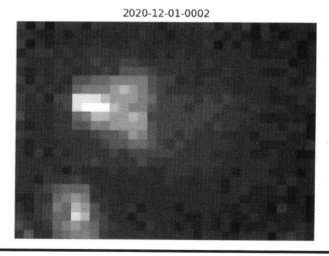

Figure 8.9 Infrared camera image resolution.

mark the images: better, worse and unchanged. The criteria for the comprehensive assessment of the pressure ulcer image included:

- Surface/size
- Classification
- Wound bed

- Wound edge
- Surrounding skin condition

The evaluation of changes in the pressure ulcer was also performed by professional nurses and used as output data for analysis. The calculations of change in pressure ulcers of the patient (using red, green and blue as the three primary colors for reference) are made through digital subtraction (area subtraction, RGB subtraction, CMYK subtraction), and with the assistance of a heat map (location verification).

Algorithm Development

The researchers analyzed the input of feature extraction to train the model to predict the main action in the video. The *Bag of Visual Words* (BoVW) model (Csurka et al., 2004) was used to classify the actions into four types: lying flat to sideways, lying sideways to laying sideways, dressing changes and other actions.

Other video features were categorized and unique clusters were selected. A fixed-length was captured from each video and the dimensions fixed for training classification as shown in Figure 8.10. Different actions were sorted using the data, and the clusters with the smallest difference were singled out to improve the accuracy, so as to strike a balance between the uniqueness and robustness of each cluster in order to train a higher-efficiency algorithm.

The subtle changes of the pressure ulcer are recorded through the combination of recording from the nursing staff and the analysis module of the individuals' position change frequency. The long short-term memory model

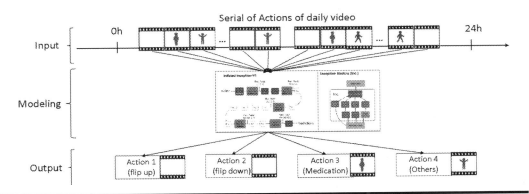

Figure 8.10 The AI-based system for pressure ulcer continuous monitoring.

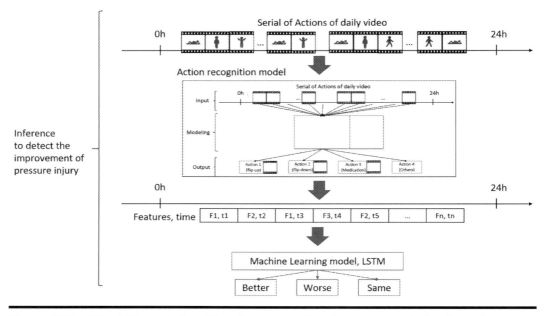

Figure 8.11 The AI-based algorithm for personalized recommendation based on pressure ulcer conditions.

was used to process the time-series data (see Figure 8.11), and the artificial intelligence deep learning method was used to analyze and calculate the changes, as well as the correlation analysis with clinical diagnosis.

Implementation Results

The significance of this project is the application of artificial intelligence in developing an algorithm for pressure ulcer prediction. This algorithm detects the need to change the patient's position to assist in the prevention and treatment of pressure ulcers, and reduce the risk of infection and other complications.

Within one year of the project, four different pressure ulcer cases were included. 824 sets of photos of pressure ulcers and 294 sets of videos of bedridden patients were collected. Through assessment of minor changes in the pressure ulcer identifying the need to further change the patients' position, a pressure ulcer change prediction model was integrated into the product. Additional data were retrieved to perform further model optimization. The overall aim was to assist healthcare professionals in caring for long-term bedridden patients, reduce care burden and balance healthcare resources and care needs by maximizing medical efficacy.

Expected Impact on Earlier Medicine Approach

The development of an AI-based pressure ulcer monitoring model not only reduces the burden on the nursing workforce, but it can also be used to establish standards for evaluating the subtle changes in pressure ulcers, providing future researchers the foundation for related research. In terms of the clinical care aspect, the AI-based pressure ulcer model helps to achieve the management of the customized needs of repositioning long-term bedridden patients.

The AI-based model, as used to interpret the images of changes in position in combination with the clinical diagnosis, improved the condition of pressure ulcers and reduced the risk of complications. This case study further achieves a balance between the well-being of patients and the distribution of medical resources, reducing the burden of a shortage of nurses or medical personnel as well as medical costs.

Conclusion

The AI-based pressure ulcer prediction model can contribute to the long-term development of a strategy for pressure ulcer prevention. Continuity of care from acute care to chronic care, combined with home care services will enable the delivery of medical care for pressure ulcers without interruption. Importantly, the AI-based model (Iqbal et al., 2020) for predicting changes in pressure ulcers will help to personalize medicine for earlier prevention and prediction. This model can also suggest best practices in the treatment of pressure ulcers, providing evidence for medical professionals regarding which treatment works best for a comparable type of ulcer. Finally, this research will empower nurses to consider a pressure ulcer virtual care model that can ultimately reduce cost and improve the quality of care delivered together with other medical professionals.

References

Agency for Healthcare Research and Quality. (2014). *Preventing pressure ulcers in hospitals*. The Agency for Healthcare Research and Quality 2014 [online]. Available at: https://www.ahrq.gov/patient-safety/settings/hospital/resource/pressureulcer/tool/index.html (Accessed 3 September 2021).

Aiken, L. H., Sloane, D. M., Bruyneel, L., Van den Heede, K., Griffiths, P., Busse, R., Diomidous, M., Kinnunen, J., Kózka, M., & Lesaffre, E. (2014). Nurse staffing and education and hospital mortality in nine European countries: A retrospective observational study. *The Lancet*, 383(9931), pp.1824–1830.

Braithwaite, J., Mannion, R., Matsuyama, Y., Shekelle, P. G., Whittaker, S., & Al-Adawi, S. (2018). *Healthcare systems: Future predictions for global care*. Boca Raton, FL: CRC Press.

Chen, C.-F., & Fu, T.-H. (2020). Policies and transformation of long-term care system in Taiwan. *Annals of Geriatric Medicine and Research*, 24(3), pp.187–194.

Csurka, G., Dance, C., Fan, L., Willamowski, J., & Bray, C. (2004). Visual categorization with bags of keypoints. In Workshop on Statistical Learning in Computer Vision, ECCV, Prague.

Dowsett, C., Protz, K., Drouard, M., & Harding, K. (2015). Triangle of wound assessment made easy. *Wounds International*, 1, p.2.

Fergus, P., Chalmers, C., & Tully, D. (2018). Collaborative pressure ulcer prevention: An automated skin damage and pressure ulcer assessment tool for nursing professionals, patients, family members and carers. arXiv, abs/1808.06503.

Fu Shaw, L., Chang, P.-C., Lee, J.-F., Kung, H.-Y., & Tung, T.-H. (2014). Incidence and predicted risk factors of pressure ulcers in surgical patients: Experience at a medical center in Taipei, Taiwan. *BioMed Research International*, 2014, p.416896. https://doi.org/10.1155/2014/416896

Haesler, E. (2014). National Pressure Ulcer Advisory Panel, European Pressure Ulcer Advisory Panel and Pan Pacific Pressure Injury Alliance. In *Prevention and treatment of pressure ulcers: Quick reference guide*. Osborne Park, Australia: Cambridge Media, pp.14–32.

Iqbal, U., Celi, L. A., & Li, Y.-C. J. (2020). How can artificial intelligence make medicine more preemptive? *Journal of Medical Internet Research*, 22(8), p.e17211.

Islam, M. M., Poly, T. N., Yang, H.-C., & Li, Y.-C. (2021). Deep into laboratory: An artificial intelligence approach to recommend laboratory tests. *Diagnostics*, 11(6), p.990.

Klassen, T. R., Higo, M., Dhirathiti, N. S., & Devasahayam, T. W. (2018). *Ageing in Asia-Pacific: Interdisciplinary and comparative perspectives*. London: Routledge.

Li, D., & Mathews, C. (2017). Automated measurement of pressure injury through image processing. *Journal of Clinical Nursing*, 26(21–22), pp.3564–3575.

Li, Y.-C. J., Lee, W.-C., Hsu, M.-H., & Iqbal, U. (2017). Taiwan: Taiwan's health information technology journey: From flash drive to health cloud. In *Health systems improvement across the globe: Success stories from 60 countries*. Boca Raton, FL: CRC Press, pp.431–438.

Lin, C. F., Huang, C. I., Kao, C. C., & Lu, M. S. (2013). The nursing shortage and nursing retention strategies in Taiwan. *Hu Li Za Zhi*, 60(3), pp.88–93.

Mervis, J. S., & Phillips, T. J. (2019). Pressure ulcers: Pathophysiology, epidemiology, risk factors, and presentation. *Journal of the American Academy of Dermatology*, 81(4), pp.881–890.

Ministry of Health and Welfare Taiwan. (2011). *Medical personnel in nursing/psychiatric rehabilitation institutions by type of practices. 2011–2020*. Taiwan: Ministry of Health and Welfare, Taiwan. [online]. Available at: https://dep.mohw.gov.tw/DOS/lp-5099-113.html (Accessed 3 September 2021).

Ministry of Health and Welfare Taiwan. (2013). *Tao-Yuan General Hospital. Ministry of Health and Welfare. Taiwan* [online]. Available at: https://www.tygh.mohw.gov.tw/?aid=302&pid=&page_name=detail&iid=146 (Accessed 3 September 2021).

Padula, W. V., & Delarmente, B. A. (2019). The national cost of hospital-acquired pressure injuries in the United States. *International Wound Journal. 16*, pp. 634–640.

Papazoglou, E. S., Zubkov, L., Mao, X., Neidrauer, M., Rannou, N., & Weingarten, M. S. (2010). Image analysis of chronic wounds for determining the surface area. *Wound Repair and Regeneration*, 18(4), pp.349–358.

Wu, K.-F., Hu, J.-L., & Chiou, H. (2021). Degrees of shortage and uncovered ratios for long-term care in Taiwan's regions: Evidence from dynamic DEA. *International Journal of Environmental Research and Public Health*, 18(2), p.605.

Zahia, S., Zapirain, M. B. G., Sevillano, X., González, A., Kim, P. J., & Elmaghraby, A. (2020). Pressure injury image analysis with machine learning techniques: A systematic review on previous and possible future methods. *Artificial Intelligence in Medicine*, 102, p.101742.

Chapter 9

Telehealth and Virtual Care

Elizabeth A. Krupinski and Kimberly D. Shea

Contents

Telehealth and the Science of Informatics	148
Definitions—Telehealth, Telemedicine and eHealth	148
Background	149
Telehealth Modalities	150
Synchronous (Real Time)	150
Audio-Videoconferencing	150
Auditory Only	151
Tele-ICU	151
Text-Based	151
Asynchronous (Store and Forward)	151
Hybrid	152
Telehealth Services	153
Nurse Roles in Telehealth	153
Information Exchange	156
Settings	157
Primary Care	158
Specialty Care	158
Emergency Services	160
Community-Based Urgent Care	160
Direct to Consumer	161
Human Factors	161
Usability	161
Technology Considerations and Room Design	162

DOI: 10.4324/9781003281016-9

Key Considerations 162
    Insurance Coverage 162
    Regulatory 163
    Training and Competencies 163
    Looking to the Future 164
References 165

Telehealth and the Science of Informatics

Telehealth and informatics are inextricably intertwined and telehealth continues to evolve within the science of informatics. The American Medical Informatics Association defines biomedical informatics as an 'interdisciplinary field that studies and pursues the effective uses of biomedical data, information, and knowledge for scientific inquiry, problem solving and decision making, motivated by efforts to improve human health' (Kulikowski et al., 2012). Following the industrial age and digitalization of data, computing power has progressed to where it is now reported that an estimated 5 zettabytes of data are stored worldwide (Gillings et al., 2016). Telehealth technologies contribute to this vast collection of stored data.

    Healthcare informatics is 'the integration of healthcare sciences, computer science, information science, and cognitive science to assist in the management of healthcare information (Saba & McCormick, 2015, p. 232). Telehealth utilizes all of these sciences with nursing as the healthcare science. Data become information and then knowledge when healthcare providers apply that knowledge to patient care. Supported by technologies developed through innovative informatics research and industries, telehealth addresses patient care by improving operational efficiencies in ways to collect, process and utilize information (Ye, 2020).

Definitions—Telehealth, Telemedicine and eHealth

There are a number of definitions of telehealth and telemedicine. The Health Resources and Services Administration (HRSA) defines telemedicine as

> the use of electronic information and telecommunications to support long-distance clinical health, patient and professional health-related education, public health and health administration.

Technologies include videoconferencing, the Internet, store-and-forward imaging, streaming media, and terrestrial and wireless communications.

(HRSA, 2019)

Telehealth is a broader term that can 'refer to remote non-clinical services, such as provider training, administrative meetings, and continuing medical education, in addition to clinical services' (HRSA, 2019).

eHealth typically refers to the use of the Internet and other telecommunications technologies to deliver healthcare and is often used only in the context of transmitting asynchronous data. mHealth refers to the use of mobile and wireless technologies (e.g., mobile phones, tablets) to provide healthcare. Terms like virtual health/care, connected health, digital health/care and remote care are often used interchangeably with telemedicine and telehealth. Remote patient monitoring/management (RPM) uses technologies to collect patient data outside the context of traditional healthcare settings and typically involves uploading or automatic data transmission to a provider or health portal for interpretation.

Background

The history of telehealth goes back farther than most people realize, with modern roots going back to 1905 when Einthoven initiated the long-distance transfer of electrocardiograms (Bashshur & Shannon, 2009). Two of the earliest applications were teleradiology and telepsychiatry (Mermelstein et al., 2017), with the modern era beginning in 1968 when the Massachusetts General Hospital (MGH) started the first hospital-based multispecialty telemedicine practice. This program offered remote clinical examinations to travelers and airport workers at Logan International Airport using MGH physicians located 2.7 miles away, with television equipment to connect the two sites. Over 1,000 patients received telemedicine examinations over the next decade and the program inspired others to start telemedicine programs. However, many programs ceased to operate by 1980 due to the high cost of equipment and other factors.

The early 1990s saw a resurgence due in part to the advent of the Internet and companies investing in telecommunications-based technologies specifically for telemedicine. Globally, tens of millions of patients have received telemedicine and telehealth services with hospitals outsourcing selected gap (e.g., nighttime and weekend coverage by teleradiology) and urgent services (e.g., tele-stroke services). Direct-to-consumer (DTC) telehealth is a more recent entrant into the marketplace (Elliott & Yopes, 2019), including primary care services that are offered at pharmacies, big box stores, walk-in clinics and directly through the Internet or mobile devices. DTC telehealth may increase utilization by increasing access and convenience although it may not reduce costs (Ashwood et al., 2017).

The COVID-19 pandemic began in late 2019 and resulted in worldwide measures such as isolation to combat its impact and resulted in an exponential rise in the use of telehealth worldwide. In the United States, the Centers for Medicare & Medicaid Services issued over 230 Medicare and over 600 Medicaid waivers to expand telehealth services and coverage (United States General Accountability Office, 2021). A recent study of 16.7 million commercially insured and Medicare Advantage enrollees from January to June 2020 revealed that 30% of all visits during the pandemic used telehealth and compared to pre-pandemic, the weekly number of visits increased 23-fold. A similar study found wide geographic variation in uptake as well as general declines over time as in-person services started to re-open (Patel et al., 2021); however, use has stabilized at a higher level today than pre-pandemic.

Telehealth Modalities

Telehealth uses a variety of technologies or modalities that have changed over time, with three main types often used in combination and across clinical specialties.

Synchronous (Real Time)

Audio-Videoconferencing

Synchronous encounters use videoconferencing technologies where providers and patients see and hear each other interactively in real time. This modality is probably the most common and most amenable to specialties like telepsychiatry and other mental/behavioral health applications, telerehabilitation, primary care and others where tasks such as assessments of medical history and basic visual exams can be done. If an encounter is scheduled between two providers (e.g., cardiologist and primary care provider) with a patient present, peripheral devices (e.g., electronic stethoscopes, ultrasound) can be used to conduct a more in-depth exam. If the patient is in their home, there are still options available to collect relevant data such as Bluetooth-enabled scales and digital blood pressure devices (Benzinger et al., 2021; Weinstein et al., 2018). In the past, these encounters were often conducted using dedicated carts with videoconferencing tools, peripherals, plug-in ports and lockable storage compartments, but state-of-the-art devices such as laptops, tablets and smartphones are more commonly used today.

Auditory Only

Telephone triage and auditory advice services (TTAS) have been around for many years (e.g., poison control centers) and are increasingly common in telehealth. It is important to note, however, that such services are not allowed in every state and may not be reimbursed. In telehealth, it is typical to have nurses, physician assistants or general practitioners support the service and interact with patients to render assessments and provide advice (Lake et al., 2017).

Tele-ICU

The tele-ICU (intensive care unit) is a synchronous service where off-site command centers staffed by intensivists and critical care nurses monitor patients remotely, having full access to monitoring and other relevant data. This service enables real-time monitoring of vital signs to alert on-site providers of changes in status, diagnoses being made, treatments ordered and even conducting interventions by controlling life support systems. Evidence shows that the tele-ICU can reduce mortality rates and length of ICU stay and potentially reduce costs (Chen et al., 2017).

Text-Based

Text-based communication using the phone and dedicated software and/or peripheral sensors are used to monitor in real-time things such as physiological measures (e.g., heart monitor harness), falls and patient location (e.g., for Alzheimer's patients) to send alerts to providers (and caretakers) when events occur or data are out of range so they can intervene.

Asynchronous (Store and Forward)

Video clips (e.g., for assessing a patient's gait), audio clips (e.g., recorded heart and lung sounds), RPM data (e.g., weight, pulse oximetry), images acquired with specialty cameras and/or smartphones (e.g., of skin conditions) and other medical images (e.g., radiographic images), virtual pathology slides, ophthalmology images) are common store-and-forward or asynchronous forms of telehealth in which data are acquired and transmitted securely for interpretation. The key feature of the asynchronous modality is that the provider typically reviews the data at a later point in time, providing diagnoses, treatment recommendations and next steps remotely (e.g., via email or through a secure portal/health record system) for the on-site provider to follow-up with the patient. Given the history of teleradiology as one of the earliest forms of telehealth, it is likely safe to say that more telehealth has occurred asynchronously than synchronously.

Hybrid

Other technologies cross the boundaries between synchronous and asynchronous for both patients and providers. mHealth applications (apps) are being developed for numerous apps primarily using smartphones as the medium. Some are Food and Drug Administration (FDA)-approved to diagnose and treat patients, but the majority are not and are available online for anyone to download and use. This capability has raised concerns regarding security and regulations (Terry, 2020) as well as the responsibility of providers to assess before acting upon non-prescribed app data that patients provide. Many of these and other tools in telehealth use artificial intelligence (AI) schemes to collate and analyze data (often in real time), send alerts to providers and patients regarding out-of-range data and even predict when an event might occur (Topol, 2019).

RPM has been available to patients for about two decades, providing ongoing assessment capabilities for patients with chronic conditions. This telehealth modality is especially beneficial for diagnoses such as congestive heart failure, chronic obstructive pulmonary disease and diabetes. Peripheral monitoring devices such as weight scales, blood pressure cuffs, glucometers and pulse oximeters can be connected via Bluetooth to a central hub and sent by Internet or satellite to a professional who is monitoring the daily vital signs. Through daily data collection, deviation from the normal range can be detected. Additionally, patients are asked routine questions such as number of pillows needed, amount of sleep or occurrence of headache, edema or other symptoms that may indicate disease exacerbation.

Telehealth Services

Services provided by registered nurses (RN) and advanced practice registered nurses (APRNs) differ in prescriptive, diagnostic and treatment authority. The use of telehealth by nurses is limited by reimbursement and state licensure that defines the APRNs' scope of practice. Practice restrictions are defined by the state boards of nursing, creating differences in practice authority among states and the inability to practice across some state lines without dual licensure.

Nurse Roles in Telehealth

The American Academy of Ambulatory Care Nursing (AAACN) supports professional nurses focusing on 'individuals, families, groups, communities, and populations in primary, specialty care, non-acute community outpatient settings' (American Academy of Ambulatory Care Nursing, 2021). Telehealth nursing exemplifies this professional practice when provided in virtual environments. AAACN defines the scope and 16 standards for telehealth nursing (American Academy of Ambulatory Care Nursing, 2018). The American Nurses Credentialing Center (ANCC) is a division of the American Nurses Association (ANA) that certifies nurses in specialty practice. Nurses interested in telehealth certification as a professional specialty must pass the Ambulatory Care Nurse Board Certification (AMB-BC) exam.

Foundational to professional telehealth nursing are the *Core Principles on Connected Health* (Table 9.1). The move to using the term '*Connected Health*' instead of '*Telehealth*' was shepherded by Partner's Healthcare. ANA acknowledges that *telehealth* is the professional certification terminology, however, they used the working definition of '*Connected Health*' as outward evidence of the importance of using technology to transform healthcare by efficiently and effectively linking patients and clinicians (American Nurses Association, 2021). A connected health approach 'facilitates remote diagnosis and treatment, continuous monitoring and adjustment of therapies, support for patient self-care, and the leveraging of providers across large populations of patients' (American Nurses Association, 2021). These core principles offer guidance to organizations providing telehealth regardless of patient location and focus on information exchange using electronic communication to improve the health of patients.

Table 9.1 Summary—American Nurses Association Telehealth Core Principles (ANA, 2021)

	Core Principles on Connected Health
Principle 1	• Connected health technology use does not alter standards of professional practice healthcare delivery, research, education • It is a healthcare professional's responsibility to provide lawful, evidence-based, high-quality personalized care regardless of delivery method
Principle 2	• Connected healthcare is subject to same healthcare laws and board oversight as in-person • Other applicable state/federal laws not applied to in-person care may apply
Principle 3	• Connected health should prioritize improving access to quality healthcare guided by best available evidence, accepted clinical standards, best practices • Services must include appropriate technological modalities that meet patient's needs, are practical, easy to use, align with patient location and care setting
Principle 4	• Healthcare professionals must meet state-specific regulatory and institutional requirements in accordance with the scope of practice • Variations in practice rules and regulations across states and facilities exist, so providers must practice respective of these variations
Principle 5	• Nursing and other healthcare professions are responsible for developing own competencies to ensure safe, effective, competent delivery of healthcare using patient- and family-centered team-based approach
Principle 6	• Connected health should be congruent with in-person care and must adhere to the best available evidence and interdisciplinary standards of care, recognizing technology limitations to ensure optimal patient-centered outcomes
Principle 7	• Integrity and therapeutic value of the patient–healthcare professional relationship should be established, maintained, promoted via connected health
Principle 8	• Transmission of electronic information and communication via health technologies must uphold the highest level of ethical conduct in secure management of patient health information, patient privacy, confidentiality, protection against unauthorized breach of information • Includes informing patients of use of third-party technology providers, risk disruption integrity of providers' data management practices, commitment to protect patients from such event
Principle 9	• Documentation requirements for healthcare services should be consistent with requirements applicable to all other patient encounters
Principle 10	• In compliance with applicable federal/state laws patients should be informed about the process, inherent risks and benefits, rights and responsibilities • Informed consent may not need to be independent from other informed consent for treatment but electronic consent should comply with applicable federal/state laws

(Continued)

Table 9.1 (Continued)   Summary—American Nurses Association Telehealth Core Principles (ANA, 2021)

	Core Principles on Connected Health
Principle 11	• Safety of patients and healthcare professionals must be ensured. Hardware and software must comply with safety/security standards. Providers must consider the appropriateness of connected health for specific patients and situations and demonstrate competence
Principle 12	• To ensure best outcomes assessment and evaluation, studying all aspects of connected health should be ongoing and systematic, include key stakeholders; resulting evidence should guide development and implementation guidelines and best practices
Principle 13	• Policies governing practices and reimbursement should be continuously updated

Combining telehealth modalities tailors communication to meet the needs of each unique situation which depend on factors such as diagnoses, treatment, technology usability and connectivity services available. A case manager from a payer source such as a government or private insurance company may initiate an assessment for potential telehealth-delivered care in the home. The patient's primary diagnosis determines the focus and goal of the treatment prescribed with relevant comorbidities considered. Assessment of available and appropriate telehealth devices for administering treatment should follow. Patient profiles are examined for travel risks such as the potential for falls and infection. Broadband, Wi-Fi and signal strength are considered for potential telehealth devices. Patient and caregiver familiarity with technology, in general, is indicative of the challenges that will be faced.

Registered nurses providing healthcare, whether within the walls of a facility or out in the community, are extremely mobile. A hallmark of nursing care is the ability to prioritize and reprioritize care based on patient needs. The ability to use text, video or audio as needed is crucial and fits with the mobile and prioritizing nature of the RN's work. Relationship building is an important part of providing care, with nurses considered a 'trusted' part of the healthcare team. A relationship can be established when the patient feels the presence of the remote nurse. This occurs when the perception of the technology disappears from the conscious attention of the patient and body language can be used to communicate. A working or therapeutic alliance follows when emotions can be evoked (Bouchard et al., 2011). Psychiatric mental health APRNs and nurses who use videoconferencing benefit from training in the development of therapeutic alliance with telehealth. Patients prefer an initial visit to be in-person, believing that a relationship can be established more readily. Once that relationship is established, telehealth visits can build rapport and trust (Bethel et al., 2021).

Touch must be substituted for when using telehealth. There are RPM tools that can provide vital signs and other data, but observation skills must be sharpened to compensate for the inability to touch. Asking the patient to move the camera in an intentional manner to function as a home visiting professional's eyes greatly enhances the opportunity to build relationships and provide a comprehensive remote assessment (Shea et al., 2021). Telehealth access into a patient's home is similar to accessing the home in-person, asking permission to walk in, taking time to engage in small talk and demonstrating concern about safety and possible risks as well as concern about the patient as a human being with a life separate from their illness.

Information Exchange

Healthcare services are dependent on the exchange of information that updates and informs the healthcare team and patients. The team is commonly led by a provider (e.g., physician or APRN (with full practice authority)) assisted by a physician's assistant (PA) or APRN (limited practice authority) who can assess, diagnose, write orders and prescribe. Other professionals are added as ordered by the provider.

How the health team uses telehealth has been classified into three types of information exchange (Figure 9.1): *Health Team Member to Health Team Member, Health Team Member to Patient*, and *Patient to Health Technology* (Tuckson et al., 2017). 'Health Team member' refers to every professional involved with care during a period of need (i.e., therapists, nurses, physicians, medical assistants and caregivers).

Healthcare Team Member to Healthcare Team Member—The healthcare team, when not in-person, exchanges information through text, audio and video, using PCs, mobile devices and telephone. If communication is required frequently, a system such as a wearable device that enables instant on speaker, wireless and hands-free voice communication can be used. A very common system uses electronic, voice-activated badges that can be spoken into while worn or used like a phone for greater privacy. These systems communicate via Wi-Fi within a hospital, long-term care or senior living center. Community-based primary care relies on mobile tablets or

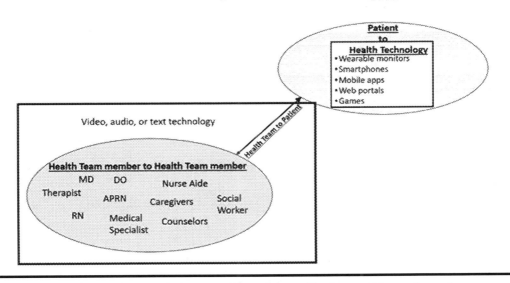

Figure 9.1   Information exchange. (Adapted from Tuckson, Edmonds and Hodgkins, 2017).

smartphone devices through cellular or Internet connection. Many devices can be configured to connect with the electronic health record (EHR) so that information can be pulled (orders or test results) and pushed (reminders, alerts) allowing the RN to be mobile and prioritize patient needs.

Health Team Member to Patient—Telehealth enables all health team members to directly interact with the patient; however, communication from many different sources at once may be confusing and overwhelming. A nurse case manager often coordinates information delivery and services, working as a communication and advocacy link between the patient and APRN, PA or physician. Video, phone, email and RPM devices provide nurses with greater access to information for exchange coordination. The telehealth benefit of *access* extends to the patient's desire to include friends and family members.

Settings

RNs and APRNs provide telehealthcare in numerous settings. The most common settings are primary care (home-based/clinic), specialty care, school nursing, emergency departments, community-based urgent care, nurse triage, DTC and health promotion.

Primary Care

The definition of primary care used for this discussion is adapted from the American Academy of Family Physicians (American Academy of Family Physicians, 2021). Primary care is the provision of integrated, accessible healthcare services given by interprofessional healthcare providers accountable for addressing personal healthcare needs, developing a sustained partnership with patients and practicing in the context of family and community. In 2007, the 'medical home' was endorsed as a primary care philosophy wherein the patient is the center of a comprehensive team approach to care, wherever the patient lives (Primary Care Collaborative, 2021). Accessibility is a distinguishing feature of the medical home philosophy with telehealth innovations providing ongoing communication with the team.

Home-based care has been revolutionized by telehealth. Prior to the 2019 pandemic, primary healthcare delivery in the home was only paid for by private insurance. Telehealth was *not* reimbursable by government-sponsored insurance (Medicare) when the patient's 'originating site' was located at home. Home healthcare services (i.e., injections, catheter changes, condition observation, wound care or management and evaluation of the care plan) from an in-person RN were only reimbursable if the patient was unable to leave their home due to an illness that could get worse or they had a disability requiring assistance of another person or medical equipment (Medicare Interactive, 2021). During the pandemic, for the safety of patient, provider and healthcare staff, reimbursable home care was able to be delivered and received from the home.

According to the American Association of Nurse Practitioners, 89% of APRNs are trained in primary care (American Association of Nurse Practitioners, 2021). The shortage of primary care physicians coupled with telehealth has dramatically paved the way for the expansion of family nurse practitioners providing telehealth services, especially in underserved and rural areas. Home health nursing has also greatly increased and this is likely to continue (American Academy of Ambulatory Care Nursing, 2021). While 'hands-on' services cannot be provided remotely, patients, family and friends can receive remote video guidance and assessment of wound, ostomy and skin care. Patients and caregivers can be educated to assess and monitor signs, and symptoms and self-performance of skills such as injection, inhaler use and ostomy management can be evaluated remotely.

Specialty Care

The shortage of specialists in rural areas compared to urban areas results in higher death and hospitalization rates, especially in patients with chronic conditions such as heart failure and diabetes. Rural dwellers who see a specialist at least once/year in addition to their primary care provider are 16.6% less likely to die from their chronic condition (Weil, 2019). In February 2021, the primary specialist claims for telehealth included psychiatry; substance use disorder treatment; rheumatology; gastroenterology; neurology; ear, nose and throat; pulmonary infectious disease; hematology; general medicine; dermatology; urology; oncology; nephrology; cardiology; dental/oral; gynecology; Poisoning/drug toxicology; neurosurgery; general surgery; orthopedic surgery and ophthalmology (Bestsennyy et al., 2021).

As mental health concerns arise, the supply of providers does not meet the demands. It is projected that by 2025, there will be almost 18,000 psychiatric-mental health nurse practitioners (National Council for Mental Wellbeing, 2017). Yet, the United States Department of Health and Human Services Health Resources and Services Administration predicts that there will be a shortage of 250,000 mental health professionals (US Department of Health and Human Services, 2016). RNs practicing in psychiatric-mental health must be good communicators and that also holds true when videoconferencing is used. Although not diagnosing or prescribing, RNs in specialty care serve as the eyes and ears of the providers. Any specialty that requires a follow-up or check-in visit can offer services provided by an RN using telehealth.

When a specialist visits remotely, a *telepresenter* is required for assessment when hand-held peripheral assessment tools (e.g., stethoscope, otoscope and ophthalmoscope) are needed (Figure 9.2). A telepresenter is a medical professional who presents a patient's problem through proper positioning for a camera or video view using digital diagnostic tools to send data to a medical provider and provide on-site human touch. RNs are often telepresenters for remote specialists and their expertise is critical to an

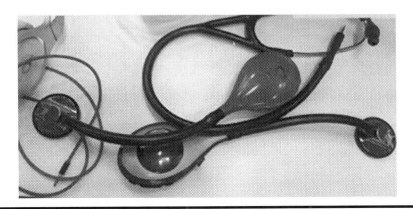

Figure 9.2 Example of an electronic stethoscope.

accurate specialist assessment as they are accustomed to providing complete patient-centered care including education and they have an understanding of physiology to be able to correctly position patients.

Emergency Services

Approximately 20% of Emergency Department (ED) visits are due to accessibility concerns such as lack of access to other providers or the preferred clinic/office is not open. The average cost of a hospital ED visit is approximately $922 and the average cost of a video telehealth visit is US$ 40–50. One out of five ED visits could be eliminated saving costs (Yamamoto, 2014) through the use of telehealth targeting population needs.

Triage nurses are the first line of care in EDs, often using telephone triage as the initial part of the process. Triage nurses within the ED or off-site prioritize the urgency of the need to determine patient disposition. Telephone triage nursing has been a service of insurance companies for quite some time. Some callers require ambulance services and others only require verbal support. Telephone triage is an art and requires training on how to properly handle emergencies. According to TriageLogic, a nurse telehealth triage training program, there are five levels for patient disposition: *911*—hang up and immediately call 911; *Urgent*—get to an ED, *make a provider appointment*—in the next 24–48 hours; *home care*—triage nurse gives clinical advice with encouragement to call provider in the next 2 weeks; and *Other*—instruct to call community-based agencies or ask for lab tests, etc. Almost half of the calls are about homecare and 29% require urgent ED intervention (TriageLogic, 2021).

Community-Based Urgent Care

Within the community, urgent care facilities are visited when illness, injuries or other needs arise and the primary care provider is not available. Most offer walk-in or telehealth services and although there can be variations in the process, there is a common workflow. The patient contacts the urgent care center and is triaged by a telephone nurse who provides instructions for the upcoming virtual visit using a Health Insurance Portability and Accountability Act (HIPAA)-compliant video platform app. Referrals to in-person assessments can be made if the remote assessment is not adequate.

Direct to Consumer

DTC is increasing in popularity, but it is not without some concern regarding potential issues such as the ability to establish a relationship between provider and patient, lack of care continuity, lack of integration with local providers and potential for fraud. A nationwide survey found that telehealth is significantly less desirable when a relationship with the provider has not been established (Welch et al., 2017). Examples of DTC services that include pharmaceuticals are sexual health, hair loss, contraception, dermatologic conditions and performance anxiety (Bollmeier et al., 2020).

DTC conditions are typically very private and there may be an embarrassment in sharing information with a known provider. The patient completes a brief, self-report, online questionnaire, followed by a virtual visit from an unfamiliar physician, APRN or PA. A prescription is then called to a pharmacy or the medication is mailed directly to the patient. Of great concern is that with a one-time interaction between a patient and the DTC provider, medication intake is not monitored for long-term safety. And primary care providers may be left out of the loop.

Human Factors

Usability

Telehealth must be easy to use for both providers and patients to ensure acceptance. One encounter with a technology glitch or failure can easily bias users against any future use. Human beings are very diverse in terms of characteristics such as size, weight, shape, perceptual and cognitive abilities, and these capabilities vary predictably with factors such as age, gender and health status. Telehealth technologies make demands on user capabilities, such as vision (text and image size, contrast), hearing (sound intensity and clarity relative to background noise), cognition (recalling which medications to take and when) and psychomotor ability (using a smartphone to enter health data). Cultural and educational differences also are important and each of these factors must be considered when building telehealth technologies in order to provide safe and effective remote care (Charness et al., 2012).

For providers, there are some simple steps that can be taken to ensure those with health and other challenges have access to telehealth. The provider should start by inventorying products, services and factors required to provide effective telehealth services and ensure they meet basic accessibility requirements for people with disabilities. The compatibility of assistive technology (e.g., alternative keyboards) should be considered, including whether these devices can work effectively with the chosen telehealth modality. It is necessary to learn about and incorporate accessibility features (e.g., close-captioning) of the software programs. One should be sure to include the patient's caregiver, family member or home health aide during telehealth visits. It is important to gain knowledge and awareness of cultural competency and linguistic sensitivity, as well as to ask patients with disabilities about their accessibility requirements.

Technology Considerations and Room Design

The environment within which telehealth encounters take place is important and can make or break a successful visit. There are numerous factors to consider and there are books, articles and even websites that provide excellent advice and tips (Charness et al., 2012; Krupinski, 2014). Some important considerations when optimizing telehealth environments include lighting sources, levels, types and angles; sound sources and quality; attire (e.g., no white lab coats or loud patterns, solid light blue works well); background (e.g., reduce clutter, keep walls bare, use basic virtual backgrounds or green screens); and camera quality, location and distance from the user. Providers can equip patients and caregivers with tips and easy steps to address key issues (e.g., lighting, camera requirements) in advance of an encounter.

Key Considerations

Insurance Coverage

At the writing of this chapter, the world is cautiously emerging from the COVID-19 pandemic. The use of telehealth has gone on fast-forward over the last two years, changing healthcare delivery and nursing processes forever. Most markedly, private and government payers for healthcare services have created policies and billing codes to reimburse all licensed healthcare practitioners for distant site telehealth services. The provider can perform services from any location, including their home, during the hours of their workday. A list of codes for telehealth services is available at https://www.cms.gov/files/zip/covid-19-telehealth-services-phe.zip. And, the number of billing codes for the delivery of telehealth has tripled.

Regulatory

When the Public Health Emergency (PHE) for the COVID-19 pandemic was declared in 2019, practice regulations were temporarily suspended to capitalize on the most beneficial and desirable aspect of telehealth—*providing patients with access to care* (Bestsennyy et al., 2021). The PHE provisions enabled rural hospitals, skilled nursing facilities and homebound patients to receive services, even though the providers were in another state. Additional suspended regulations were those limiting medical exams that nurse practitioners could perform as a surrogate for a medical provider and prescriptive privileges via telehealth. Adherence to the scope of practice regulations will most likely return to pre-pandemic standards following the conclusion of this PHE, however, it appears that telehealth is here to stay.

Training and Competencies

There are a number of groups developing telehealth competencies for nursing. Carius et al. (2016) developed a holistic competency model for telenursing practice that identified four categories: social (e.g., soft skills like friendliness and empathy), personal (e.g., reliability and willingness to learn), methodological (e.g., anamnesis skills, analytical thinking, coping with abstraction) and professional competencies (e.g., medical knowledge and experience). Social competencies were viewed as especially important, particularly with respect to having strong communication skills and those skills related to establishing effective relationships with patients in a virtual environment. Being able to convey empathy and sensitivity and having good active listening skills are important attributes as they contribute to a nurse's ability to make solid clinical decisions backed by clear critical thinking skills that are necessary when trying to understand the patient's needs, which may not be expressed well virtually.

During the development of these competencies, the research team interviewed both nurses involved in telenursing and employers. Overall, there was good agreement between the two groups with several exceptions. Employers felt that legal knowledge and knowledge of the healthcare market were important, while nurses did not feel these were as relevant. The nurses also raised an interesting challenge—often they still serve only as gatekeepers between physicians and patients. No matter how skilled they are, or how much telenursing experience they have, patients frequently want to ask the doctor directly for advice.

Table 9.2 Competencies for Initiating a Telehealth Program

Four Ps of a Telehealth Program	Competencies to be Completed for Initiating a Telehealth Program
Plans	• How will this program define telehealth? • For what age and cultural population with what type of health conditions will this program provide services? What is the setting? • What are the regulations and reimbursements for our services? • What are the benefits and barriers? • What type of technology and personnel is required?

Preparation	• Determine
	  • Guiding protocols for delivery of services
	  • Remote consenting processes with confidentiality of information
	  • Equipment, technology and space needed to deliver services
	  • Skills required for each professional delivering care

Provision	• Professional visits will include initiation, assessment, charting and follow-up for each encounter

Performance	• Evaluation of impact
	  • Access to care
	  • Financial
	  • Satisfaction of patient and providers
	  • Usefulness

The Four P's of telehealth: planning, preparing, providing and performance evaluation, were used to establish nursing knowledge skills and abilities/attitudes for competent delivery of remote healthcare (Rutledge et al., 2021). The resulting telehealth competencies were derived from an extensive literature review with refinement by 12 APRNs with backgrounds in telehealth. Table 9.2 shows the competencies for initiating a telehealth program. Using the Four Ps as a framework for interprofessional curriculum development and clinical practice assures a comprehensive process for assessing and meeting healthcare system needs when transitioning to telehealthcare.

Looking to the Future

It is clear that telehealth will continue to grow, evolve and become an integral part of healthcare in the future. Ideally, the lessons learned and increased awareness of the capabilities of telehealth, as well as limitations that occurred during the COVID-19 pandemic will pave the way toward further regulatory and financial support. Ideally, the prefix 'tele' will be dropped and it will become the practice of healthcare, caring for patients despite the technology, tools or distance.

New technologies will be developed to further enhance the telehealth experience and reduce some of the challenges evident today. For example, Haptic sensors are being used to provide feedback during remote palpation (e.g., for appendicitis) and other technologies can provide tactile information of surface textures (e.g., bumps on the skin) and temperature. Virtual and augmented reality devices are being evaluated and sensors are being developed and tested for remote monitoring. These and many other telehealth advances will define the future of healthcare and potentially reduce health disparities and improve patient care and population health overall.

References

American Academy of Ambulatory Care Nursing. (2018). *Scope and standards of practice for professional telehealth nursing.* Wolters Kluwer [online]. Available at: https://www.wolterskluwer.com/en/solutions/ovid/scope-and-standards-of-practice-for-professional-telehealth-nursing-12529 (Accessed 18 August 2021).

American Academy of Ambulatory Care Nursing. (2021). About AAACN. *Many settings. Multiple roles. One unifying speciality* [online]. Available at: https://www.aaacn.org/about/about-aaacn (Accessed 18 August 2021).

American Academy of Family Physicians. (2021). Primary Care. *Policies* [online]. Available at: https://www.aafp.org/about/policies/all/primary-care.html (Accessed 18 August 2021).

American Association of Nurse Practitioners. (2021). *Nurse practitioners in primary care.* AANP's Positions and Papers [online]. Available at: https://www.aanp.org/advocacy/advocacy-resource/position-statements (Accessed 18 August 2021).

American Nurses Association. (2021). *ANA core principles on connected health* [online]. Available at: https://www.nursingworld.org/~4a9307/globalassets/docs/ana/practice/ana-core-principles-on-connected-health.pdf (Accessed 18 August 2021).

Ashwood, J. S., Mehrotra, A., Cowling, D., & Uscher-Pines, L. (2017). Direct-to-consumer telehealth may increase access to care but does not decrease spending. *Health Affairs*, 36(3), pp.485–491. https://doi.org/10.1377/hlthaff.2016.1130

Bashshur, R. L., & Shannon G. W. (2009). *History of telemedicine: Evolution, context, and transformation.* New Rochelle, NY: Mary Ann Liebert, Inc.

Benzinger, C. P., Huffman, M. D., Sweis, R. N., & Stone, N. J. (2021). The telehealth ten: A guide for a patient-assisted virtual physical exam. *American Journal of Medicine*, 134(1), pp.48–51. https://doi.org/10.1016/j.amjmed.2020.06.015

Bestsennyy, O., Gilbert, G., Harris, A., & Rost, J. (2021). *Telehealth: A quarter-trillion-dollar post-COVID-19 reality?* McKinsey and Company: Healthcare Systems & Services Practice [online]. Available at: https://connectwithcare.org/wp-content/uploads/2021/07/telehealth-a-quarter-trillion-dollar-post-covid-19-reality.pdf (Accessed 17 August 2021).

Bethel, C., Towers, V., Crist, J., Silva, G. E., & Shea, K. D. (2021). *A guide for intentional home telehealth assessment: Patient and caregiver perceptions.* CIN: Computers, Informatics, Nursing, Advance Publication [online]. Available at: http://ovidsp.ovid.com/ovidweb.cgi?T=JS&PAGE=reference&D=ovftw&NEWS=N&AN=0002665-900000000-99264. https://doi.org/10.1097/CIN.0000000000000779. (Accessed 17 August 2021).

Bollmeier, S. G., Stevenson, E., Finnegan, P., & Griggs, S. K. (2020). Direct to consumer telemedicine: Is healthcare from home best? *Missouri Medicine*, 117(4), pp.303–309.

Bouchard, S., Dumoulin, S., Michaud, M., & Gougeon, V. (2011). Telepresence experienced in videoconference varies according to emotions involved in videoconference sessions. *Studies in Health Technology and Informatics*, 167, pp.128–132.

Carius, C., Zippel-Schultz, B., Schultz, C., Schultz, M., & Helms, T. M. (2016). Developing a holistic competency model for telenursing practice: Perspectives from telenurses and managers of telemedicine service centres. *Journal of the International Society for Telemedicine and eHealth*, 4(e22), pp.1–17.

Charness, N., Demiris, G., & Krupinski, E. (2012). *Designing telehealth for an aging population: A human factors perspective.* New York: CRC Press.

Chen, J., Sun, D., Yang, W., Liu, M., Zhang, S., Peng, J., & Ren, C. (2017). Clinical and economic outcomes of telemedicine programs in the intensive care unit: A systematic review and meta-analysis. *Journal of Intensive Care Medicine*, 33(7), pp.383–393. https://doi.org/10.1177%2F0885066617726942

Gillings, M. R., Hilbert, M., & Kemp, D. J. (2016). Information in the biosphere: Biological and digital worlds. *Trends Ecology & Evolution*, 31 (3), pp.180–189. https://doi.org/10.1016/j.tree.2015.12.013

Health Resources and Services Administration. (n.d.). What is telehealth? How is telehealth different from telemedicine?' [online]. Available at: https://www.healthit.gov/faq/what-telehealth-how-telehealth-different-telemedicine (Accessed 23 April 2021).

Hunter, K. M., & Bickford, C. J. (2015). The practice specialty of nursing informatics. In Saba, V. K., & McCormick, K. A. (Eds.), *Essentials of Nursing Informatics.* 6th ed. San Francisco, CA: McGraw Hill Education, pp.232.

Krupinski, E. A. (2014). Telemedicine workplace environments: Designing for success. *Healthcare*, 2(1), pp.115–122. https://doi.org/10.3390/healthcare2010115

Kulikowski, C. A., Shortliffe, E. H., Currie, L. M., Elkin, P. L., Hunter, L. E., Johnson, T. R., Kalet, I. J., Lenert, L. A., Musen, M. A., Ozbolt, J. G., Smith, J. W., Tarczy-Hornoch, P. Z., & Williamson, J. J. (2012). AMIA Board white paper: Definition of biomedical informatics and specification of core competencies for graduate education in the discipline. *JAMIA*, 19(6), pp.931–938. https://doi.org/10.1136/amiajnl-2012-001053

Lake, R., Georgiou, A., Li, J., Li, L., Byrne, M., Robinson, M., & Westbrook, J. I. (2017). The quality, safety and governance of telephone triage and device services: An overview of evidence from systematic reviews. *BMC Health Services Research*, 17, p.614. https://doi.org/10.1186/s12913-017-2564-x

Medicare Interactive. (2021). The homebound requirement. *Get answers.* [online] Medicare Rights Center. Available at: https://www.medicareinteractive.org/get-answers/medicare-covered-services/home-health-services/the-homebound-requirement (Accessed 1 January 2022).

Mermelstein, H., Guzman E., Rabinowitz, T., Krupinski, E., & Hilty, D. (2017). The application of technology to health: The evolution of telephone to telemedicine and telepsychiatry: A historical review and look at human factors. *Journal of Technology in Behavioral Science*, 2, pp.5–20. https://link.springer.com/article/10.1007/s41347-017-0010-x

National Council of Mental Wellbeing. (n.d.). *The psychiatric shortage: Causes and solutions.* In Medical Directors Institute National Council of Behavioral Health report [online]. Available at: https://www.thenationalcouncil.org/wp-content/uploads/2017/03/Psychiatric-Shortage_National-Council-.pdf?daf=375ateTbd56 (Accessed 17 August 2021).

Patel, S. Y., Mehrotra, A., Huskamp, H. A., Uscher-Pines, L., Ganguli, I., & Barnett, M. L. (2021). Trends in outpatient care delivery and telemedicine during the COVID-19 pandemic in the US. *JAMA Internal Medicine*, 181(3), pp.388–391 [online]. Available at: http://jamanetwork.com/article.aspx?doi=10.1001/jamainternmed.2020.5928 (Accessed 17 August 2021)

Primary Care Collaborative. (2021). Defining the Medical Home. *About us* (published ahead of print)

Rutledge, C. M., O'Rourke, J., Mason, A. M., Chike-Harris, K., & Behnke, L. et al. (2021 Sep-Oct 01). Telehealth competencies for nursing education and practice: The Four P's of Telehealth. *Nurse Educator*, 6(5), pp. 300–305. https://doi.org/10.1097/nne.0000000000000988. PMID: 33481494; PMCID: PMC8395962

Shea, K. D., Towers, V., Koon, M., & Silva, G. (2021). Development of an intentional telehealth viewing guide for home-based patient assessment. *Telemedicine Reports*, 2(1), pp.32–38. https://doi.org/10.1089/tmr.2020.0017

Terry, N. P. (2020). Assessing the thin regulation of consumer-facing health technologies. *Journal of Law Medicine Ethics*, 38(1), pp.94–102. https://doi.org/10.1177%2F1073110520917034

Topol, E. (2019). *Deep Medicine: How Artificial Intelligence Can Make Healthcare Human Again.* New York: Basic Books.

TriageLogic. (2021). The 5 levels of telephone nurse triage. Telehealth [online]. Available at: https://triagelogic.com/the-5-levels-of-telephone-nurse-triage/ (Accessed 17 August 2021).

Tuckson, R. V., Edmunds, M., & Hodgkins, M. L. (2017). Telehealth. *New England Journal of Medicine*, 377(16), pp.1585–1592. https://doi.org/10.1056/NEJMsr1503323

United States Department of Health and Human Services. (2016). Behavioral health practitioners: 2013–2025. *National projections of supply and demand* [online]. Available at: https://bhw.hrsa.gov/sites/default/files/bureau-health-workforce/data-research/behavioral-health-2013-2025.pdf (Accessed 18 August 2021).

United States Government Accountability Office. (2021). *Medicare and medicaid COVID-19 program flexibilities and considerations for their continuation. GAO-21-575T* [online]. Available at: https://www.gao.gov/assets/gao-21-575t.pdf (Accessed 18 June 2021).

Weil, A. R. (2019). Rural health. *Health Affairs*, 38(12), p.1963. https://doi.org/10.1377/hlthaff.2019.01536

Weinstein, R. S., Krupinski, E. A., & Doarn, C. R. (2018). Clinical examination component of telemedicine, telehealth, mHealth, and connected health practices. *Medical Clinics*, 102(3), pp.533–544. https://doi.org/10.1016/j.mcna.2018.01.002

Welch, B. H., O'Connell, N. S., & McElligott, J. T. (2017). Patient preferences for direct-to-consumer telemedicine services: A nationwide survey. *BMC Health Services Research*, 17(1), p.784.

Yamamoto, D. (2014). Assessment of the feasibility and cost of replacing in-person care with acute care telehealth services. *Medicare acute care telehealth feasibility* [online]. Available at: https://connectwithcare.org/wp-content/uploads/2014/12/Medicare-Acute-Care-Telehealth-Feasibility.pdf (Accessed 17 August 2021).

Ye, J. (2020). The role of health technology and informatics in a global public health emergency: Practices and implications from the COVID-19 pandemic. *JMIR Medical Informatics*, 8(7), p.e19866. https://doi.org/10.2196/19866

Chapter 10

Simulations-Based Care Delivery

Cynthia Sherraden Bradley, Joanne Donnelly and Nellie Munn Swanson

Contents

Introduction 170
    Background of Simulation 170
    Nursing-Led Innovation in Healthcare Simulation................................... 170
    Safety and Quality Initiatives 172
Simulation Training for Healthcare Providers and Teams............................ 172
    Provider Training and Assessment... 172
    Technical Skills Training... 173
    Nontechnical Skills Training 175
    Team-Based Crisis Simulation 175
    Continuing Education.. 177
    Discrete Event Simulation 177
Simulation Research and Assessment... 177
Healthcare Systems—Meeting the Needs of the Future................................ 179
    Testing New Space Design and Care Processes 179
    Testing New Products.. 179
Cost and ROI 180
Conclusion 181
References 181

Introduction

Simulation is an active learning pedagogy that has proliferated in use across academic and practice settings to improve the confidence and competence of individual care providers and to strengthen team performance in clinical situations. Despite numerous safety initiatives, preventable medical error remains the third leading cause of death, a statistic that may not be completely accurate because many errors are not reported. Simulation training has demonstrated positive outcomes, supporting the need for continued exploration of innovative strategies to reduce preventable errors throughout care delivery organizations. This chapter describes the evolution of simulation-based activities in patient care delivery settings and provides examples of the significant role of nursing in improving patient safety and the quality of care delivered by individuals, teams and organizations.

Background of Simulation

The first documented use of simulation was in aviation to train pilots in the technical skills needed to fly using instruments. During World War II, simulation training was used for teams to practice piloting, navigating and operating bomber aircrafts. Because of its success, simulation was used prominently for pilot training by the late 1970s, which accelerated the development of industry standards for simulation training to ensure consistency in both the training process and evaluation of outcomes. Novice and experienced pilots routinely practice emergency procedures in simulators to continually improve flight safety.

The improved safety outcomes of aviation simulation-based training served as the impetus for translating simulation pedagogy to healthcare settings. Anesthesia providers were early adopters in the 1960s, but it was not until the 1990s that the benefits of simulation-based training were more widely accepted (Gaba, 2007). Issenberg and colleagues (2005) first reported the positive effects of high-fidelity simulation (HFS)-based education when used as a complement to traditional training in patient care settings, then later identified best practices of simulation-based activities in academic settings (McGaghie et al., 2011).

Nursing-Led Innovation in Healthcare Simulation

Nursing has a rich history of using role-play and task trainers to prepare new nurses (Nehring & Lashley, 2009). During the late 1990s, HFS slowly pervaded the early nursing adopters, which began a progression of innovative pioneering to build empirical evidence underpinning a lasting integration of simulation into clinical education. The National League for Nursing conducted an HFS pilot study in 2005, followed by the National Council for State Boards of Nursing (NCSBN) landmark multi-site National Simulation Study which found that the learning outcomes of nursing students were no different when 50% of clinical hours were substituted with simulation (Hayden et al., 2014). By 2019, over half of the State Boards of Nursing reported documented regulations for the use of simulation to replace clinical hours in prelicensure nursing programs (Bradley et al., 2019).

While the purpose of simulation in academic settings is to improve the confidence and competence of new healthcare professionals as they enter the workforce, simulation is used in practice settings as a mechanism for achieving broader organizational goals related to safety initiatives, quality improvement and system design. As the use of simulation proliferated across both academic and practice settings, the mounting evidence of its effectiveness also increased. This development resulted in Standards of Best Practice (SOBP) being published by the International Nursing Association for Clinical Simulation and Learning and revised several times as the pedagogy matures (INACSL Standards Committee[SM], 2016). The eight SOBP are intended to be used to guide simulation facilitators through best practices of simulation design, outcomes and objectives, facilitation, debriefing, participant evaluation, professional integrity, simulation-enhanced interprofessional education and operations.

In addition to INACSL, professional simulation organizations have grown in quantity and quality as a support mechanism for simulation educators in all environments nationally and internationally. This includes the Society for Simulation in Healthcare, the Association for Standardized Patient Educators and many regional simulation networking groups. These organizations are unified in broadening the impact of simulation education across settings and populations, as well as deepening the rigor of the pedagogy by upholding best practices throughout the development of sustainable simulation curricula. These best practices include the design of scenarios and the facilitation of simulation-based activities.

The simulation professional organizations are a resource for training in simulation facilitation and debriefing, as recommended by the SOBP (INACSL Standards Committee, 2016). As the most important aspect of simulation learning, debriefing is recommended after every simulation experience. Debriefing is a collaborative discussion among a debriefer and participants to facilitate reflective thinking, provide feedback and apply learning from the simulation scenario to future similar situations participants have not yet encountered with live patients (Dreifuerst, 2015). Although formal training and competence assessment in debriefing is recommended as best practice, few report consistent training processes in academic or practice settings (Bradley, 2019).

Safety and Quality Initiatives

In patient care delivery areas, the key driver of the use of simulation is ultimately the patient. The Triple Aim to improve population health, reduce per capita costs and enhance patient experiences is a guiding framework for improving healthcare systems (Berwick et al., 2008). Organizations are also driven to meet regulatory requirements including conditions of participation set by the Centers for Medicare and Medicaid Services and accreditation through The Joint Commission (TJC), which closely tracks National Patient Safety Goals to reduce adverse events (TJC, 2021). These requirements include ensuring competency and retention of skills to provide high-quality resuscitation and rescue care (Garvey & Dempsey, 2020). One example of a regulatory requirement is simulation-based team training in pediatric trauma centers, which is associated with reduced risk-adjusted patient mortality measures compared to similar centers that do not utilize simulation (Jensen et al., 2019).

Simulation-based activities are used in patient care areas to improve the overall safety and quality deliverables of a healthcare system, which is achieved through systematic analyses both prospectively and retrospectively (Paige et al., 2018). Prospective approaches can include simulation-based activities to assess current system processes that identify specific breakdown leading to current issues without manipulating the typical system flow. The goal of this approach is to reduce error, thereby improving patient safety and quality of care, through reproducing system failures that may lead to error, while seeking to generate solutions to correct process deficiencies (Dube et al., 2019). Alternatively, retrospective approaches use simulation to provide insight through a root cause analysis of sentinel events (Paige et al., 2018).

Simulation Training for Healthcare Providers and Teams

Provider Training and Assessment

While historical models of training relied on an apprentice style of learning and practicing skills on patients under the supervision of faculty and preceptors, simulation offers a new teaching-learning method that eliminates the potential for patient harm during the learning process. The steep learning curve of practice professions, combined with inconsistent learning opportunities and the risk of patient complications, has shaped the advent of simulation training in healthcare education. The paradigm of providing learners and clinicians consistent and standardized skill training and deliberate practice is a valuable benefit of simulation-based training. Simulation is an effective mechanism for training in high-risk low-frequency events, as well as repeated practice in high-frequency patient situations.

Technical Skills Training

Simulation-based training of technical skills with HFS or task trainers is used by a broad range of professions including medicine and nursing, particularly in the specialty areas of emergency, critical care, anesthesiology, endoscopy, perioperative care and cardiology. The theory of deliberate practice underpins the use of simulation-based learning to achieve mastery of skills (Ericsson et al., 2019). Deliberate practice is not merely a repetition of skill practice but requires intentional practice with focused effort to improve performance through immediate formative feedback from an expert who observed the skill performance.

Fitts and Posner's three-stage theory of motor skill acquisition (Fitts & Posner, 1967) supports deliberate practice to achieve muscle memory, characterized by three sequential stages: cognitive, associative and autonomous (Taylor & Ivry, 2012). Deliberate practice of technical skills offers several advantages: (1) learning can be focused on trainee needs, (2) learners can focus on whole procedures or specific components, (3) learners have the opportunity to perform a procedure many times in quick succession, (4) learners have a safe environment wherein they are allowed to learn from their mistakes rather than be rescued by their supervisor to keep the patient safe and (5) computerized simulators can provide objective evidence of performance, offering a formative and summative assessment.

Trends in technical training encompass an escalating approach from task trainers to HFS. HFS, defined as a replication of a clinical scenario using a full-body computerized manikin (Lioce et al., 2020), is typically staged in realistic patient care environments and used in scenario training. Task trainers are used to teach a specific technical skill, allowing for repetitive practice and the development of muscle memory. The two approaches, not always mutually exclusive, are often used in scaffolded approaches. For example, the transition of single task intubation with task trainers to the management of the difficult airway with HFS has been widely reported (Komasawa & Berg, 2017). This unique approach allows for nuanced feedback from the high-fidelity manikin related to the complexity of the procedure and competency of the clinician. Simulation sessions focused on practicing approved treatment algorithms aid clinicians in learning best practice, which leads to improved patient outcomes. In fact, data has shown a direct correlation with simulation training of complex procedures and adherence to standardized treatment algorithms (Hubert et al., 2014). These findings hold promise of improving widespread outcomes and national metrics of health (D'Alton et al., 2019).

Simulated skills training for high-risk procedures has demonstrated positive outcomes for both novice and experienced clinicians and provides the context for an expert to observe and use objective evaluation tools that support certifying skill competency (Laack et al., 2014). The Objective Structured Clinical Examination (OSCE) is commonly used across the health sciences as a method of assessment of specific technical skills and behaviors (Lioce et al., 2020). During OSCEs, trainees are observed by experts while performing a determined task or a set of skills using objective measurements to determine competency. OSCE assigns a standardization of practice and a model for evaluation as observers can provide feedback for improvement (Mileder et al., 2020).

Assessment tools developed to measure a specific skillset have been well reported in the literature, and often include procedure-specific checklists or global rating tools (Ilgen et al., 2015). Objective Structured Assessment of Technical Skills (OSATS) is one example of published checklists, which represent a procedure-specific tool used by an evaluator who rates skills as performed, not performed, poorly performed or well performed (Martin et al., 1997). Such assessment tools are used widely to assess surgical skills (Atesok et al., 2017; D'Angelo et al., 2015). The ease of use of checklists rests on the phenomenon that checklists require observation of either performance or omission of performance. Recent comparisons of global rating scales (GRS) versus skills checklists reveal that the checklists may prove easier to use, diminishing rater training requirements (Ilgen, 2015). In contrast, GRSs are advantageous by requiring raters to judge participants' overall performance or provide global impressions of performance on sub-tasks. GRSs can be used across multiple tasks, obviating the need for task-specific instrument development and simplifying application-specific validation.

Nontechnical Skills Training

As the complexity of healthcare continues to increase, the nontechnical skills (NTS) assessed and achieved through simulation continue to significantly impact patient outcomes. In healthcare, NTS represent the social (communication and teamwork) and cognitive (analytical and personal behavior) skills necessary for providing high-quality and safe interprofessional care (Gordon et al., 2015). Decision-making, communication, collaboration, teamwork and conflict resolution can all be practiced and assessed in simulation environments. Because coordination of care delivery was identified as a common contributor of medical error (McDonald et al., 2014), improving team processes and communication have been the focus of many mitigating interventions, including simulation (Beneria et al., 2020; Rosen et al., 2018). Simulation has also been found to improve communication across interprofessional healthcare teams (Blackmore et al., 2018), specifically in intensive care units (Wang et al., 2018), in obstetric emergency teams (Fransen et al. 2017) and among delivery room teams (Dadiz et al., 2013).

Communication errors account for approximately 80% of adverse events in healthcare (Joint Commission International, 2018) and therefore are crucial NTS. Simulation provides a safe environment for identifying and examining communication gaps and other nontechnical skill deficiencies. A recent systematic review illustrated the numerous specialty-specific NTS assessment tools available and highlighted the need for further research to determine if a more generic tool would be appropriate for assessing NTS across disciplines during simulation (Higham et al., 2019).

Team-Based Crisis Simulation

Team-based crisis simulation integrates the practice of complex technical and behavioral skills applied within critical patient care scenarios and can be facilitated in either a dedicated simulation center or in situ. In the current complex and dynamic healthcare environment, HFS is used to blend technical and nontechnical skills to practice low-frequency-high-risk scenarios to prepare teams for emergency responses (Bischoff, 2021; Boudiche et al., 2020; Colman et al., 2019; Di Nardo et al., 2018; Lee et al., 2019) and improve critical thinking and decision-making (Lewis et al., 2019). Crew Resource Management (CRM) is one example of team-based simulation aimed at rehearsing scenarios focused on complex dynamics in teamwork and communication, rather than a single task or event training. Training and evaluating the tenets of high reliability in simulated settings have been well established by other high-risk industries including aviation and nuclear power (Veazie, 2019). In healthcare, CRM techniques have also been applied in simulation training to teach and reinforce shared leadership and communication skills needed for highly functioning teams to provide complex, high stakes care (Armstrong, 2021; D'Asta et al., 2019; Man et al., 2020; Kuzma et al., 2020).

In-situ simulation (ISS) provides a unique opportunity to practice and develop key team behavioral skills in an actual patient care environment. ISS can be used to improve reliability and safety, especially in high-risk, high-stress care settings. This mode of simulation is an attractive alternative for those lacking access to a dedicated simulation center and may provide a greater sense of realism for interprofessional teams, thereby improving team collaboration (Bapteste et al., 2020; Lie et al., 2020; Skelton, 2016). Additionally, ISS has been valuable in the rapid training of critical patient care processes in response to the global COVID-19 pandemic (Balmarks et al., 2021; Delamarre et al., 2021; Lee et al., 2021; Sharara-Chami et al., 2020). Further research is needed to assess the direct impact of ISS training on clinical outcomes (Kurup, 2017).

While there are many barriers to delivering safe care, communication and team dynamics are leading challenges. High-reliability organizations focus on strengthening systems to achieve resilience and safety (Paige et al., 2018). Objectives of simulation-based scenarios to support high-reliability address clinical issues known to disrupt specific teams, for example, obstetric hemorrhage in the labor and delivery suite. Team simulations are focused on communication across all gradients, requiring non-hierarchical and closed-loop communication. Team-based crisis simulations focus on the underpinnings of high-reliability including clear task assignments and roles, team input at decision points and care implemented as a team (Reising et al., 2017). Scenario development is intended to be specific to clinical situations that may be encountered by specialty teams, allowing for the pre-brief and debrief sessions to be focused on the tenets of effective communication and teamwork.

Team communication and effective dynamics can be practiced in simulation environments using Kolb's (1984) experiential learning theory as a vehicle for both short-term and long-term effects. Reflecting and constructing new meaning through debriefing (Kolb's 'reflective observation' and 'abstract conceptualization' stages), and repeated practice of tasks and skills in sequential simulation (Kolb's 'active experimentation' stage) demonstrate that by employing all stages of Kolb's learning cycle, learning is strongly influenced and more likely to be sustained (Kolb, 1984).

Continuing Education

Ongoing professional practice evaluation (OPPE) activities, required by the Joint Commission for accreditation, consist of a quantitative and qualitative, competency-based evaluation of providers' clinical performance. Hospitals require scalable assessment tools that measure clinical competencies and minimize impact on the clinician's daily routine. Gorrindo et al. (2013) reported the benefit of web-based simulation requiring participants to conduct a risk assessment and implement therapeutic actions as a method of conducting OPPE. While few healthcare specialties (Holley & Ketel, 2014) have reported the use of simulation for either OPPE or as an approach to address clinical deficiencies, the benefits of using simulation to assess and reinforce professional practice activities may be feasible if coupled with peer-review.

Discrete Event Simulation

An essential component of patient safety is the analysis of discrete, adverse patient events. Discrete event review is a complex process that depends on the work of safety experts with highly specialized knowledge and skills in adverse event investigation. Simulation offers the opportunity to recreate adverse events, offering a more comprehensive evaluation of systems, an investigative perspective of system gaps and the ability to scale learning across healthcare teams and systems (Macrae, 2018). One method for reviewing adverse events is ISS, which can be used as a tool to first review, then implement system changes to positively impact patient safety. Employing simulation for discrete event review offers both a retrospective approach to explore the underlying causes of incidents and a prospective approach to developing and testing mitigating safety strategies (Riley et al., 2016; Macrae, 2018).

Simulation Research and Assessment

Research investigating the use of simulation has proliferated simultaneously with advances in best practice for simulation, simulation societies and interest groups and an increased number of peer-reviewed journals focused on simulation (Nestel et al., 2019). Simulation is a form of translational science, following the bench to bedside approach consistent with the biomedical sciences (McGaghie et al., 2011). While there are academic studies focused on the T1 level (performance measured in simulation), more research is needed at the higher levels as there are few reports at T4 (translation to communities) levels; much simulation research reports outcomes at the T2 (improved patient care practice) and T3 (improved patient outcomes) levels. In a current systematic review, 10% of articles outlining simulation research were focused on teams, human factors, patient safety, theory and validation while 6% addressed medical knowledge, patient outcomes and patient care (Scerbo, 2016). Most research was reported in clinical areas that had high levels of resources, and long traditions of using simulation, with practicing clinicians and residents as the population of interest rather than health science students.

Further research is needed to test the use of simulation as clinical education in the health sciences, specifically in nursing. While the NCSBN National Simulation Study determined an initial benchmark for all State Boards of Nursing (BON) to allow up to 50% of clinical education to be substituted with simulation (Bradley et al., 2019), this study has yet to be replicated, nor has new research extended the study findings by examining a substitution greater than 50%. Before the COVID-19 pandemic, many state BONs limited programs to the historic clinical model and would not approve of a 25% substitution; pandemic-induced challenges temporarily changed these restrictions, yet new nurses matriculated and successfully entered a pandemic practice environment. Follow-up research is needed to determine the amount of respective simulation and in-person clinical hours needed for competent transition into practice. Indeed, as nursing navigates an unknown post-pandemic environment with increasing care complexity, academia demands solutions for corresponding shortages of qualified faculty in addition to less access to appropriate clinical sites amid escalating nursing shortages.

Simulation is used to assess systems, environments, teams and individuals to measure the strengths and weaknesses of an institution, thereby allowing appropriation of resources to improve processes and cost. Hospital systems commonly use simulation to assess their system processes including those that rely on clinician behavior, team collaboration and leadership to deliver safe care. Through simulation, organizations can reproduce system errors to gain insight into individual and team dynamics, thereby targeting processes to correct deficiencies. Examples include quality improvement initiatives to determine adherence to protocols for infection prevention (Drew et al., 2016; Phrampus et al., 2016), sterile procedures (Golden et al., 2020) and team response to mock codes (Barbeito et al., 2015). Simulation may not replicate the extent of chaos experienced by clinicians in codes, but has the potential to target team training in areas of greatest need (Sachedina et al., 2019). Simulation is a valuable tool to measure the effectiveness of targeted training (Oner, 2018; Perry, 2018), and to assess interprofessional team performance (Jonsson et al., 2021), increasing the likelihood that team members will be empowered to speak up to challenge unsafe practices. Simulation has been used to understand and foster safety culture in organizations by developing quality improvement skills in executive leadership (Rosen et al., 2015).

Healthcare Systems—Meeting the Needs of the Future

Testing New Space Design and Care Processes

As healthcare organizations develop and expand services, a simulation approach offers unique opportunities to test new spaces and processes without impacting patient care. Simulation facilitates design thinking as it allows teams to test existing procedures and workflow, trial new processes and correct problems before infrastructures are built (Petrosoniak et al., 2020). It can also be used to assess readiness to move to a new patient care unit, as it allows testing critical processes and correction of safety threats (Bender, 2018; Ventre, 2014). In low-frequency, high-risk scenarios such as magnetic resonance imaging for critically ill patients, ISS has been used to identify multiple latent safety threats, which equipped clinicians in developing safety checklists and protocols to ensure safety and improve teamwork (Wong et al., 2021). Telehealth simulation has been used to test processes and technologies while creating opportunities for socialization of new teams (Bond et al., 2019), which is important for delivering services to underserved populations through the interface of high-tech equipment and functioning teams. In each of these examples, simulation enabled organizations to proactively identify and correct issues, then prepare clinicians for major change.

Testing New Products

Simulation facilitates the testing of new equipment that directly impacts patient care and safety. During the COVID-19 pandemic, health systems experienced global supply chain shortages of critical equipment including personal protective equipment (PPE). The need to rapidly integrate unfamiliar isolation garments posed significant challenges and risks due to potential contamination. HFS patient encounters were used to train staff in the proper use of new bio isolation gowns and determine actual contamination using Glo-germ (Shavit, 2020).

Computational modeling and simulations (CM&S) are accepted by the Food and Drug Administration (FDA) to validate and verify new medical devices (Morrison et al., 2017). CM&S is used in device development and design optimization and could also be used for root-cause analyses, and subsequently used again to address the failures and re-establish an improved performance profile. Further research is needed to advance the use of CM&S for medical devices, virtual physiological patients and clinical trial simulations.

Cost and ROI

The return on investment for simulation is difficult to quantify with traditional financial tools. The direct benefits of simulation on patient experience may be difficult to measure, and not all benefits of improved care quality may be monetized (Asche, 2018). However, the cost of a medical error occurring among individuals, healthcare organizations, systems and society is substantial. Medication error-related adverse events alone may result in significantly increased healthcare costs, ranging from US$ 11,000 to US$ 17,000 per patient (Hebbar et al., 2018).

Simulation has been used as a quality improvement intervention to implement standardized safety processes for medication administration, for example, which has demonstrated efficacy in leading practice change for medication error reduction and cost savings (Hebbar, 2018; Zimmerman & House, 2016). Cost avoidance is not the only monetary value of simulation; qualitative and quantitative benefits must also be considered. Bukhari (2017) suggests a framework that integrates traditional ROI, value measurement methodology and other variables to better capture both financial and intangible costs and benefits of simulation in healthcare. Additional quality indicators such as error and readmission rates may be reduced through improved systems of care and higher functioning teams (Asche, 2018).

Simulation costs vary widely based on factors including the fidelity of simulators, physical space and labor costs. Few published examples detail the costs and outcomes of simulation programs in hospitals, making it difficult to analyze the overall financial impact of simulation in practice (Hippe, 2020). Healthcare leaders have found cost-effective strategies to justify the expense of developing and sustaining simulation. It is common to maintain a database to manage details of simulation events, learners, evaluations, and costs to translate the investments and outcomes of simulation programs into reports for administrative and fiscal review (Mobley, 2014). In one example, a simulation program investment of US$ 3.6 million over three years resulted in a 25% reduction in adverse events and conservatively saved US$ 12.6 to US$ 28 million dollars for the organization, an ROI of US$ 9.1 to US$ 24.4 million (Moffatt-Bruce et al., 2017). When detailed cost accounting is paired with simulation outcomes, simulation has the potential to drive significant ROI through increasing patient safety, thereby improving patient experiences.

Conclusion

The use of simulation-based activities continues to increase in patient care delivery settings because of the positive outcomes demonstrated with individual care providers as well as among teams. The evidence yielded through simulation training strengthens healthcare organizations dedicated to improving patient safety and quality of care. As the pedagogy of simulation matures through broader use and depth of rigor, refining best practices will continually improve the process in which individuals and organizations prepare for simulation, use it within organizations and evaluate its outcomes. Rigorous empirical testing is needed to further investigate innovative uses of simulation to improve the delivery of healthcare at all levels, from individual provider care to team care and across organizational system processes.

References

Armstrong, P., Peckler, B., Pilkinton-Ching, J., McQuade, D., & Rogan, A. (2021). Effect of simulation training on nurse leadership in a shared leadership model for cardiopulmonary resuscitation in the emergency department. *Emergency Medicine Australasia*, 33, pp.255–261.

Asche, C. V., Kim, M., Brown, A., Golden, A., Laack, T. A., Rosario, J., Strother, C., Totten, V. Y., & Okuda, Y. (2018). Communicating value in simulation: Cost–benefit analysis and return on investment. *Academic Emergency Medicine*, 25(2), pp.230–237.

Atesok, K., Satava, R. M., Marsh, J. L., & Hurwitz, S. R. (2017). Measuring surgical skills in simulation-based training. *Journal of the American Academy of Orthopaedic Surgeons*, 25(10), pp.665–672.

Balmaks, R., Gramatniece, A., Vilde, A., Lulla, M., Dumpis, U., Gross, I. T., & Šlēziņa, I. (2021). A simulation-based failure mode analysis of SARS- CoV-2 infection control and prevention in emergency departments. *Simulation in Healthcare* [online]. Available at: https://journals.lww.com/simulationinhealthcare/Abstract/9000/A_Simulation_Based_Failure_Mode_Analysis_of.99436.aspx (Accessed 19 August 2021).

Bapteste, L., Bertucat, S., & Balanca, B. (2020). Unexpected detection of latent safety threats by in situ simulation: About two cases in an adult intensive care unit. *Clinical Simulation in Nursing*, 47, pp.6–8.

Barbeito, A., Bonifacio, A., Holtschneider, M., Segall, N., Schroeder, R., & Mark, J. (2015). In situ simulated cardiac arrest exercises to detect system vulnerabilities. *Simulation in Healthcare*, 10, pp.154–162.

Bender, G. J., & Maryman, J. A. (2018). Clinical macrosystem simulation translates between organizations. *Simulation in Healthcare*, 13(2), pp.96–106. htpps://doi.org/10.1097/SIH.0000000000000263

Beneria, A., Arnedo, M., Contreras, S., Pérez-Carrasco, M., Garcia-Ruiz, I., Rodríguez-Carballeira, M., Raduà, J., & Rius, J. B. (2020). Impact of simulation-based teamwork training on COVID-19 distress in healthcare professionals. *BMC Medical Education*, 20(1), pp.1–6.

Berwick, D. M., Nolan, T. W., & Whittington, J. (2008). The triple aim: Care, health, and cost. *Health Affairs (Project Hope)*, 27(3), pp.759–769.

Bischoff, M. (2021). Prepare for the rare: Innovation simulation for managing abdominal wall defects. *Neonatal Network*, 40(2), pp.98–102. https://doi-org.ezp2.lib.umn.edu/10.1891/0730-0832/11-T-685

Blackmore, A., Kasfiki, E. V., & Purva, M. (2018). Simulation-based education to improve communication skills: A systematic review and identification of current best practice. *BMJ Simulation and Technology Enhanced Learning*, 4(4), pp.159–164.

Bond, W., Barker, L., Cooley, K., Svendsen, J., Tillis, W. P., Vincent, A. L., Vozenilek, J. A., & Powell, E. S. (2019). A simple low-cost method to integrate telehealth interprofessional team members during in situ simulation. *Simulation in Healthcare*, 14, pp.129–136.

Boudiche, S., Zelfani, S., Hammamia, M. B., Mghaieth, F., Ouaghlani, K., Halima, M. B., Manai, H., Ziadi, J., Rekik, B., Rajhi, M., Gharsallaoui, O., Farhati, A., Ouali, S., Larbi, N., Denguir, R., Daghfous, M., & Mourali, M. S. (2020). Simulation training for continuing professional development of nurses in cardiology and cardiovascular surgery. *LaTunisie Medicale*, 98(2), pp.116–122.

Bradley, C. S. (2019). Impact of training on use of debriefing for meaningful learning. *Clinical Simulation in Nursing*, 32, pp.13–19.

Bradley, C. S., Johnson, B. K., Dreifuerst, K. T., White, P., Conde, S. K., Meakim, C. H., Curry-Lourenco, K., & Childress, R. M. (2019). Regulation of simulation use in United States prelicensure nursing programs. *Clinical Simulation in Nursing*, 33, pp.17–25.

Bukhari, H., Andreatta, P., Goldiez, B., & Rabelo, L. (2017). A framework for determining the return on investment of simulation-based training in health care. *INQUIRY: The Journal of Health Care Organization, Provision, and Financing*, 54, pp.1–7.

Colman, N., Patera, A., & Hebbar, K. B. (2019). Promoting teamwork for rapid response teams through simulation training. *Journal of Continuing Education in Nursing*, 50, pp.523–528.

Dadiz, R., Weinschreider, J., Schriefer, J., Arnold, C., Greves, C. D., Crosby, E. C., Wang, H., Pressman, E. K., & Guillet, R. (2013). Interdisciplinary simulation-based training to improve delivery room communication. *Simulation in Healthcare*, 8(5), pp.279–291.

D'Alton, M. E., Friedman, A. M., Bernstein, P. S., Brown, H. L., Callaghan, W. M., Clark, S. L., Grobman, W. A., Kilpatrick, S. J., O'Keeffe, D. F., Montgomery, D. M., Srinivas, S. K., Wendel, G. D., Wenstrom, K. D., & Foley, M. R. (2019). Putting the "M" back in maternal-fetal medicine: A 5-year report card on a collaborative effort to address maternal morbidity and mortality in the United States. *American Journal of Obstetrics and Gynecology*, 221(4), pp.311–317, e1.

D'Angelo, A. L. D., Cohen, E. R., Kwan, C., Laufer, S., Greenberg, C., Greenberg, J., Wiegmann, D., & Pugh, C. M. (2015). Use of decision-based simulations to assess resident readiness for operative independence. *The American Journal of Surgery*, 209(1), pp.132–139.

D'Asta, F., Homsi, J., Sforzi, I., Wilson, D., & de Luca, M. (2019). "SIMBurns": A high-fidelity simulation program in emergency burn management developed through international collaboration. *Burns: Journal of the International Society for Burn Injuries*, 45(1), pp.120–127.

Delamarre, L., Coarraze, S., Vardon-Bounes, F., Marhar, F., Fernandes, M., Legendre, M., Houze-Cerfon, C. H., Rigal, R., Pizzuto, R., Mathe, O., & Larcher, C. (2021). Mass training in situ during COVID-19 pandemic: Enhancing efficiency and minimizing sick leaves. *Simulation in Healthcare* [online]. Advance on-line publication.

Di Nardo, M., David, P., Stoppa, F., Lorusso, R., Raponi, M., Amodeo, A., Cecchetti, C., Guner, Y., & Taccone, F. S. (2018). The introduction of a high-fidelity simulation program for training pediatric critical care personnel reduces the times to manage extracorporeal membrane oxygenation emergencies and improves teamwork. *Journal of Thoracic Disease*, 10(6), pp.3409–3417.

Dreifuerst, K. T. (2015). Getting started with debriefing for meaningful learning. *Clinical Simulation in Nursing*, 11(5), pp.268–275.

Drew, J., Turner, J., Mugele, J., Hasty, G., Duncan, T., Zaiser, R., & Cooper D. (2016). Beating the spread: Developing a simulation analog for contagious body fluids. *Simulation in Healthcare*, 11, pp.100–105.

Dube, M., Reid, J., Kaba, A., Cheng, A., Eppich, W., Grant, V., & Stone, K. (2019). PEARLS for systems integration: A modified PEARLS framework for debriefing systems-focused simulations. *Simulation in Healthcare*, 14, pp.333–342.

Ericsson, K. A., & Harwell, K. W. (2019). Deliberate practice and proposed limits on the effects of practice on the acquisition of expert performance: Why the original definition matters and recommendations for future research. *Frontiers in Psychology*, 10, p.2396.

Fitts, P. M., & Posner, M. I. (1967). *Human performance*. Belmont, CA: Brooks/Cole.

Fransen, A. F., van de Ven, J., van Tetering, A. A., Oei, S. G., Schuit, E., & Mol, B. W. (2017). Simulation-based team training for multi-professional obstetric care teams to improve patient outcome: A multicentre, cluster randomised controlled trial. *BJOG: An International Journal of Obstetrics and Gynaecology*. 124(4), pp.641–650.

Gaba, D. M. (2007). The future vision of simulation in healthcare. *Simulation in Healthcare*, 2(2), pp.126–135.

Garvey, A. A., & Dempsey, E. M. (2020). Simulation in neonatal resuscitation. *Frontiers in Pediatrics*, 8, p.59.

Golden, A., Alaska, Y., Levinson, A., Davignon, K., & Lueckel, S. (2020). Simulation-based examination of arterial line insertion method reveals interdisciplinary practice differences. *Simulation in Healthcare*, 15, pp.89–97.

Gordon, M., Baker, P., Catchpole, K., Darbyshire, D., & Schocken, D. (2015). Devising a consensus definition and framework for non-technical skills in healthcare to support educational design: A modified Delphi study. *Medical Teacher*, 37(6), pp.572–577. https://doi.org/10.3109/0142159X.2014.959910

Gorrindo, T., Goldfarb, E., Birnbaum, R. J., Chevalier, L., Meller, B., Alpert, J., Herman, J., & Weiss A. (2013). Simulation-based ongoing professional practice evaluation in psychiatry: A novel tool for performance assessment. *The Joint Commission Journal on Quality and Patient Safety*, 39, pp.319–323.

Hayden, J. K., Smiley, R. A., Alexander, M., Kardong-Edgren, S., & Jeffries, P. R. (2014). The NCSBN national simulation study: A longitudinal, randomized, controlled study replacing clinical hours with simulation in prelicensure nursing education. *Journal of Nursing Regulation*, 5(2), pp.S3–S40.

Hebbar, K. B., Colman, N., Williams, L., Pina, J., Davis, L., Bost, J. E., Jones, H., & Frank, G. (2018). A quality initiative: A system-wide reduction in serious medication events through targeted simulation training. *Simulation in Healthcare*, 13, pp.324–330.

Higham, H., Greig, P. R., & Rutherford, J. (2019) Observer-based tools for non-technical skills assessment in simulated and real clinical environments in healthcare: A systematic review. *BMJ Quality & Safety*, 28, pp.672–686.

Hippe, D. S., Umoren, R. A., McGee, A., Bucher, S. L., & Bresnahan, B. W. (2020). A targeted systematic review of cost analyses for implementation of simulation-based education in healthcare. *SAGE Open Medical*, 8, pp.1–9.

Holley, S. L., & Ketel, C. (2014). Ongoing professional practice evaluation and focused professional practice evaluation: An overview for advanced practice clinicians. *Journal of Midwifery Womens Health*, 59(4), pp.452–459.

Hubert, V., Duwat, A., Deransy, R., Mahjoub, Y., & Dupont, H. (2014). Effect of simulation training on compliance with difficult airway management algorithms, technical ability, and skills retention for emergency cricothyrotomy. *Anesthesiology*, 120(4), pp.999–1008.

Ilgen, J. S., Ma, I. W., Hatala, R., & Cook, D. A. (2015). A systematic review of validity evidence for checklists versus global rating scales in simulation-based assessment. *Medical Education*, 49(2), pp.161–173.

INACSL Standards Committee. (2016). INACSL standards of best practice: Simulation^SM: Simulation design. *Clinical Simulation in Nursing*, 12(S), pp.S5–S12.

Issenberg, B. S., Mcgaghie, W. C., Petrusa, E. R., Lee Gordon, D., & Scalese, R. J. (2005). Features and uses of high-fidelity medical simulations that lead to effective learning: A BEME systematic review. *Medical Teacher*, 27(1), pp.10–28.

Jensen A. R., McLaughlin C., Subacius H., McAuliff K., Nathens A. B., Wong C., Meeker D., Burd, R. S., Ford, H. R., & Upperman, A. S. (2019). Simulation-based training is associated with lower risk- adjusted mortality in ACS pediatric TQIP centers. *The Journal of Trauma and Acute Care Surgery*, 87, pp.841–848.

Joint Commission International. (2018). *Communicating clearly and effectively to patients how to overcome common communication challenges in health care. White Paper* [online]. Available at: https://store.jointcommissioninternational.org/assets/3/7/jci-wp-communicating-clearly-final_(1).pdf (Accessed 15 May 2021).

Jonsson, K., Hultin, M., Hargestam, M., Lindkvist, M., & Brulin, C. (2021). Factors influencing team and task performance in intensive care teams in a simulated scenario. *Simulation in Healthcare*, 16, pp.29–36.

Kolb, D. A. (1984). *Experiential learning: Experience as the sources of learning and development*. Upper Saddle River, NJ: Prentice Hall.

Komasawa, N., & Berg, B. W. (2017). Simulation-based airway management training for anesthesiologists: A brief review of its essential role in skills training for clinical competency. *The Journal of Education in Perioperative Medicine*, 19(4), p.E612.

Kurup, V., Matei, V., & Ray, J. (2017). Role of in-situ simulation for training in healthcare: Opportunities and challenges. *Current Opinion in Anaesthesiology*, 30(6), pp.755–760.

Kuzma, G., Hirsch, C. B., Nau, A. L., Rodrigues, A. M., Gubert, E. M., & Soares, L. (2020). Assessment of the quality of pediatric cardiopulmonary resuscitation using the in situ mock code tool. *Revista Paulista de Pediatria*, 38, p.e2018173.

Laack, T. A., Dong, Y., Goyal, D. G., Sadosty, A. T., Suri, H. S., & Dunn, W. F. (2014). Short-term and long-term impact of the central line workshop on resident clinical performance during simulated central line placement. *Simulation in Healthcare* 9(4), pp.228–233.

Lee, H. L., Liu, P. C., Hsieh, M. C., Chao, A. S., Chiu, Y. W., & Weng, Y. H. (2019). Comparison of high-fidelity simulation and lecture to improve the management of fetal heart rate monitoring. *Journal of Continuing Education in Nursing*, 50, pp.557–562.

Lee, M., Chen, S., Tosif, S., & Gordon, J. (2021). "Talk-Through Walk-Through": A simulation approach adapted during preparation for COVID-19. *Simulation in Healthcare* [online]. Advance on-line publication.

Lewis, K. A., Ricks, T. N., Rowin, A., Ndlovu, C., Goldstein, L., & McElvogue, C. (2019). Does simulation training for acute care nurses improve patient safety outcomes: A systematic review to inform evidence-based practice. *Worldviews on Evidence-Based Nursing*, 16, pp.389–396.

Lie, S., Wong, L. T., Chee, M., & Chong, S. (2020). Process-oriented in situ simulation is a valuable tool to rapidly ensure operating room preparedness for COVID-19 outbreak. *Simulation in Healthcare*, 15, pp.225–233.

Lioce, L., Lopreiato J., Downing, D., Chang, T. P., Robertson, J. M., Anderson, M., Diaz, D. A., Spain, A. E., & Terminology and Concepts Working Group (2020). *Healthcare simulation dictionary*, 2nd ed. Rockville, MD: Agency for Healthcare Research and Quality.

Macrae, C. (2018). Imitating incidents: How simulation can improve safety investigation and learning from adverse events. *Simulation in Healthcare*, 13(4), pp.227–232.

Man, A. P. N., Lam, C. K. M., Cheng, B. C. P., Tang, K. S., & Tang, P. F. (2020). Impact of locally adopted simulation-based crew resource management training on patient safety culture: Comparison between operating room personnel and general health care populations pre and post course. *American Journal of Medical Quality*, 35, pp.79–88.

Martin, J. A., Regehr, G., Reznick, R., Macrae, H., Murnaghan, J., Hutchison, C., & Brown, M. (1997). Objective structured assessment of technical skill (OSATS) for surgical residents. *British Journal of Surgery*, 84(2), pp.273–278.

McDonald, K. M., Schutz, E., Albin, L., Pineda, N., Lonhart, J., Sundaram, V., Smith-Spangler, C., Brustrom, J., Malcolm, E., Rohn, L., & Davies, S. (2014). Care coordination measures atlas update. Agency for Healthcare Research and Quality [online]. Available at: https://www.ahrq.gov/ncepcr/care/coordination/atlas.html (Accessed 28 May 2021).

McGaghie, W. C., Issenberg, S. B., Cohen, E. R., Barsuk, J. H., & Wayne, D. B. (2011). Does simulation-based medical education with deliberate practice yield better results than traditional clinical education? A meta-analytic comparative review of the evidence. *Academic Medicine*, 86(6), pp.706–711.

Mileder, L. P., Schüttengruber, G., Prattes, J., & Wegscheider, T. (2020). Simulation-based training and assessment of mobile pre-hospital SARS-CoV-2 diagnostic teams in Styria, Austria. *Medicine*, 99(29), p.e21081.

Mobley, B., Adler, M., & McNerney, D. (2014). Board #316: Technology innovation a lower cost solution to track simulation activity for ROI reports-submission #8338. *Simulation in Healthcare*, 9, p.490.

Moffatt-Bruce, S. D., Hefner, J. L., Mekhjian, H., McAlearney, J. S., Latimer, T., Ellison, C., & McAlearney, A. S. (2017). What is the return on investment for implementation of a Crew Resource Management program at an academic medical center? *American Journal of Medical Quality*, 32(1), pp.5–11.

Morrison, T. M., Dreher, M. L., Nagaraja, S., Angelone, L. M., & Kainz, W. (2017). The role of computational modeling and simulation in the total product life cycle of peripheral vascular devices. *Journal of Medical Devices*, 11(2), pp.024503.1–024503.5.

Nehring, W. M., & Lashley, F. R. (2009). Nursing simulation: A review of the past 40 years. *Simulation & Gaming*, 40(4), pp.528–552. https://doi.org/10.1177/1046878109332282

Nestel, D., Scerbo, M. W., & Kardong-Edgren, S. E. (2019). A contemporary history of healthcare simulation research. In D. Nestel, J. Hui, K. Kunkler, M. W. Scerbo, & A. W. Calhoun, eds., *Healthcare simulation research*. Switzerland: Springer International Publishing, pp.9–14.

Oner, C., Fisher, N., Atallah, F., Son, M., Homel, P., Mykhalchenko, K., & Minkoff, H. (2018). Simulation-based education to train learners to "Speak Up" in the clinical environment: Results of a randomized trial. *Simulation in Healthcare*, 13, pp.404–412.

Paige, J., Terry Fairbanks, R., & Gaba, D. (2018). Priorities related to improving healthcare safety through simulation. *Simulation in Healthcare*, 13(S), pp.S41–S50.

Perry, M., Seto, T., Vasquez, J., Josyula, S., Rule, A., & Kamath-Rayne, B. D. (2018). The influence of culture on teamwork and communication in a simulation-based resuscitation training at a community hospital in Honduras. *Simulation in Healthcare*, 13, pp.363–370.

Petrosoniak, A., Hicks, C., Barratt, L., Gascon, D., Kokoski, C., Campbell, D., White, K., Bandiera, G., Lum-Kwong, M. M., Nemoy, L., & Brydges, R. (2020). Design thinking- informed simulation: An innovative framework to test, evaluate, and modify new clinical infrastructure. *Simulation in Healthcare*, 15, pp.205–213.

Phrampus, P., O'Donnell, J., Farkas, D., & Abernethy, D. (2016). Rapid development and deployment of Ebola readiness training across an academic health system: The critical role of simulation education, consulting, and systems integration. *Simulation in Healthcare*, 11, pp.82–88.

Reising, D. L., Carr, D. E., Gindling, S., & Barnes, R. (2017). An analysis of interprofessional communication and teamwork skill acquisition in simulation. *Journal of Interprofessional Education & Practice*, 8, pp.80–85.

Riley, W., Begun, J. W., Meredith, L., Miller, K. K., Connolly, K., Price, R., Muri, J. H., McCullough, M., & Davis, S. (2016). Integrated approach to reduce perinatal adverse events: Standardized processes, interdisciplinary teamwork training, and performance feedback. *Health Services Research*, 51(Supplement 3), pp.2431–2452.

Rosen, M., Goeschel, C., Che, X.-X., Fawole, J., Rees, D., Curran, R., Gelinas, L., Martin, J. N., Kosel, K. C., Pronovost, P. J., & Weaver, S. J. (2015). Simulation in the executive suite: Lessons learned for building patient safety leadership. *Simulation in Healthcare*, 10, pp.372–377.

Rosen, M. A., Diaz Granados, D., Dietz, A. S., Benishek, L. E., Thompson, D., Pronovost, P. J., & Weaver, S. J. (2018). Teamwork in healthcare: Key discoveries enabling safer, high-quality care. *American Psychologist*, 73(4), p.433.

Sachedina, A., Blissett, S., Remtulla, A., Sridhar, K., & Morrison, D. (2019). Preparing the next generation of code blue leaders through simulation: What's missing? *Simulation in Healthcare*, 14, pp.77–81.

Scerbo, M. W. (2016). Simulation in healthcare: Growin'up. *Simulation in Healthcare*, 4, pp.232–235.

Sharara-Chami, R., Sabouneh, R., Zeineddine, R., Banat, R., Fayad, J., & Lakissian, Z. (2020). In situ simulation: An essential tool for safe preparedness for the COVID-19 pandemic. *Simulation in Healthcare*, 15, pp.303–309.

Shavit, D., Feldman, O., Hussein, K., Meir, M., Miller, A., Gutgold, A., Idelman, R., Kvatinsky, N., Cohen, D. M., & Shavit, I. (2020). Assessment of alternative personal protective equipment by emergency department personnel during the SARS-CoV-2 pandemic: A simulation-based pilot study. *Simulation in Healthcare*, 15, pp.445–446.

Skelton, T., Nshimyumuremyi, I., Mukwesi, C., Whynot, S., Zolpys, L., & Livingston, P. (2016). Low-cost simulation to teach anesthetists non-technical skills in Rwanda. *Anesthesia & Analgesia*, 123, pp.474–80.

Taylor, J. A., & Ivry, R. B. (2012). The role of strategies in motor learning. *Annals of the New York Academy of Sciences*, 1251, p.1.

The Joint Commission. (2021). *Standards* [online]. Available at: https://www.jointcommission.org/standards/ (Accessed 15 May 2021).

Veazie, S., Peterson, K., & Bourne, D. (2019). *Evidence brief: Implementation of high reliability organization principles.* United States Department of Veterans Affairs [online]. Available at: https://www.ncbi.nlm.nih.gov/books/NBK542883/ (Accessed 15 May 2021).

Ventre, K. M., Barry, J. S., Davis, D., Baiamonte, V. L., Wentworth, A. C., Pietras, M., Coughlin, L., & Barley, G. (2014). Using in situ simulation to evaluate operational readiness of a children's hospital-based obstetrics unit. *Simulation in Healthcare*, 9(2), pp.102–111.

Wang, Y. Y., Wan, Q. Q., Lin, F., Zhou, W. J., & Shang, S. M. (2018). Interventions to improve communication between nurses and physicians in the intensive care unit: An integrative literature review. *International Journal of Nursing Sciences*, 5(1), pp.81–88.

Wong, J., Kalaniti, K., Castaldo, M., Whyte, H., Lee, K. S., Schroff, M., & Campbell, D. (2021). Utilizing simulation to identify latent safety threats during neonatal magnetic resonance imaging procedure. *Simulation in Healthcare*, 16(3), pp.170–176 [online]. Available at: https://journals.lww.com/simulationinhealthcare/Citation/2021/06000/Utilizing_Simulation_to_Identify_Latent_Safety.3.aspx (Accessed 19 August 2021).

Zimmerman, D. M., & House, P. (2016). Medication safety: Simulation education for new RNs promises an excellent return on investment. *Nursing Economics*, 34(1), pp.49–51.

Chapter 11

Case Studies in Applied Informatics during COVID-19

Brenda Kulhanek

Contents

Case Study: Disaster Documentation for Decreased Documentation Burden 190
    Introduction 190
    Background 190
    Changes 190
    Case Summary 191
Case Study: Rapid Telehealth Implementation 192
    Introduction 192
    Background 192
    Changes 193
    Case Summary 193
Case Study: Collaboration for COVID-19 Information Sharing 194
    Introduction 194
    Background 194
    Changes 195
    Case Summary 196
Case Study: Workflow Efficiency to Address COVID-19 Needs 196
    Introduction 196
    Background 196
    Changes 197
    Case Summary 198
Conclusion 198
References 199

DOI: 10.4324/9781003281016-11

Case Study: Disaster Documentation for Decreased Documentation Burden

Introduction

Numerous studies have pointed to the impact of electronic documentation on nurses, physicians and other care providers. The burden of documentation has produced increased levels of physician burnout (Colicchio et al., 2019), and has emerged as a major factor in nurses leaving the profession due to compassion fatigue and burnout (Khairat et al., 2020; Jouparinejad et al., 2020). A heightened degree of documentation burden is not only causing fatigue and burnout for care providers but also poses efficiency challenges and safety risks due to incomplete or fragmented nursing documentation (McIlreevy et al., 2021). Although many organizations have attempted to scale back the amount of electronic documentation by reducing unnecessary charting elements, this work has been slow to progress and has been hampered by internal and external policy, regulatory requirements, risk mitigation and nursing tradition (Englebright et al., 2014).

Background

In 2020, healthcare organizations struggled to cope as they were flooded with large numbers of patients infected with COVID-19, resulting in short-staffed patient care units and grossly overworked nurses (Lucchini et al., 2020). To add to the stress of caring for desperately ill patients, nurses were faced with documentation requirements that took precious time away from patient care. Over one-quarter of nurses reported high levels of challenges with record-keeping during pandemic patient care, and four in ten nurses reported moderate levels of challenges documenting patient care when caring for COVID-19 patients (Babu & Rajakumari, 2020). Extensive documentation requirements may also produce data showing declines in capturing nurse-sensitive indicators due to the many fields linked to data collection that may not be completed during an extreme patient surge such as during the COVID-19 pandemic (Stifter et al., 2021).

Changes

One forward-thinking organization used the pandemic as impetus to create a new process for documenting on COVID-19 patients so that the nurses caring for this patient population would benefit from streamlined documentation practice. The new documentation screens would provide necessary information while minimizing data collection to enable more nursing time to care for the flood of patients needing intensive care in hospitals. The informatics team found that many requirements of typical nursing documentation such as care plans, screening and referral tools and other assessment tools did not apply to this urgent patient population and admission documentation requirements that were discharge-focused were not immediately relevant when attempting to stabilize these patients. The organization reviewed the team's findings and identified the elements that must be collected, enabling the team to place those elements within a minimum dataset focused solely on COVID-19 patients and assessments.

Leadership concerns about the impact of these documentation changes on other patient populations were addressed by retaining all current electronic health record (EHR) documentation so that the data could continue to be captured and used for patients with other non-COVID-19 conditions. The traditional EHR workflow containing processes, referrals and screenings remained unchanged and available for non-COVID-19 patients.

In addition to scaling down electronic documentation to a minimum dataset for COVID-19 patients, the informatics team also developed a predictive analytics tool by repurposing a sepsis/infection risk model to better identify patients developing COVID-19 symptoms. The predictive analytics process focused on current inpatients so that timely testing, isolation and treatment for inpatients developing symptoms of COVID-19 could occur. Adding to improved efficiency, the COVID-19 predictive analytics data populated an EHR dashboard to facilitate rapid staff awareness of any changes. Screens were redesigned so that key information could easily be seen by care providers without taking time to search through the electronic chart (Padden, 2020).

Case Summary

Based on a specific patient population, nursing documentation was restructured to best reflect the documentation needs of this specific and fairly homogenous COVID-19 patient population. With the reduced documentation burden, nurses were able to focus more time on patient care, and essential elements of patient information were used to trigger predictive analytics capabilities and facilitate more rapid identification and treatment of emerging infectious processes. Additionally, no changes were made to the usual electronic documentation processes, allowing for minimal to no disruption for care providers working with non-COVID-19 patients within the facility.

Case Study: Rapid Telehealth Implementation

Introduction

Since the earliest recorded use of technology to remotely provide healthcare in the late 1800s, telehealth has been advancing, fueled by improvements in technology (Baumann & Scales, 2016). However, prior to the pandemic of 2020, realization of the full benefits of telehealth progressed slowly and widespread use was limited (see Chapter 9 for an overview of telehealth). Factors such as differing state regulations and requirements for telehealth have inhibited the use of this technology across widespread geographical areas. Adding to the list of barriers, telehealth regulatory requirements for reimbursement have also limited the use of telehealth technology to very specific circumstances to assure payment (Lee et al., 2020). Reimbursement for telehealth services has typically been minimal, reducing the incentive for healthcare providers to use telehealth as a regular service for care (NEJM Catalyst, 2018).

Background

Prior to the COVID-19 pandemic, healthcare was primarily delivered through in-person visits with care providers at clinics, urgent care, emergency rooms and in the hospital. With the introduction of a highly infectious coronavirus in early 2020, healthcare organizations sought to reduce COVID-19 transmission risk within the healthcare environment. To improve safety, in-person elective surgeries and maintenance visits in many organizations were quickly reduced or eliminated. Early state-by-state changes to healthcare delivery reflected the varying regional spread of COVID-19, ranging from a 15% decrease in weekly visits to more than a 75% decrease in several states (Patel et al., 2021).

In addition to managing patients with chronic illness and performing health maintenance, healthcare organizations were preparing for a deluge of patients infected with the coronavirus. This potential influx necessitated a shift in the manner of care delivery for many different patient populations including such diverse specialties as urology, geriatrics, neurology, pediatrics, ophthalmology and ambulatory pharmacy (Williams et al., 2020; Thorakkattil et al., 2021; Schuman, 2020; Rodler et al., 2020; Dewar et al., 2020). To meet the continuing need for healthcare in light of declining in-person visits, informatics practitioners were deployed to identify ways to best address the healthcare needs of these diverse patient populations.

Changes

When a stay-at-home order was issued in the state of Colorado, an interdisciplinary team of informaticists, educators and project managers at UCHealth worked together to fully implement a telehealth program in just two weeks. Although telehealth functionality was currently present in the existing EHR system, the technology had rarely been used and most staff were not familiar with the product, or the workflow and processes for performing telehealth visits. The use of existing telehealth capabilities required education about the technology, training on how to best provide care using telehealth, communication about best practices for working from home and evidence-based communication skills for performing these virtual visits.

To support the rapid changes that were needed, a virtual command center was formed with the purpose of providing coordinated management of the move to telehealth services along with multiple other rapid and urgent changes occurring at the medical center. Using virtual technology, the informatics team educated over 1,500 healthcare providers in less than two weeks through easily accessible online webinars and educational materials made available in an electronic library managed by the informatics team. Within 14 days of training and preparation, the UCHealth system increased the number of telehealth visits performed by providers by 5700%, to a total of over 20,000 visits per week, seamlessly addressing the urgent and ongoing healthcare needs of the patients (Lin et al., 2020).

Case Summary

A patient population sheltering at home needed ongoing healthcare even though in-person visits were reduced or eliminated to prevent the spread of coronavirus. The UCHealth system mobilized an interdisciplinary group to meet this informatics challenge. The previously existing telehealth technology was implemented and heavily utilized to provide ongoing healthcare to patients in the UCHealth system while minimizing infection risk, resulting in dramatic increases in the use of telehealth technology within a short period of time. Although the health system is now past the largest wave of the pandemic at the time of this writing, telehealth services remain a favorable option for accessing healthcare for many patients. As time moves forward and more is known about ongoing reimbursement and policy support for telehealth visits, this technology, which has proven to be a satisfactory and effective means of providing safer healthcare for patients during a pandemic, may continue with strong usage (Knierim et al., 2021).

Case Study: Collaboration for COVID-19 Information Sharing

Introduction

Although the COVID-19 pandemic has affected almost every healthcare facility in the United States and globally, efforts to explore elements of the impact of the pandemic and share clinical and data solutions have been fragmented. Health risk information and communication strategies are critical for effective management of public health emergencies (Kim & Kreps, 2020). When multiple stakeholders and entities are involved in communicating and managing a global pandemic, it can be challenging to produce a coordinated effort to manage health risk information. One example of an effective health risk strategy occurred in the Kingdom of Saudi Arabia where a collaboration of healthcare, educational sector, technology and government resources worked together to produce an effective system for managing information sharing during a global pandemic (Hassounah et al., 2020).

Background

Saudi Arabia is a nation with nearly 500 public and private hospitals, equaling just over two hospital beds per 1,000 people, ranking higher in healthcare outcomes than neighboring countries and the more distant nations of Australia, Canada and the United States. The Saudi Arabian healthcare workforce is made up of citizens and imported healthcare labor, resulting in a mixture of many cultures and languages (Al-Hanawi et al., 2019). The Kingdom of Saudi Arabia had prior experience managing a pandemic during the 2009 H1N1 pandemic, resulting in an awareness of the need for a national risk communication infrastructure (Al-Sayyad et al., 2014). Armed with information gained from the prior pandemic, healthcare stakeholders were prepared to efficiently manage and combat the global COVID-19 pandemic (Hassounah et al., 2020).

Changes

The Kingdom of Saudi Arabia identified digital technology as a tool to address healthcare and communication needs related to the COVID-19 pandemic. Stakeholders involved in the effort to coordinate pandemic management included public health, healthcare organizations, education, telecommunications, industry and risk experts. As a result of this unique collaboration, a combination of nineteen web-based platforms and apps were launched to support education, telecommunications, mobile technology, risk communication using social media and text messaging. Within the healthcare sector, multiple informatics tools were implemented to enable sharing of public health information with individuals and the healthcare community. In the public health realm, newly launched informatics tools included a secure appointment app that funneled all healthcare appointments through a single, centralized intake point. This scheduling app was not only used to guide individuals with COVID-19 symptoms to established COVID-19 clinics, but the app also offered general health education, gamification and health challenges for communities to develop and maintain healthy habits.

In addition to patient health management, an electronic surveillance system was used to consolidate data from all COVID-19 laboratory tests in the Kingdom and facilitate COVID-19 contact tracing. A newly released smartphone app was made available for use by residents to access specific coronavirus health information including clinical guidelines and symptom tracking. The app also included location tracking for those in lockdown, adding another valuable layer of surveillance to contact tracing.

Another unique app was developed that could identify a person's location and use de-identified data to notify them when close contact occurred with a confirmed COVID-19 case. A central service center managed medications and provided the ability to deliver prescriptions to patients' homes when needed, thus avoiding additional risk for COVID-19 exposure.

A key component of pandemic risk management is communication. The Kingdom of Saudi Arabia used social media to distribute health education information and materials in multiple languages. Text messages were sent to all citizens to reinforce best practices during the pandemic, and false information and rumors about the pandemic were quickly addressed and dispelled through rigorous social media monitoring (Hassounah et al., 2020).

Case Summary

The Kingdom of Saudi Arabia was able to promote collaboration of diverse stakeholders to quickly respond to the complex factors involved in a global pandemic. Almost 20 apps and digital platforms were created or reformatted to provide information resources such as patient education, pandemic communication, tracking of COVID-19 positive patients, contact tracing, medication and care management and to support a social media campaign. Additionally, the apps and digital platforms allowed for minimal disruptions to daily life and included education, telehealth, remote work and other key functions. Although the multiple apps and platforms facilitated a well-coordinated approach to the pandemic and healthcare management, a decrease in the number of apps and platforms enabled by integrating the technology would provide greater efficiency and visibility for a future digital pandemic risk communication approach.

Case Study: Workflow Efficiency to Address COVID-19 Needs

Introduction

The lack of nursing involvement in workflow design can result in a cumbersome and frustrating workflow for nurses, leading to inefficiency, frustration and dissatisfaction (Dykes & Chu, 2020). Nursing involvement in workflow design allows for representation of the true work of nurses and eliminates or reduces unnecessary processes while reinforcing key connections and collaborations (Schoenbaum & Carroll, 2020). During the COVID-19 pandemic, the importance of efficient workflow for nurses and other caregivers increased in priority. Informatics teams were tasked with creating new workflows that supported the addition of extensive use of personal protective equipment (PPE) into daily routines, and reduction of time spent in the rooms of COVID-19 infected patients. Nurse informaticians are well-equipped to address workflow changes and maintain a patient-centered experience by aligning both in-person and virtual visits with the health and communication needs of the caregiver and patient (Johnson, 2020).

Background

Ever since Emory University Hospital was at the center of the 2014 United States Ebola epidemic, the organization has been alert and ready to develop workable solutions for any upcoming crisis. Faced with nursing workflow challenges during the COVID-19 pandemic, the Atlanta-based medical center assembled a quality improvement (QI) team to address issues such as staff and patient safety, the use and conservation of PPE in the hospital and nursing workflow. The interdisciplinary QI team consisted of epidemiologists, a clinical nurse specialist and a group of infection preventionists. The primary concern was associated with the number of times that nurses on the COVID-19 units had to don and doff PPE to care for patients—a process that took time away from patient care and exposed nurses to the risk of infection.

When the team was assembled, the medical center was geographically cohorting suspected and confirmed COVID-19 patients in designated areas. Over time, the geographical units became fully populated with confirmed COVID-19 patients, and those suspected of having a COVID-19 infection were kept in a separate geographical area until their infection was confirmed. This cohorting model necessitated an average of 40 episodes of donning and doffing PPE per nurse, per 12-hour shift.

Changes

Based on data input from the QI team, the geographical cohorting of COVID-19 patients was discontinued and COVID-19 patient care areas were divided into 'hot,' 'warm' and 'cold' zones within the COVID-19 patient care unit. The hot zone was the patient room, the warm zone was the side of the hallway adjacent to the patient room doorways and the cold zone was the remaining half of the patient hallway. Within the hot zone, the nurses required PPE protection. In the warm zone, the nurses could move from room to room using the same PPE when indicated. The cold zone was the area where normal traffic could proceed, and supplies could be easily obtained and delivered. This new zoning model enabled nurses to decrease donning and doffing from 40 gowns per nurse, per shift, to an average of 22 gowns per nurse, per shift, saving both time and PPE supplies. Nurses also reported greater efficiency and work satisfaction as a result of these changes.

As with most changes in healthcare, the informatics team must be involved to ensure that technology effectively supports the new workflow. Changes to other workflow processes included obtaining blood product co-signatures remotely using technology; frequent remote rounding using tele-ICU functionality; providing nursing with alerts when patient pumps were ready for refill; coordination of medication refills with the pharmacy via distance technology; and remote monitoring for continuous renal replacement therapy. Communication with infectious patients was also enhanced by adding baby monitors in hot zones so that nursing communication could continue even with the door closed. The addition of the new technical solutions reduced the need for direct-care nurses to don PPE and enter patient rooms unless necessary (Omess et al., 2021).

Case Summary

Although changes in workflow and disruption of routine can create discomfort and frustration for nurses, Emory nurses expressed a positive attitude toward these workflow changes. When faced with extremely sick patients and the prospect of donning and doffing PPE up to 40 times in a 12-hour shift, nurses appreciated an almost 50% reduction in the activity, which ultimately reduced the risk of contamination and created more time for patient care. The role of informatics was essential in this innovative workflow enhancement by automating and enhancing communication and other routine processes such as refilling IV medications, monitoring pumps and requirements for co-signatures that previously would have required additional time and effort.

Conclusion

The COVID-19 pandemic has generated numerous opportunities for informatics nurses to improve patient safety, increase efficiency for healthcare providers, support caregivers, facilitate better communication and deliver healthcare in new and innovative ways. These four case studies illustrate the important role of informatics in decreasing the documentation burden during a pandemic, implementing telehealth, using technology to improve risk communication, adding efficiency and safety to workflow and improving patient safety and the patient/nurse experience. In addition to the case studies presented here, there are other untold stories that could highlight the important role of informatics and applied technologies in healthcare.

Applied technologies have improved healthcare in multiple and unique ways. Wearable devices have been reconfigured to transmit patient vital signs from home for nurse remote monitoring, resulting in timely intervention from healthcare providers (Lin et al., 2020). Informaticians have rapidly assessed changes within multiple EHR systems to support emerging challenges. They have implemented countless telehealth systems, facilitated installation of video communication systems and tested numerous technology changes to ensure seamless operation for care providers (Tyler, 2020).

While devastating in nature, the COVID-19 pandemic has provided unprecedented opportunities for informatics nurses to collaborate with others to use health information and communication technologies to better serve our patients and stakeholders while enhancing safety for our staff and patients. The use of new and existing technology has expanded exponentially, highlighting the vital role that informatics has played throughout the pandemic, with the anticipation that working together, we will evolve state-of-the-art innovative technology into the future.

References

Al-Hanawi, M. K., Khan, S. A., & Al-Borie, H. M. (2019). Healthcare human resource development in Saudi Arabia: Emerging challenges and opportunities: A critical review. *Public Health Reviews*, 40(1).

Al-Sayyad, A. S., Al-Haddad, S. A., Erzaiqat, F. A., AlReqraq, F. J., Al-Dar, M. M., & Al Rebeh, Y. A. (2014). Knowledge and practice among the population of Saudi Arabia eastern province during the H1N1 pandemic 2009. *Bahrain Medical Bulletin*, 36(1), pp.72–80.

Babu, M., & Rajakumari, S. (2020). Record-keeping: Level of challenges experienced by nurses during COVID-19 pandemic. *International Journal of Applied Research*, 6(8), pp.352–355.

Baumann, P. K., & Scales, T. (2016). History of information communication technology and telehealth. *Academy of Business Research Journal*, 3, pp.48–52.

Colicchio, T. K., Cimino, J. J., & Del Fiol, G. (2019). Unintended consequences of nationwide electronic health record adoption: Challenges and opportunities in the post-meaningful use era. *Journal of Medical Internet Research*, 21(6), p.e13313.

Dewar, S., Lee, P. G., Suh, T. T., & Min, L. (2020). Uptake of virtual visits in a geriatric primary care clinic during the COVID –19 pandemic. *Journal of the American Geriatrics Society*, 68(7), pp.1392–1394.

Dykes, S., & Chu, C. H. (2020). Now more than ever, nurses need to be involved in technology design: Lessons from the COVID-19 pandemic. *Journal of Clinical Nursing* [online]. Available at: https://onlinelibrary.wiley.com/doi/10.1111/jocn.15581 (Accessed 19 August 2021).

Englebright, J., Aldrich, K., & Taylor, C. R. (2014). Defining and incorporating basic nursing care actions into the electronic health record. *Journal of Nursing Scholarship*, 46(1), pp.50–57.

Hassounah, M., Raheel, H., & Alhefzi, M. (2020). Digital response during the COVID-19 pandemic in Saudi Arabia. *Journal of Medical Internet Research*, 22(9), pp.e19338.

Johnson, C. B. (2020). The day in the life of an informatics nurse: The informatics nurse's role in creating a patient-centered virtual experience. *Journal of Informatics Nursing*, 5(3), pp.24–29.

Jouparinejad, S., Foroughameri, G., Khajouei, R., & Farokhzadian, J. (2020). Improving the informatics competency of critical care nurses: Results of an interventional study in the southeast of Iran. *BMC Medical Informatics and Decision Making*, 20(1), p.220.

Khairat, S., Xi, L., Liu, S., Shrestha, S., & Austin, C. (2020). Understanding the association between electronic health record satisfaction and the well-being of nurses: Survey study. *JMIR Nursing*, 3(1), p.e13996.

Kim, D. K. D., & Kreps, G. L. (2020). An analysis of government communication in the United States during the COVID-19 pandemic: Recommendations for effective government health risk communication. *World Medical & Health Policy*, 12(4), pp.398–412.

Knierim, K., Palmer, C., Kramer, E. S., Rodriguez, R. S., Vanwyk, J., Shmerling, A., Smith, P., Holmstrom, H., Bacak, B. S., Brown Levey, S. M., Staton, E. W., & Holtrop, J. S. (2021). Lessons learned during COVID-19 that can move telehealth in primary care forward. *The Journal of the American Board of Family Medicine*, 34(Supplement), pp.S196–S202.

Lee, I., Kovarik, C., Tejasvi, T., Pizarro, M., & Lipoff, J. B. (2020). Telehealth: Helping your patients and practice survive and thrive during the COVID-19 crisis with rapid quality implementation. *Journal of the American Academy of Dermatology*, 82(5), pp.1213–1214.

Lin, C.-T., Bookman, K., Sieja, A., Markley, K., Altman, R. L., Sippel, J., Perica, K., Reece, L., Davis, C., Horowitz, E., Pisney, L., Sottile, P. D., Kao, D., Adrian, B., Szkil, M., Griffin, J., Youngwerth, J., Drew, B., & Pell, J. (2020). Clinical informatics accelerates health system adaptation to the COVID-19 pandemic: Examples from Colorado. *Journal of the American Medical Informatics Association*, 27(12), pp.1955–1963.

Lucchini, A., Giani, M., Elli, S., Villa, S., Rona, R., & Foti, G. (2020). Nursing activities score is increased in COVID-19 patients. *Intensive and Critical Care Nursing*, 59, pp.102876.

McIlreevy, J., Rylee, T. L., Shields-Tettamanti, T., & Gee, P. M. (2021). Interdisciplinary optimization of admission documentation: Reducing the bloat. *CIN: Computers, Informatics, Nursing*, 39(5), pp.248–256.

NEJM Catalyst. (2018). What is telehealth? *NEJM Catalyst* [online]. Available at: https://catalyst.nejm.org/doi/full/10.1056/CAT.18.0268 (Accessed 19 August 2021).

Omess, S., Kaplow, R., Green, A., Kingsley-Mota, W., Mota, S., Wilson, K., & Paris, L. (2021). Implementation of a warm zone model during the COVID-19 pandemic. *AJN American Journal of Nursing*, 121(1), pp.48–54.

Padden, J. S. (2020). Informatics X-men evolution to combat COVID-19. *Nurse Leader*, 18(6), pp.557–560.

Patel, S. Y., Mehrotra, A., Huskamp, H. A., Uscher-Pines, L., Ganguli, I., & Barnett, M. L. (2021). Trends in outpatient care delivery and telemedicine during the COVID-19 pandemic in the US. *JAMA Internal Medicine*, 181(3), p.388.

Rodler, S., Apfelbeck, M., Stief, C., Heinemann, V., & Casuscelli, J. (2020). Lessons from the coronavirus disease 2019 pandemic: Will virtual patient management reshape uro-oncology in Germany? *European Journal of Cancer*, 132, pp.136–140.

Schoenbaum, A., & Carroll, W. (2020). Nursing informatics key role in defining clinical workflow, increasing efficiency and improving quality. *HIMSS* [online]. Available at: https://www.himss.org/resources/nursing-informatics-key-role-defining-clinical-workflow-increasing-efficiency-and (Accessed 19 August 2021).

Schuman, A. J. (2020). COVID-19: A battle plan for pediatricians. *Contemporary Pediatrics*, 37(6), pp.21–23.

Stifter, J., Sermersheim, E., Ellsworth, M., Dowding, E., Day, E., Silvestri, K., Margwarth, J., Korkmaz, K., Walkowiak, N., Boudreau, L., Hernandez, L., Harbert, B., Ambutas, S., Abraham, A., & Shaw, P. (2021). COVID-19 and nurse-sensitive indicators. *Journal of Nursing Care Quality*, 36(1), pp.1–6.

Thorakkattil, S. A., Nemr, H. S., Al-Ghamdi, F. H., Jabbour, R. J., & Al-Qaaneh, A. M. (2021). Structural and operational redesigning of patient-centered ambulatory care pharmacy services and its effectiveness during the COVID-19 pandemic. *Research in Social & Administrative Pharmacy*, 17(1), pp.1838–1844.

Tyler, D. D. (2020). The day in the life of an informatics nurse: Informatics nurses and COVID-19. *Journal of Informatics Nursing*, 5(2), pp.21–23.

Williams, A. M., Kalra, G., Commiskey, P. W., Bowers, E. M. R., Rudolph, B. R., Pitcher, M. D., Dansingani, K. K., Jhanji, V., Nischal, K. K., Sahel, J.-A., Waxman, E. L., & Fu, R. (2020). Ophthalmology practice during the coronavirus disease 2019 pandemic: The university of Pittsburgh experience in promoting clinic safety and embracing video visits. *Ophthalmology and Therapy*, 9(3), pp.1–9.

Index

A

Activities of daily living (ADL), 24, 27
Activity-based pressure injury prediction (APIP), 135
ADL, *see* Activities of daily living
Advanced practice registered nurses (APRNs), 153, 156, 158
Agency for Healthcare Research and Quality (AHRQ), 133
AGI, *see* Artificial General Intelligence
AHRQ, *see* Agency for Healthcare Research and Quality
AI-based pressure ulcer model, 143
AI health technologies (AIHTs), 96, 97
AIHTs, *see* AI health technologies
Alberta Health Services corporate approach, 29–30
Alzheimer's disease, 90
American Medical Association (AMA), 11
American Medical Informatics Association, 148
American Nurses Association Telehealth Core Principles, 153–155
ANI, *see* Artificial Narrow Intelligence
APIP, *see* Activity-based pressure injury prediction
Applied data science
    data biases effect, 90–91
    framework, 83–84
    home healthcare risk factor categories, 88, 89
    machine learning, 84
    model transferability and adoption, 91–92
    nursing notes, identify patients risk, 87–88
    open-access nursing sensitive software, 88
    overview of, 81–83
    regression and clustering, 84–85
    score matching, model health trajectories, 86–87
    symptom information identification, 88, 90
Applied Healthcare Data Science Roadmap, xxix
Applied informatics, case studies during COVID-19
    COVID-19 information sharing
        background, 194–195
        changes, 195
        overview, 194
    disaster documentation
        background, 190
        changes, 190–191
        overview, 190
    rapid telehealth implementation
        background, 192–193
        changes, 193
        overview, 192
    workflow efficiency
        background, 196–197
        changes, 197–198
        overview, 196
APRNs, *see* Advanced practice registered nurses
AR, *see* Augmented reality
Artificial General Intelligence (AGI), 105
Artificial intelligence (AI), xxx, 7–9, 105–106

204 ■ Index

application, 106–107
data, statistics and algorithms, 97–100
ethics, 107–108
into future, 108–110
machine learning (ML), 97, 98, 100–101
    deep learning, 101–103
    machine learning models, 103
    neural networks, 101–103
    reinforcement learning, 103–104
    supervised learning, 103
    unsupervised learning, 103
overview of, 96–97
Artificial intelligence (AI), nursing and healthcare
    augmented reality (AR), 122
        applications, 122–123
        cautions, 123
    machine learning (ML), 116–117
        applications, 117–118
        cautions, 118–119
    mobile technology, 119
        applications, 119–120
        cautions, 120–121
    robotics, 114–115
        applications, 115–116
        cautions, 116
    virtual reality (VR), 121–122
        applications, 122–123
        cautions, 123
Artificial Narrow Intelligence (ANI), 105
Artificial Superintelligence (ASI), 105
Asynchronous modalities, 151–152
Audio-videoconferencing, 150–151
Augmented reality (AR), 122
    applications, 122–123
    cautions, 123

B

Bag of Visual Words (BoVW) model, 141
Big data, 71, 82
BoVW, *see* Bag of Visual Words model

C

Canadian Health Outcomes for Better Information and Care (C-HOBIC)
    case study
        Alberta Health Services corporate approach, 29–30
        Health Prince Edward Island, 31–32
        Vancouver Coastal Health, 30–31
    challenges, 26–27
    evolution of, 20–22
    implementation history
        Pilot Project with CIHI, 24–25
        projects demonstration in Canada, 23–24
        transition synoptic report, 24
    International Classification for Nursing Practice® (ICNP), 22–23
    National Nursing Data Standards (NNDS) Initiative, 32–33
    nursing data standards, 19–20
    nursing in Canada, 18–19
    nursing practice in future, 33–34
    opportunities, 27–28
    Systematized Nomenclature of Medicine-Clinical Terms (SNOMED CT), 22–23
    transitions report, 33, 34
    value of linking with national datasets, 26
Canadian Institute for Health Information (CIHI), 24
    Pilot Project with, 24–25
Canadian Nurses Association (CNA), 21, 22
Centers for Disease Control and Prevention (CDC), 6
Centers for Medicare and Medicaid Services (CMS), 6
CGHD, *see* Consumer-generated health data
CIHI, *see* Canadian Institute for Health Information
CIS, *see* Clinical Information System
Clinical data standards, 19
Clinical Information System (CIS), 29
Cloud layer, 69, 71
CMS, *see* Centers for Medicare and Medicaid Services
CM&S, *see* Computational modeling and simulations
CNA, *see* Canadian Nurses Association
CNN, *see* Convolutional neural network

Cold zone, 197
Community-based urgent care, 160
Community Health Network, 8
Computational modeling and simulations (CM&S), 180
Consumer-generated health data (CGHD), 40, 41
Consumer-generated whole-person health data
    eHealth literacy, 40–41
    health literacy, 40–41
    interoperability, 41–42
    knowledge representation, 41–42
    mHealth, 40–41
    MyStrengths+MyHealth (MSMH), 46–48
        circulation signs and symptoms, 48–50
        clinical conversations, 50, 52
        exploring resilience, 53
        international collaboration, 53–54
        older adults, 50, 51
        social media studies, 53
    simplified Omaha system terms, 46
    standardized, interoperable data, 41
    whole-person health, 43–46
Convolutional neural network (CNN), 136, 137
COVID-19 information sharing
    background, 194–195
    changes, 195
    overview, 194
COVID-19 pandemic, 6, xxx, 19; see also Applied informatics, case studies during COVID-19
Crew Resource Management (CRM), 175, 176

D

DAD, see Discharge Abstract Database
Data biases effect, 90–91
Data science, 83, 87; see also Applied data science
    definition, 82
    projects, 91
Deep learning, 101–103
Digital health, 3, 4
Direct-to-consumer (DTC) telehealth, 150, 161

Disaster documentation
    background, 190
    changes, 190–191
    overview, 190
Discharge Abstract Database (DAD), 25
Discrete event simulation, 177
DTC, see Direct to consumer

E

ED, see Emergency Department
eHealth, 149
eHealth literacy, 40–41
Electronic health record (EHR), 3, 5, 9, 11, 18, 26, 81, 191
    key challenges, 32
Emergency Department (ED), 160
European Pressure Ulcer Advisory Panel (EPUAP), 133

F

Food and Drug Administration (FDA), 152

G

Global rating scales (GRS), 174
GAO, see US Government Accountability Office (GAO) report
GRS, see Global rating scales

H

Health and Human Services (HHS), 67
Health literacy, 40–41
Health Outcomes and Better Information for Care (HOBIC), 20, 21
Health Prince Edward Island, 31–32
Health Resources and Services Administration (HRSA), 148
HFS, see High-fidelity simulation
HHS, see Health and Human Services
High-fidelity simulation (HFS), 170, 173–175, 180
HOBIC, see Health Outcomes and Better Information for Care
Hot zone, 197

206 ■ Index

HRSA, *see* Health Resources and Services Administration
Hybrid modalities, 152

I

IA, *see* Intelligence amplification
ICES, *see* Institute for Clinical Evaluative Sciences
ICNP, *see* International Classification for Nursing Practice®
Immobility, 115
INACSL, *see* International Nursing Association for Clinical Simulation and Learning
Informatics trends, next decade
    artificial intelligence (AI), 7–9
    emerging trends and nursing's role, 2–4
    mobile device integration, 11–12
    overview of, 1–2
    personalized healthcare, 4–5
    predictive analytics, 10
    telehealth, 5–6
    voice technology, 9
Information exchange, 156–157
Information value loop, 67–68
Infrared image capturing system, 138, 140
Innovation, 3, 4, 119
Innovative model development, 135–136
Inpatient nursing, 69–71
In-situ simulation (ISS), 176
Institute for Clinical Evaluative Sciences (ICES), 21
Integrated Care Management Program, 77
Intelligence amplification (IA), 109
International Classification for Nursing Practice® (ICNP), 22–23
International Nursing Association for Clinical Simulation and Learning (INACSL), 171
Internet of Things (IoT)
    building blocks
        networks, 65–66
        sensors, 62–65
        standards, 66–67
    future, 77
    information value loop, 67–68
    nursing practice
        inpatient nursing, 69–71
        outpatient nursing, 72–77
    overview of, 61–62
    themes driving future adoption, 78
ISS, *see* In-situ simulation

J

The Joint Commission (TJC), 172

K

Kingdom of Saudi Arabia, 194–196

L

Local area networks (LAN), 66
Logistic regression model, 85
Long short-term memory model (LSTM), 136

M

Machine learning (ML), 7, 84, 88, 97, 98, 100–101, 107, 116–117
    applications, 117–118
    cautions, 118–119
    deep learning, 101–103
    machine learning models, 103
    neural networks, 101–103
    reinforcement learning, 103–104
    supervised learning, 103
    unsupervised learning, 103
Machine learning models, 103
Massachusetts General Hospital (MGH), 149
MEMS sensors, 65
Mercy Virtual Care Center (MVCC), 72, 76, 77, 79
MGH, *see* Massachusetts General Hospital
mHealth, 40–41, 46, 119–121, 149
Ministry of Health and Welfare, 132
ML, *see* Machine learning
Mobile device integration, 11–12
Mobile technology, 119
    applications, 119–120
    cautions, 120–121
Model transferability, 91

MSMH, *see* MyStrengths+MyHealth
MVCC, *see* Mercy Virtual Care Center
MyStrengths+MyHealth (MSMH), 46–48
    circulation signs and symptoms, 48–50
    clinical conversations, 50, 52
    exploring resilience, 53
    international collaboration, 53–54
    older adults, 50, 51
    social media studies, 53

N

NAIL, *see* Nursing and Artificial Intelligence Leadership Collaborative
National Institute of Nursing Research (NINR), 5
National Institute of Standards and Technology (NIST), 90
National Institutes of Health (NIH), 5
The National League for Nursing, 171
National Nursing and Midwifery Digital Health Capability Framework, 3
National Nursing Data Standards (NNDS) Initiative, 32–33
Natural language processing (NLP), 8, 9, 87, 90, 102–104
    open-access nursing sensitive software, 88
Networks, 65–66
Neural networks, 101–103
NIH, *see* National Institutes of Health
NimbleMiner, 88, 90
NINR, *see* National Institute of Nursing Research
NIST, *see* National Institute of Standards and Technology
NLP, *see* Natural language processing
NNDS, *see* National Nursing Data Standards Initiative
Nontechnical skills (NTS), 175
Nursing and Artificial Intelligence Leadership (NAIL) Collaborative, 8, 91
Nursing data standards, 19–20
Nursing informatics, 2, 69
Nursing value, 19–20

O

Objective Structured Assessment of Technical Skills (OSATS), 174
Objective Structured Clinical Examination (OSCE), 174
OEM, *see* Original equipment manufacturer
Omaha system, 45, 47
Ongoing professional practice evaluation (OPPE), 177
Open-access nursing sensitive software, 88
OPPE, *see* Ongoing professional practice evaluation
Original equipment manufacturer (OEM), 66
OSATS, *see* Objective Structured Assessment of Technical Skills
OSCE, *see* Objective Structured Clinical Examination
Outpatient nursing, 72–77

P

Personal area networks (PAN), 66
Personalized healthcare, 4–5
Personal protective equipment (PPE), 197
PHE, *see* Public Health Emergency
PPE, *see* Personal protective equipment
Predictive analytics, 10
Pressure ulcer changes monitoring, Taiwan
    algorithm development, 141–142
    camera monitoring set up, 137–139
    classification, 139–141
    current pressure ulcer prevention standard, 133
    earlier medicine approach, impact on, 143
    implementation results, 142
    infrared image capturing system, 138, 140
    innovative model development, 135–136
    overview of, 132–134
    photo-taking method, 137, 138
    standard settings, 136–137
    virtual care model, 133, 135
Primary care, 158
Public Health Emergency (PHE), 163
Python, 104

Q

Quality improvement (QI), 197

R

Rapid telehealth implementation
   background, 192–193
      changes, 193
      overview, 192
Recurrent neural network (RNN), 136
Registered nurses (RN), 153, 155, 159
Reinforcement learning, 103–104
Remote patient monitoring/management (RPM), 149, 152, 156
Return on investment (ROI), 180–181
RN, *see* Registered nurses
RNN, *see* Recurrent neural network
Robotics, 114–115
   applications, 115–116
   cautions, 116
ROI, *see* Return on investment
RPM, *see* Remote patient monitoring/management

S

Saudi Arabia, 194, 195
Saudi Arabian healthcare workforce, 194
Sensors, 62–65
Simplified Omaha system terms (SOST), 46, 47
Simulations-based care delivery
   costs, 180–181
   future needs
      new space design and care processes testing, 179
      testing new products, 179–180
   nursing-led innovation, 170–172
   research and assessment, 177–179
   return on investment (ROI), 180–181
   safety and quality initiatives, 172
   simulation, 170
   training for healthcare providers
      continuing education, 177
      discrete event simulation, 177
      nontechnical skills (NTS), 175
      team-based crisis simulation, 175–177
      technical skills training, 173–174
      training and assessment, 172–173
SNOMED CT, *see* Systematized Nomenclature of Medicine—Clinical Terms
SNT, *see* Standardized nursing terminologies
SOST, *see* Simplified Omaha system terms
Standardized nursing terminologies (SNT), 42
Superintelligence, 105
Supervised learning, 103
Symptom information identification, 88, 90
Synchronous modalities, 150–151
Systematized Nomenclature of Medicine—Clinical Terms (SNOMED CT), 22–23

T

Team-based crisis simulation, 175–177
Telehealth, 5–6
Telehealth and virtual care
   background, 149–150
   definition, 148–149
   future, 164–165
   human factors
      technology considerations, 162
      usability, 161–162
   information exchange, 156–157
   insurance coverage, 162
   modalities, 150
      asynchronous modalities, 151–152
      hybrid modalities, 152
      synchronous modalities, 150–151
   nurse roles, 153, 155–156
   regulatory, 163
   services, 153
   settings
      community-based urgent care, 160
      direct to consumer (DTC), 161
      emergency services, 160
      primary care, 158
      specialty, 158–160
   training and competencies, 163–164
Tele-ICU (intensive care unit), 151
Telephone triage, 160
Telephone triage and auditory advice services (TTAS), 151

Telepresenter, 159
Text-based communication, 151
TigerPlace, 11
TJC, see The Joint Commission
Training, healthcare providers
    continuing education, 177
    discrete event simulation, 177
    nontechnical skills (NTS), 175
    team-based crisis simulation, 175–177
    technical skills training, 173–174
    training and assessment, 172–173
Transition synoptic report (TSR), 24
TTAS, see Telephone triage and auditory advice services

U

UCHealth system, 193
Unsupervised learning, 103
US Government Accountability Office (GAO) report, 7
US Office of the National Coordinator for Health Information Technology (ONC), 66

V

Value, 82
Vancouver Coastal Health, 30–31
Variability, 82
Variety, 82
Velocity, 82
vEngagement Program, 77
Veracity, 82
Virtual ICU (vICU), 72, 77
Virtual reality (VR), 121–122
    applications, 122–123
    cautions, 123
Voice technology, 9
Volume, 82
VR, see Virtual reality

W

WAN, see Wide area networks
Warm zone, 197
WHO, see World Health Organization
Whole-person health, 43–46
Wide area networks (WAN), 66
Wired networks, 66
Wireless networks, 65
Workflow efficiency
    background, 196–197
    changes, 197–198
    overview, 196
World Health Organization (WHO), 119

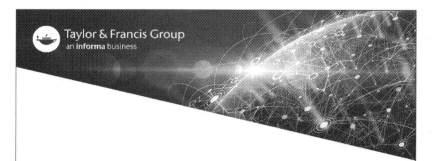

Printed in the United States
by Baker & Taylor Publisher Services